P9-EDH-106

THE LIBERTIES OF AN AMERICAN

Leo Pfeffer, associate general counsel for the American Jewish Congress, has written many briefs submitted to the United States Supreme Court in civil-liberties cases. He is the author of CHURCH, STATE, AND FREEDOM, *published in 1953 by the Beacon Press. Protestants and Other Americans United for Separation of Church and State (POAU) awarded Mr. Pfeffer its 1955 citation for meritorious contributions to religious liberty.*

The *Liberties* of an AMERICAN

The Supreme Court Speaks

by Leo Pfeffer

THE BEACON PRESS

Library of Congress catalog card number: 56–7174

Printed in U.S.A.

To
Justine Wise Polier
a courageous fighter for American liberties

Contents

Preface

This book is about our most precious heritage, a heritage so precious that for its preservation we have been prepared to risk collective extermination in a thermonuclear Armageddon. Our nation was born in liberty; we declared our independence of the English monarch because he denied to us the liberties we deemed the rightful possession of all free men. Since then our tradition has been liberty; but, even more, our popular instinct has been liberty. Like all instincts, it is generally imperfectly articulated, but its manifestations are unmistakable. Take, for example, the spontaneous response likely to be given by most Americans to a remark that a particular candidate for public office does not attend church: "That's his private business." Or the equally spontaneous exclamation when someone suggests that an unpopular street orator be silenced: "He's got a right to talk." Or the response likely to greet a derogatory statement concerning a public figure: "But can you prove it?" Or the widespread indignation, particularly in the North, evoked by the Eustace Till kidnapping-murder incident in Mississippi. In America liberty truly is of the people.

The precipitous decline and fall of Senator Joseph R. McCarthy furnish good evidence that the American instinct for liberty is still a vital force with which ambitious politicians must reckon. Yet it would be fatuous and futile to claim that the state of our liberties is healthy. We have often been warned that in our struggle against totalitarianism we have been adopting its methods and thus abandoning the liberties we are struggling so valiantly to preserve. The gods would surely laugh at their cruel joke if when the atomic holocaust erupted you could not tell the totalitarians from the libertarians.

The reason, I think, for the serious condition of our liberties is that instinct alone is not enough. The trouble with instinct is that it can be overpowered by a stronger instinct. Fear is a more potent motivating force than generosity, and the instinct for security is more potent than the instinct for liberty. Instinct, moreover, is irrational;

otherwise, why would we destroy what we are risking our lives to preserve?

To illustrate what I mean let us go back to the unpopular street orator and the American who exclaimed: "He's got a right to talk." The response might be: "But he's a Communist!" In this case I venture to suggest that it would be unlikely that the reply would be "That's his business"; even less likely that it would be "Can you prove it?"; and most unlikely that it would be "He's still got a right to talk." Here are three of our basic liberties — freedom of belief, freedom of speech, and the right to a fair trial — instinctively adjudged irrelevant when the specter of Communism haunts the land.

The probability of this reaction was sadly evidenced in 1954 by the irrationality of the most articulate anti-McCarthy Senators in shouting and voting for enactment of a bill to outlaw Communists, so Draconian that even Senator McCarthy could not accept it. Truly the end of wisdom is the fear of Communists.

Or take the suburban Northerner who expresses vociferous and sincere indignation at the Till murder or at the indignities suffered by Autherine Lucy in her efforts to gain admission to the University of Alabama. Fear bordering on panic is likely to strike the same Northerner should he learn that a Negro is negotiating for the house next door. It is more than a reasonable probability that he will hastily confer with his neighbors and his lawyer on the means to avert the threatened catastrophe.

Instinct for liberty is not enough. It must be reinforced by understanding — an understanding as widespread as the instinct. An American who understands why "He's got a right to talk," is less likely to accept "But he's a Communist" or "He is an atheist" as a sufficient reason for denying that right. The American is more likely to see that liberty is one boat and that, unless the hole under the seat occupied by the Communist or atheist is plugged up, the sea will ultimately engulf all the occupants — even those who sit on the extreme right side of the boat and fear the Communist or detest the atheist. And the same is true with respect to the Northern suburbanite. If the American understands what American liberty is, he can reasonably be expected to recognize that it is indivisible.

My hope in writing this book is to help provide some of that understanding. I believe that, given light, the American people can be counted on in the long run to find their way. I have tried in this book to shed some light on what the liberties of an American are and what they mean. I have chosen as my method an account of the leading decisions of the United States Supreme Court which interpret and apply the Bill of Rights of our Constitution. I have chosen this method because under our system the Supreme Court is the ultimate arbiter and interpreter of our liberties, and an examination of its major decisions is therefore a convenient way to obtain an understanding of these liberties.

For convenience the various liberties of Americans are treated separately and more or less independently. But it must always be kept in mind that these liberties are interdependent and overlapping. Consider, for example, the refusal of a municipality to allow a member of Jehovah's Witnesses to address a group in a park and distribute a religious pamphlet published by him, although clergymen of other faiths are permitted to do so. This one act of the municipality has infringed upon at least the following liberties of Americans: free exercise of religion, freedom of speech, freedom of the press, freedom of assembly, and the equal protection of the laws.

This book is intended primarily for the general reader. I lay no claim to either originality or profundity; my purpose is expository and my objective is clarity. While I have striven for accuracy, I have dispensed with footnotes, long quotations from original sources, and other accouterments of scholarship. For the reader's convenience the text of the relevant constitutional provisions is set forth in the Appendix. (I have there retained the archaic punctuation and capitalization of the original Constitution; but I have employed modern punctuation and capitalization where provisions of the Constitution are quoted in the text of the book.) For the reader desiring to consult the original sources, I have listed the legal cases discussed in the book, together with their appropriate citations and dates. I have also included a suggested reading list, prepared by my associate Will Maslow. For this and for his many helpful suggestions I acknowledge my indebtedness and appreciation. To my wife, Freda Pfeffer, there is due at least an acknowledgment and expression of gratitude for reading proofs and preparing the index, laborious tasks of which she uncomplainingly relieved me.

L. P.

CHAPTER 1. *American Liberties and the Supreme Court*

A DECLARATION OF LIBERTIES

The men at Philadelphia had done their work well — well, but unlawfully. They had come together in 1787 under a mandate to propose amendments to the Articles of Confederation. When they adjourned four months later they had drafted an entirely new instrument, a constitution to replace the Articles. Moreover, they decided not to transmit the fruit of their labors to the Congress under whose authority they had convened, but directly to the people. Their conduct was as unlawful and revolutionary as had been the conduct of those who in the same city some eleven years earlier had declared their independence of George III. Thus the two basic documents of American history upon which our government rests — the Declaration of Independence and the Constitution — were both the products of men who, in the phrase so common in present-day anti-subversion laws, sought to change the existing form of government "by unlawful means."

The lawlessness in Philadelphia in 1787 was no spontaneous accident. Everything about it gave proof of premeditation and design. The alacrity with which a majority of the delegates voted to flout the law and disregard the limitations upon their authority indicates pretty clearly that they had given long thought to the matter and had come to Philadelphia with unlawful intent. If further evidence is needed it is supplied by the secrecy surrounding the meetings. Press and public were barred; no official minutes were taken; the delegates undertook not to disclose to outsiders what went on in the secret sessions. (Lest the aging Ben Franklin unwittingly divulge any of the secrets in the course of his social dinners, a delegate was assigned to accompany him everywhere and keep him in check.)

Everything about the meeting gave proof of unlawful conspiracy, not excluding the " dupe " or " innocent " — Luther Martin of Maryland — who withdrew in anger when his eyes were opened to the true nature of the conspiracy against the existing government.

What is particularly shocking about this unlawful conspiracy is the character of the conspirators. They were no wild-eyed radicals or youthful visionaries. They were mostly staid and reputable members of the community, successful in their private affairs and conservative in their outlook. Of the fifty-five who attended the sessions regularly, only eight had been signers of the Declaration of Independence, and these had long since lost their revolutionary fervor. The radicals were conspicuously absent. Thomas Jefferson was in Paris as minister to France. Patrick Henry had been chosen to serve; but, on learning the identity of his co-delegates and their political and economic philosophies, he " smellt a rat " and refused to go. Sam Adams was not even chosen, and Tom Paine had left for Europe to start another phase in his lifelong personal war against tyranny.

It is hardly surprising that on basic principles the delegates were united. Above all they wanted a strong, central government. Shays's rebellion was too recent, and the helplessness of Congress to suppress that uprising of impoverished debtors too frightening, to be forgotten, and the men at Philadelphia were determined that the government which they would fashion would not lack adequate powers to deal with a recurrence. The principal if not sole purpose of this strong, central government was to protect men of substance and property from the predatory designs of the populace.

There were, of course, differences as to detail and method, differences so serious that they occasionally threatened to result in a breakup of the assembly. Agreement on basic principle, however, led to adjustment of these differences. The competing demands of the large and small States in respect to representation in the national government and taxation were adjusted by means of ingenious compromises improvised on the moment. The more serious conflict between the commercial free economy of the North and the agrarian slave economy of the South was simply postponed four score and seven years for ultimate bloody determination at Gettysburg and Antietam. In the meantime, the moral objections of two lonely radicals in the convention, Luther Martin and George Mason, to any sanction of slavery were met by carefully avoiding use of the words "slaves" or "slavery," words which might be "odious to the ears of Americans," and substituting for them such euphemisms as persons "held to service or labor."

The delegates to the convention could hardly be described as overly solicitous for the liberties of the people. On the contrary, most of them felt that the people had too much liberty. "Your people," said Alexander Hamilton on one occasion, "is a beast." While the majority of the delegates were not prepared to go as far as Hamilton in restricting the powers of "the beast," they generally agreed that what the country was suffering from was an "excess of democracy." Thus it was hardly surprising that they evinced little enthusiasm for the proposal by Mason, the author of the Virginia Bill of Rights, to preface the constitution with a declaration of the liberties of the people. Roger Sherman of Connecticut was all "for securing the rights of the people when requisite." But was it really requisite here? After all, the States themselves had declarations of rights in their constitutions, and, said Sherman, the "State declarations of rights are not repealed by this Constitution; and being in force are sufficient."

Mason pointed out quite logically that under the proposed new constitution the laws of the United States were to be paramount and therefore would override any provision in a State bill of rights. But the argument was of little avail. The debate was short, and when the motion to appoint a committee to draft a bill of rights came to a formal vote, not a single State delegation could muster a majority in favor and the motion was lost, ten States to none.

As the men at Philadelphia should have anticipated, Mason's argument could not be disposed of so simply. At least "We, the people," who were later called upon to approve and adopt the new constitution, did not accept the unanimous negative vote as a satisfactory disposition of the matter. Actually, the delegates themselves were unwilling to place full trust in the States. They did not rely on the States in respect to laws impairing the obligations of contracts and expressly prohibited the States from making any such laws — which is quite understandable. Moreover, in respect to certain civil liberties the delegates indicated quite clearly that they were not prepared to place all their trust in the State bills of rights. The constitution they drafted expressly forbade both Congress and the States to enact retroactive or ex post facto laws, or laws condemning without trial, known as bills of attainder. It forbade suspension of the writ of habeas corpus except in cases of rebellion or invasion by a foreign enemy. It guaranteed the right to trial by jury in all Federal criminal cases, and required that the trial of a criminal case be held in the State in which the crime had been committed. It defined treason narrowly as levying war against the United States or aiding or comforting its enemies, required that it be proved by the testimony of at least two witnesses to the same overt act or the defendant's confession in open court, and prohibited punishment of the defendant's family or forfeiture of his estate. Finally, it forbade forever any religious test as a requirement or qualification for public office under the new government.

These provisions were just the kind of liberties Mason wanted declared in a bill of rights. Indeed, when the Bill of Rights was later added to the Constitution, the provision for a jury trial to be held in the State where the crime had been committed was again included, in somewhat more detail. The express specification of some liberties in the Constitution deprived of all logical force Sherman's argument that the State declarations of rights, not being repealed by the Constitution, were sufficient.

Actually, the prevalence of bills of rights in the various State constitutions should have been a warning to the men at Philadelphia that omission of a similar declaration of liberties from the document they fashioned would lead to trouble. The last quarter of the eighteenth century was an era of high idealism, of appeals to the opinions of mankind, to reason and to nature. It was an era of declarations and pronouncements, of petitions and memorials and remonstrances. It was an era of long preambles justifying the action taken, with liberal invocations of nature and natural rights. Those who had assembled at Philadelphia eleven years earlier needed but one sentence to establish the independence of the United States and assert its sovereignty; but they used more than three dozen sentences to relate not only why they established this independence and sovereignty but also why they felt it necessary to declare to " a candid world " why they did so. The Virginia Statute for Religious Liberty, enacted a year before the meeting at Philadelphia to draft a constitution, consisted of one operative sentence of medium length sandwiched between a preamble seven times as long as the statute itself and an epilogue which, though substantially shorter, nevertheless exceeded the statute itself in length. Not only did the State constitutions enacted during this period contain elaborate declarations of rights, but in some — Massachusetts and New York for instance — the declaration of rights constituted the major part of the constitution.

It therefore should have been expected that there would be widespread dissatisfaction with a long constitution preceded by a one-sentence preamble in which securing " the blessings of liberty " was listed last, almost as an afterthought, among the purposes of the constitution. But the ground for dissatisfaction was far more than suspicion of a government fashioned by persons who gave such scant consideration to liberty. The social contract of Locke and Rousseau was generally accepted as the true basis of governments. Men are created free and with inalienable natural rights; they institute governments among themselves for the sole purpose of securing these rights; whenever a government fails to secure these rights, men are entitled to alter or abolish it. That was the moral justification for the dissolution of the political bands that connected the colonies with Great Britain. Certainly any government formed out of that severance should contain a declaration of these inalienable natural rights and a solemn undertaking not to deny or abridge them.

To meet the storm of criticism aroused by the omission of a specific bill of rights, the champions of the Constitution, particularly Hamilton and James Madison, argued that a separate bill of rights was not only unnecessary but even dangerous. It was unnecessary because the powers of the new government were limited to those specifically delegated to it in the Constitution, and no power to abridge or deny liberties had been delegated to it. " Why," asked Hamilton, " declare that things shall not be done which there is no power to do? " Why, for example, forbid Congress to abridge freedom of religion when it was quite clear that Congress had been given no power to intermeddle with religion at all, and that religion was completely outside its jurisdiction?

The inclusion of a separate bill of rights was dangerous because it was likely to become self-defeating. A prohibition to be effective must be phrased in language as encompassing as total absence of power, and this is impossible. A future Congress seeking to abridge a particular right would have little difficulty in reading in exceptions to the prohibition and could argue with cogency that the constitutional prohibition implicitly conferred a power to abridge the right to the extent not specifically prohibited.

An excellent example is the interpretation urged in respect to the banning, in the Bill of Rights ultimately adopted, of laws " respecting an establishment of religion "; this will be considered in the next chapter and need not detain us here. Another example is the Supreme Court's interpretation of this provision in the Bill of Rights: " A well regulated militia, being necessary to the securing of a free state, the right of the people to keep and bear arms shall not be infringed." If this natural and inalienable right of self-defense had not been specifically expressed, it might reasonably be argued that no power had ever been conferred on Congress to infringe it in any case. But because the Bill of Rights prohibited infringement of the right and gave an explanation of the reason for the prohibition, Congress was implicitly authorized to infringe the right in those cases where the reason for the prohibition is inapplicable. Therefore, said the Supreme Court in *United States* v. *Miller* (1939), Congress may prohibit the bearing in interstate commerce of unregistered shotguns with barrels less than eighteen inches in length — for the possession of such arms has no reasonable relationship to the maintenance and efficiency of a well-regulated militia.

Or take one last example, to be considered in more detail shortly. The Bill of Rights provides that *Congress* shall not abridge freedom of religion, speech, press, assembly, or petition. If there were no Bill of Rights, it could validly be argued that no part of the Federal government has been given power to abridge these freedoms; but since the Bill says only that Congress shall not abridge them, is it not reasonable to infer that the President or the Federal Judiciary was given implied power to abridge them?

A further and corollary danger arises out of the fact that it is impossible to list all the possible rights of the people. " Who," asked James Wilson of Pennsylvania, " will be bold enough to enumerate all the rights of the people? " If an attempt to enumerate them is made it must be remembered that if the enumeration is not complete, everything not expressly mentioned will be presumed to be purposely omitted. The Bill of Rights, to cite one instance, specifies freedom of speech, but it does not specify freedom of silence. Is it not therefore inferable that silence is not a liberty of Americans?

These arguments appear cogent, and the fears expressed later turned out to have been prophetic. But at the time the American people were not convinced. (When the Bill of Rights was ultimately written, avoidance of the danger was attempted by declaring that the enumeration of certain rights should not be construed to deny the existence of others not enumerated, and that the powers not specifically delegated to the national government in the Constitution are retained by the States and the people.) The people wanted no constitution without a bill of rights, and ratification was achieved only after the champions vowed that, as soon as the Constitution was ratified, a bill of rights would be added by amending the Constitution in accordance with the procedure set forth therein.

Madison, though mildly favoring a bill of rights, had been skeptical as to its real value. His own opinion, he wrote Jefferson, had always been in favor of a bill of rights, provided it could be so framed as not to create the implication of an intent to confer powers not enumerated. On the other hand he did not think its omission from the Constitution a particularly serious defect. "Experience," he continued, "proves the inefficacy of a bill of rights on those occasions when its control is most needed. Repeated violations of these parchment barriers have been committed by overbearing majorities in every State." In Virginia he had "seen the bill of rights violated in every instance where it had opposed a popular current." Actually, "the danger of oppression lies in the interested majorities of the people rather than in the usurped acts of the government," and as to oppression by the people a bill of rights would afford little help.

Nevertheless, Madison agreed, a bill of rights does have some modest value. In respect to abuses by the government, a bill of rights would "be a good ground for an appeal to the sense of the community." Moreover, if a bill of rights is inserted in the Constitution, "independent tribunals of justice will consider themselves in a peculiar manner the guardians of those rights." And even in respect to action by tyrannical majorities, liberties solemnly declared in the national charter "acquire by degrees the character of fundamental maxims and as they become incorporated with the national sentiment, counteract the impulses of interest and passion." In any event a bill of rights, if properly framed, could not do any harm, and good faith required compliance with the covenant in reliance upon which the people had been induced to ratify the Constitution.

Accordingly, when the Constitution was finally ratified and the first Congress met, Madison, who had been elected to the House of Representatives, undertook to draft a bill of rights. He based his draft on the various proposals submitted by a number of State conventions at the time they ratified the Constitution. The draft proposed by Madison was subject to extended debate in both Houses of Congress. After approval by the requisite two-thirds of each House it was submitted to the States for ratification. Finally, on December 15, 1791, the first ten Amendments became part of the Constitution when Virginia, the eleventh State to act favorably, ratified them and thus made up the required three-fourths of the States.

These ten Amendments are generally called our Bill of Rights. For convenience we will so use the term, although it is not completely accurate. In the first place, as we have seen, some rights — such as habeas corpus, trial by jury in criminal cases, and freedom from ex post facto laws and bills of attainder — had been included in the Constitution itself. Other rights — such as freedom from slavery or unequal treatment by government — came later, after the Civil War. All these together really constitute our Bill of Rights. All are set forth at the end of this book, and the reader may wish to turn to the Appendix and read them before going any further.

Briefly, the First Amendment forbade Congress to enact laws establishing religion or prohibiting its free exercise, or abridging freedom of speech, press, assembly, and petition. The Second Amendment guaranteed the right to bear arms. The Third prohibited the quartering of soldiers in private homes in peacetime without the owners' consent. The Fourth outlawed unreasonable searches and seizures. The Fifth guaranteed prosecution of felonies by indictment, forbade double jeopardy, compulsory self-incrimination, deprivation of life, liberty, or property without due process of law, and the taking of private property for public use without just compensation. The Sixth guaranteed a speedy, impartial, public, and local jury trial in all criminal prosecutions, and guaranteed the right of compulsory process to obtain witnesses as well as assistance of legal counsel. The Seventh provided for jury trials in civil actions, and the Eighth prohibited excessive bail, excessive fines, and cruel and unusual punishments. The Ninth provided that rights not specifically enumerated should not be therefore deemed denied, and the Tenth that powers not expressly delegated to the Federal government are retained by the States and the people.

THE BILL OF RIGHTS, THE PRESIDENT, AND THE COURTS

The first thing we notice in examining the Bill of Rights is that it begins with the words "Congress shall make no law . . ." Does that mean that only Congress is restrained and that the President or the Judiciary may freely deprive Americans of their liberties? This idea is startling if not shocking, and could hardly have been what the people intended when they adopted the Bill of Rights, if for no other reason than because some of the rights specified are ordinarily subject to infringement only by the President or the Judiciary. Thus the responsibility for quartering soldiers would ordinarily lie not with Congress but with the President, in his capacity as commander in chief of the armed forces. Or, to take another example, the responsibility for fixing bail would ordinarily lie with the courts rather than with Congress. Fortunately, no difficulty arises with respect to these rights because the Amendments after the First are worded in the passive rather than the active tense; they state merely that the right to bear arms "shall not be infringed," that a person shall not "be deprived of life, liberty or property without due process of law," etc. These Amendments do not specify against whom they are directed, and therefore there is no difficulty in holding that all branches of the Federal government are subject to them.

But what about the freedoms of religion, speech, press, assembly, and petition guaranteed by the First Amendment? These freedoms are preceded by the phrase, "Congress shall make no law . . ." There is nothing in the Bill of Rights to prohibit the President or the courts from abridging these freedoms.

Here the Ninth and Tenth Amendments come into play. The fact that the First Amendment by its terms forbids only Congress from abridging the named freedoms is not to be construed as implicitly authorizing the President or the courts to abridge them. Even though the First Amendment specifically mentions only Congress, the President and the courts are equally without constitutional authority to abridge these freedoms. A Federal judge, for example, may not hold a newspaper publisher in contempt for criticizing the judge's decision, for that would be an abridgment of freedom of the press. So too, President Jefferson refused to issue proclamations of prayers or fasts because he thought that such proclamations violated the prohibition "respecting the establishment or free exercise of religion," even though the language of the prohibition is directed only at Congress.

THE BILL OF RIGHTS AND THE STATES

It is therefore safe to say that the Bill of Rights prohibits abridgment of freedoms by the President and the Federal courts to the same extent that it prohibits such abridgments by Congress. But no such easy solution is available in respect to abridgments by the States. The Ninth and Tenth Amendments do not help here, because these say only that the fact that the Constitution prohibits the *Federal* government from abridging certain enumerated freedoms is not to be construed to mean that the *Federal* government is authorized to abridge the freedoms not enumerated. Since the Ninth and Tenth Amendments do not restrict the States' powers and the First Amendment refers only to Congress, it is clear that the rights enumerated therein are not protected by the Bill of Rights from infringement by the States. In fact, Madison had proposed an amendment which would have expressly forbidden the States to infringe upon freedom of religion, speech, and press; but although the House of Representatives accepted it the Senate refused to do so, and it never became part of the Constitution.

As far as the First Amendment is concerned, therefore, there is nothing to prevent a State from abridging freedom of religion, speech, press, petition, or assembly. The same is true of the right to a jury trial in non-criminal cases guaranteed by the Seventh Amendment, which specifically refers to "any court of the United States," i.e., any Federal court. But the same is not so obvious in respect to the rights guaranteed in the other provisions of the original Bill of Rights. The other Amendments do not refer specifically either to Congress or to any other branch of the Federal government. They use passive verbs without specifying the actor.

Take, as an illustration, the Fifth Amendment, which concludes: ". . . nor shall private property be taken for public use, without just compensation." May it not be argued (as indeed it has been in a highly controversial book published a few years ago by Professor Crosskey of the University of Chicago) that the prohibition extends to the States as well as the Federal government? After all, are there not certain basic rights which may not be infringed by any government, State as well as Federal, even though they are not expressly referred to in the Constitution? Moreover, Article IV of the Constitution expressly guarantees to every State in the Union a "republican form of government," and can a government which appropriates the property of its citizens without compensation truly be called "republican?"

Time and time again these arguments were presented to the United States Supreme Court, and time and time again they were rejected. Beginning with *Barron* v. *Baltimore,* a decision by Chief Justice John Marshall in 1833, the Court consistently held that no part of the original Bill of Rights (i.e., the first Ten Amendments) restricted the States in any way or prohibited them from infringing upon the liberties secured therein.

Thus the situation stood until the Civil War. After the War, and as a direct result of it, three amendments were adopted which expressly prohibited the States from abridging liberties secured in those amendments. The Thirteenth Amendment prohibited slavery anywhere "within the United States," and thus barred States from imposing slavery. The Fourteenth Amendment provided that all persons born in the United States are citizens of the United States and that "No State shall make or enforce any law which shall abridge the privileges or immunities of citizens of the United States; nor shall any State deprive any person of life, liberty, or property without due process of law; nor deny to any person within its jurisdiction the equal protection of the laws." The Fifteenth Amendment provides that the right to vote shall not be abridged on racial grounds "by the United States or by any State."

The meanings of the Thirteenth and the Fifteenth Amendments are clear enough; the Thirteenth abolished slavery and the Fifteenth secured the right of Negroes to vote. The meaning of the Fourteenth Amendment, however, is not so clear. Everyone agrees that it conferred the right of citizenship upon Negroes, but beyond that there is much controversy. There is good evidence that some of the Congressional leaders responsible for the drafting and adoption of the Fourteenth Amendment intended that it should abrogate John Marshall's 1833 decision and make the Bill of Rights applicable to the States. They used the term "privileges or immunities of citizens of the United States " to mean the rights secured by the first eight Amendments, and by prohibiting the States from abridging those " privileges or immunities " they intended that the Constitution should guarantee the liberties of Americans against hostile action by States to the same extent as against hostile action by the Federal government. On the other hand, there is equally good evidence that many other members of Congress assumed that the Amendment dealt only with Negroes and did no more than confer the equal rights of citizenship upon Negroes.

Five years after the Fourteenth Amendment was adopted, the question of the meaning of " privileges or immunities " reached the Supreme Court for the first time in the Slaughter-House Case — a case having nothing to do with Negroes, but involving the power of a State to regulate business. The legislature of Louisiana enacted a law making operation of slaughterhouses in New Orleans unlawful except by a single corporation, which was required to serve all at rates fixed by law. A suit was brought to declare the law unconstitutional on the ground that the right to engage in a lawful calling, such as butchering, was one of the " privileges or immunities " protected by the Fourteenth Amendment against State abridgment.

The majority of the Court upheld the Louisiana law and in doing so gave the term " privileges or immunities " a very narrow construction. It held that the only privileges and immunities secured by the Fourteenth Amendment against infringement by States were rights or privileges that owe their existence to the Federal government, i.e., rights and privileges growing out of the relationship of an American citizen to the Federal government. Examples of these are the right to vote in Federal elections, the right to petition the Federal government, the right of access to Federal buildings, offices, and courts of justice, etc. The right to engage in the slaughterhouse business or other lawful occupation (not connected with the Federal government) was a natural right, not created by the Federal government, and therefore was not protected by the " privileges or immunities " clause.

While this case did not expressly hold that the " privileges or immunities " clause did not encompass the rights specifically enumerated in the first eight Amendments, the narrow interpretation of the clause spelled its death knell as an effective means of obtaining protection by the Federal government against State impairment of the liberties of Americans. The attempt to employ the clause for this purpose, however, was not given up. Numerous efforts were made to reverse the Court's narrow interpretation. For example, the anarchists who were charged with responsibility for the 1886 Haymarket Square riots in Chicago were tried by a jury which included men who candidly admitted before serving that they had made up their minds that the defendants were guilty. The Sixth Amendment guarantees the right to trial "by an impartial jury," and in *Spies* v. *Illinois* counsel for the anarchists argued before the Supreme Court that this was a privilege or immunity which could not be infringed by the State of Illinois. But they argued in vain.

In another case, *Ex parte Kemmler*, it was unsuccessfully argued that the electric chair was "cruel and unusual punishment" which a State could not impose, since the Eighth Amendment's prohibition of such punishment is a privilege or immunity within the protection of the Fourteenth Amendment. In other cases it was unsuccessfully argued that the right of prosecution by indictment (Fifth Amendment), freedom of the press (First Amendment), security against unreasonable searches and seizures (Fourth Amendment) and self-incrimination (Fifth Amendment) were privileges and immunities within the purview of the Fourteenth Amendment. While some of these cases were decided on other grounds (e.g., execution by electrocution was held not to be "cruel and unusual punishment" within the meaning of the Eighth Amendment), the Court steadfastly refused to broaden the scope of the "privileges or immunities" clause so as to give it any significant meaning in the protection of American liberties against State encroachment.

Yet the demand for Federal protection against State deprivation of liberties did not abate. Local passions and prejudices require resort to a higher tribunal sufficiently strong and removed to resist them; otherwise the Bill of Rights would become, to use Madison's phrase, no more than a "parchment barrier." True enough, all the States have bills of rights in their own constitutions; but Madison, as we have seen, observed that the Virginia bill of rights had been "violated in every instance where it has been opposed to a popular current." A tragic Civil War had to be fought and thousands of lives lost because the States would not give effect to the self-evident truth that all men are created equal. The Thirteenth, Fourteenth, and Fifteenth Amendments were adopted solely because the people did not believe that the States could at all times be relied upon to secure the liberties of their inhabitants.

And so the legal struggle continued. Lawyer after lawyer appealed to the Supreme Court to upset some action taken by a State court or a State legislature which infringed upon the liberties of his client. Finally, a half-century after the Fourteenth Amendment was adopted, a crack appeared in the wall that had been erected between the liberties protected by the Federal government and those in whose protection the States had the last say. The crack did not appear in the " privileges and immunities " clause; the Slaughter-House decision had effectively sealed off that approach. The crack that ultimately split the wall appeared in that part of the Fourteenth Amendment which prohibited the States from depriving any person of " life, liberty or property without due process of law."

In fact, astute lawyers had previously invoked the jurisdiction of the Supreme Court with the claim that a State's impairment of a right specifically enumerated in the first eight Amendments constituted a deprivation of life, liberty or property " without due process of law " within the ban of the Fourteenth Amendment. Thus, the Fifth Amendment requires that all serious crimes shall be prosecuted only after a grand jury has handed down an indictment. In 1879 California adopted a new constitution for the purpose of modernizing its government. One of the changes was to allow a trial of a felony charge simply after an examination and commitment by a magistrate. After a man named Hutardo had been tried, convicted, and sentenced to hang for murder, his lawyer appealed to the United States Supreme Court on the claim that the right to grand-jury consideration of an accusation of a felony was a liberty of which an American could not be deprived by a State any more than by the Federal government itself.

The Court, in *Hurtado* v. *California,* rejected the appeal, but stated that arbitrary and unreasonable deprivations of liberty by the States could be brought to the Court under the " due process " clause. If, as an illustration, the legislature of California had passed a law saying that Hurtado was so clearly guilty that it would be a waste of the taxpayers' money to conduct a trial and therefore declaring him guilty and ordering him hanged, that would have been a deprivation of life and liberty without due process of law which the Supreme Court would hold unconstitutional. But, the Court held, the procedure of information rather than indictment adopted by California was not unreasonable or arbitrary.

In 1923, in *Moore* v. *Dempsey,* the Court upset the conviction of five Negroes by a mob-dominated judge and jury on the ground that a trial under those conditions did not constitute " due process of law." In the same year the Court, in *Meyer* v. *Nebraska,* held unconstitutional under the " due process " clause a Nebraska law, passed during the World War I period, prohibiting the teaching of the German language. In doing so, the Court said that the term " liberty " in the Fourteenth Amendment " denotes not merely freedom from bodily restraint, but also the right of an individual to contract, to engage in any of the common occupations of life, to acquire useful knowledge, to marry, establish a home and bring up children, to worship God according to the dictates of his own conscience, and, generally, to enjoy those privileges recognized at common law as essential to the orderly pursuit of happiness by free men."

In 1925, in *Gitlow* v. *New York,* the Court, while upholding the conviction of Ben Gitlow under a New York law punishing the advocacy of criminal anarchy, accepted his contention that the term " liberty " in the " due process " clause of the Fourteenth Amendment included freedom of speech and press.

With the advent of the Roosevelt Court in the late 1930's and the 1940's, the crack in the wall barring approach to the Supreme Court for redress from State infringement of liberties became a breach. In rapid succession the Court held that the " due process " clause of the Fourteenth Amendment protected freedom of religion and of assembly, the separation of church and state, the right to counsel in criminal cases, freedom from brutality and other " third degree " methods in extorting confessions, freedom from conviction based on testimony known by the prosecution to be perjured, and many other liberties of Americans. The effect of these decisions was to imbue into the " due process " clause much of the vitality and meaning that had been taken out of the " privileges or immunities " clause by the Slaughter-House decision.

Do these decisions now give effect to the intention of those Congressional leaders who looked to the Fourteenth Amendment as a means to impose upon the States the restrictions imposed upon the Federal government by the first eight Amendments? In other words, does the " due process " clause prohibit a State from doing anything that the first eight Amendments prohibit the Federal government from doing?

Yes and no. Yes, as far as the First Amendment is concerned; no, as far as the other seven Amendments are concerned. The First Amendment deals with the freedoms inherent in a democratic society — religion, speech, press, assembly, and petition. The others, by and large, seek to provide for a fair administration of justice. Their purpose is to protect the individual against arbitrary arrest and punishment. In the language of the lawyer, they provide *procedural safeguards* while the First Amendment secures *substantive rights.*

Under the recent decisions of the Supreme Court the restrictions of the First Amendment apply equally to the Federal government and to the States. An act of Congress abridging freedom of speech, press, or religion would be unconstitutional; such a measure would be equally unconstitutional if enacted by a State legislature. But this is not the case with respect to the other Amendments. The Seventh Amendment requires a jury trial in every action for damage involving more than twenty dollars. This applies in the Federal courts (although, of course, the parties may waive a jury trial); but it does not necessarily mean that every State court must allow a jury trial in similar circumstances. The Sixth Amendment guarantees a jury trial in all criminal cases in the Federal courts; but in many States misdemeanors are tried by a Court of Special Sessions, consisting of three judges without any jury, and the Supreme Court has held this procedure to be constitutional.

The test is simply this: The Federal government is bound by the express terms of the Second through Eighth Amendments. Hence a Federal civil damages case for twenty-five dollars or a Federal prosecution for a misdemeanor must be tried by a jury. The States, on the other hand, are required only to act with " due process of law." Due process of law means Anglo-American concepts of fair play; it means that the State must conform to what is implied in the concept of ordered liberty; it means that a State may not act in such a way that shocks the American sense of justice. So long as the State keeps within the requirements of fair administration of justice, it does not violate the Fourteenth Amendment even though its action would be inconsistent with a specific prohibition of one of the first eight Amendments.

There is nothing outrageous or shocking in having petty crimes tried by a court of three judges instead of twelve laymen. Nor is there anything outrageous or shocking in allowing a judge or district attorney to comment to the jury on the fact that the defendant in a criminal case has elected to exercise the privilege of not taking the stand and testifying in his own defense. Such conduct in a State court is therefore not unconstitutional even though similar action in a Federal court might be.

Certain conduct may, of course, be unconstitutional whether committed by the Federal government or by a State. In 1952, for example, State policemen, having received a tip that a man named Rochin was engaged in unlawfully selling narcotics in violation of a State law, entered his home without a warrant and forced their way into his bedroom. They rushed toward Rochin and pointed to two capsules lying on the night table near his bed, demanding, "Whose stuff is this?" Rochin seized the capsules and swallowed them. Quickly handcuffing Rochin, the policemen took him to a hospital, where a stomach pump and emetic were forcefully imposed upon him, causing him to vomit up the capsules. The capsules were analyzed by the police, found to contain morphine, and introduced into evidence against Rochin. The Supreme Court, in *Rochin* v. *California*, reversed the conviction on the ground that the police officials' conduct shocked the American sense of fair play. If the prosecution had been in a Federal court for violation of the Federal narcotics law, the result would have been the same on the ground that the policemen's conduct violated the prohibition against unreasonable searches and seizures in the Fourth Amendment and the prohibition against compulsory self-incrimination in the Fifth Amendment.

This does not mean that the Federal government may do anything not expressly forbidden by the Second through Eighth Amendments. The Fifth Amendment contains a "due process" clause similar to that contained in the Fourteenth Amendment. The Federal government, therefore, may not act in such a way as to shock the American sense of fair play, or outside the scope of ordered liberty, even if not expressly forbidden by a specific provision in the first eight Amendments. Generally speaking it may be said that neither the Federal government nor a State may transgress the bounds of fair play and ordered liberty; within those bounds, the States are free to experiment with their systems for the administration of justice, while the Federal government must also keep itself within the confines set by the specific provisions of the Amendments from the Second through the Eighth. The First Amendment applies equally to the Federal government and to the States.

THE BILL OF RIGHTS AND PRIVATE ACTION

The first eight Amendments apply to and restrict every organ of the Federal government: the President, Congress, the Judiciary, and all agencies created by them. Similarly the Fourteenth Amendment applies to and restricts every organ of State government: legislative, executive, judicial, and administrative. Neither, however, applies to or restricts the actions of private individuals. Generally constitutions speak to governments while laws or statutes speak to individuals. True enough, the Thirteenth Amendment prohibits slavery not only by the Federal or State governments, but also by individuals, and the Eighteenth Amendment, while it was in force, prohibited the sale or manufacture of intoxicating liquors by individuals as well as States or the Federal government. But these are exceptions. By and large, the provisions of the Constitution and the Bill of Rights govern conduct by governments and do not apply to conduct by individuals. Nothing in the Constitution prohibits an individual from restricting another individual's freedom of religion or speech or press (although there may be *statutes* which prohibit him from doing so).

One of the most difficult problems in constitutional law is to decide whether certain action is governmental action or private action. Consider two illustrative cases which have reached the Supreme Court. The First and Fourteenth Amendments prohibit a city or town (which are deemed parts of the State) from forbidding the distribution of religious literature to passers-by in the streets. This, the Court has held, would be an interference with the free exercise of religion. But suppose a housing development, consisting of buildings, stores, streets, and parks, is owned in full by a private corporation. And suppose that this corporation forbids the distribution of religious literature in the streets. And suppose a missionary preacher violates this regulation and is arrested for trespass or ejected from the company town by a State trooper. Has there been a violation of the First and Fourteenth Amendments? The Supreme Court, in

Marsh v. *Alabama,* decided in 1946, held that there was because it found no substantial distinction between a company town and an ordinary town. But in *Watchtower Bible and Tract Society* v. *Metropolitan Life Insurance Company* two years later, it refused to find a violation where the missionary preacher was prevented from distributing his literature in the lobbies and corridors of a large apartment house.

A second illustration arises from the liberty of freedom of speech, which, as we will see later, may include freedom not to listen. An employer may, if he wishes, require his workers to listen to speeches attacking labor unions and the principle of collective bargaining. So long as the speeches are delivered on company time and the workers may, if they wish, resign from their jobs and thus avoid listening, no constitutional right is infringed upon. But suppose the political speeches are broadcast in a railroad station or in trolley cars and buses, and the public or a part of it has no other means of transportation, and the reason is that the State or municipality has given a franchise to operate a trolley or bus system to but one company, which is supervised and regulated by the State or municipality. Is the company in such a case merely a private individual not subject to constitutional restrictions? No, said the Supreme Court in *Public Utilities Commission* v. *Pollak;* in these circumstances, the company is an agency or instrumentality of the State or municipality, and its conduct is subject to the restrictions of the Bill of Rights.

These are two illustrative cases that have reached the Court. As we shall see later, the question of whether certain conduct is governmental or private is most important and is most frequently raised in cases concerning racial discrimination. The distinction between governmental and private action, however, is not limited to the liberty of equality but pervades the whole Bill of Rights.

THE ROLE OF THE SUPREME COURT

It should now be clear to the reader that the Supreme Court is the ultimate authority for the meaning of our liberties. The Constitution is the supreme law of the land, but, as Charles Evans Hughes once remarked, "the Constitution is what the Supreme Court says it is." This remark has become almost a platitude among political scientists. Like most facile and pithy platitudes, it is a good deal of an oversimplification. Nevertheless, it contains much truth, and is a realistic appraisal of the actual situation.

How the Court achieved the role of ultimate guardian and interpreter of the Constitution has been often told and need not be repeated here. Whether this role was contemplated by all or most of the men who gathered in Philadelphia in 1787 is far from clear. It is even less clear that the role was contemplated by most of the men in the States whose votes ratified the Constitution and put it into effect. The Court's assertion, in the 1803 case of *Marbury* v. *Madison,* of its right to declare acts of Congress unconstitutional and invalid was a master stroke of statecraft on the part of John Marshall, although the Court did not attempt to exercise the claimed right for a half-century after its assertion. However, its right to declare *State* acts unconstitutional was assumed and exercised at an early date. The highest Federal court had the right and duty to set aside decisions of lower Federal courts that infringed upon constitutional liberties, and the supremacy clause (i.e., that the Constitution is the supreme law of the land) gave it a similar right and duty in respect to decisions of State courts. The Supreme Court's assertion of power over the Executive was more strenuously contested; but President Truman's unquestioning acceptance of its decision in 1952 that his seizure of the steel mills to prevent a shutdown during the Korean war was invalid, and his compliance with its direction to return the mills to private control, showed clearly the Court's supremacy over the President in interpreting the Constitution and in defining the liberties of Americans.

What is remarkable about this universal acceptance of the Court's claim of final authority to nullify the acts of all other instrumentalities of our governments, Federal and State, is that the Court has no practical means of enforcing its decisions. It has no control over the nation's revenues as does Congress, nor over the nation's armed forces as does the President. If Mr. Truman had said of the decision in the steel-seizure case what President Jackson is reputed to have said a little more than a century earlier about a decision he did not like — " John Marshall made the decision, let John Marshall enforce it " — there would have been nothing the Supreme Court could have done. Yet Mr. Truman dutifully complied with the decision.

To paraphrase the word of the Lord unto Zerubbabel, not by

might nor by power but by its spirit does the Court prevail. The President, Congress, and the States accept the Court's word as final because the people so accept it, and in a democracy the ultimate power is public opinion. Therein lies the ultimate authority of the Court — public opinion. Because the people look to the Court as the ultimate guardian of their Constitution, because they look to the Court as the supreme arbiter, the President, Congress, and the States must accept it as such.

It is questionable that the Court was born with this supremacy. Nor was supremacy thrust upon it. The Court's supremacy was acquired by its own statesmanship, greatly aided by the demands of America's evolutionary nationalism and industrialism. The supremacy was in large measure achieved through trial and error. The assertion of supremacy in 1803 was greatly threatened by the Court's blunder fifty-four years later in the Dred Scott decision, which declared the Missouri Compromise unconstitutional. It was again threatened by the Court's reluctance in the 1930's to recognize the profound influence of the great depression upon American economic and political thinking, a temporary blindness which resulted in Franklin Roosevelt's plan for reorganizing the Court. Both crises were directly attributable to the fact that the Court alienated itself from the source of its authority — the people's conscience and public opinion. The Court recovered in both instances because it was able to rediscover and accept the sovereignty of the people's conscience and the people's opinion. Mr. Dooley's aphorism, "The Court follows the election returns," is, like Hughes's remark, an oversimplification; but, likewise, it is basically true. The Court has learned that to survive as supreme arbiter it must continue to follow the election returns.

If the Supreme Court's strength lies in its attunement to the conscience and opinion of the people, therein too lies its limitation as the guardian of America's liberties. The Court is effective in making the Bill of Rights more than a parchment barrier to encroachments upon the liberties of the people by the Legislature or the Executive. But it is really effective only when these encroachments seriously offend the conscience and opinion of the people. When the encroachments reflect rather than oppose the popular will, the Court's effectiveness as the guardian of the people's liberties is severely limited. If the overwhelming majority of Americans believe deeply and passionately that advocacy of Communism should be prohibited, the Court cannot be expected to bar effectuation of the people's will. Freedom, like democracy, must be willed from within; it cannot be imposed from without.

Limited as is the Court's effectiveness when it would act counter to the popular current, it is by no means insubstantial. The Court does not merely reflect the public conscience but helps to fashion it. The Court does not merely follow the people; it also leads them. Even as it says to the people, "Thy will be done," it can declare to them the evil and immorality of their will.

In this respect the dissenting opinion plays an important role. The dissenting opinion may in the long run be more important than the majority's decision. The dissents of Holmes and Brandeis in the twenties became in the forties not only the voice of the Court but, more important, the conscience of the American people. It is not unreasonable to suggest that our surprisingly good record in preserving civil liberties during World War II — at least as compared with World War I — is in no small measure attributable to the eloquence of the Holmes-Brandeis dissents. Nor is it unreasonable to predict that the dissents of Black and Douglas in the period following World War II may serve a similar function in the future.

But the contribution of the Supreme Court to the preservation of civil liberties is far greater than the moral teachings of its dissenting opinions. The Court's structure and prestige enable it to resist to a considerable degree the passing passions and prejudices of the people. It can set limits beyond which the people cannot go without departing from the democratic system. While the Court's decisions reflect the will of the people, "the people" is an amorphous thing and its "will" is rarely clearly defined or immutable. Within limits, the Court has a great deal of mobility. The Court need not wait until all of the people agree that racial discrimination and segregation are immoral; it can act with considerable effectiveness notwithstanding vehement opposition by a large part of "the people." The Court, even if it wished to, could not perhaps assure the right of proved Communists to work for the government, particularly in so-called sensitive positions; but its authority in our system is sufficiently strong and secure to assure that government employees will receive a fair trial of charges that they are Communists.

The criticism that has been legitimately pointed at the Court in eras of attack on civil liberties is not that it has failed to do the impossible in stemming the attack on civil liberties, but that it has failed to do much that was possible. The near-disasters of the Dred Scott decision and the great depression decisions have understandably made the Court cautious in frustrating the people's will. Yet, unless the Court is prepared to offer some resistance to the passions and prejudices of the moment it has no just claim to the office of supreme protector of a Constitution designed to ride out storms of passion and prejudice. There is no practicable way of assuring total security for the Court's status and prestige; but it is not unreasonable to expect the Court to assume some risk in the cause of constitutional liberty. That the Court recognizes this is evidenced by its courageous decision in the school segregation case, notwithstanding outcries in the South that implementation of the decision would be vigorously resisted. It is safe to predict that when the Court feels the time ripe it will act similarly in the field of political liberties; and recent statements by the Court and particularly Chief Justice Warren indicate that the time may become ripe a good deal sooner than many have dared to expect.

The foregoing discussion seems to indicate that the Court is free to determine for itself when it will decide a particular constitutional controversy and how it will decide it. This may surprise those who assume that the Court must decide a particular issue when it is presented to it by litigants seeking a decision and must decide it in accordance with the text of the Constitution and precedents established in previous cases.

Both assumptions are in large measure incorrect. The Supreme Court, unlike any other court in the land, decides for itself what cases it will hear and what cases it will not. The fact that a lower court has incorrectly decided a particular case is not of itself sufficient reason for the Supreme Court to agree to review the decision. Many factors enter into the Court's decision to review or not to review a particular case. Generally the Court need not and does not say why it refuses to hear a particular case, and the reason is left to the speculation of constitutional students and lawyers. It is generally agreed, however, that timing is one of the most important considerations, particularly in controversies over civil liberties. The issue must be ripe for the Court, and the country must be ripe for the Court's decision.

Even more surprising, if not shocking, is the fact that the Court is pretty much its own master as to how it will decide a particular civil-liberties case. The Bill of Rights speaks in majestic generalities, and their application to a particular lawsuit is not a simple matter of matching the lawsuit to the Constitution; if it were there would be no need for a Supreme Court. The fact that so many constitutional-law cases are decided by sharply divided Courts, and the fact that dissenting opinions are legion in civil-liberties cases, prove that a constitutional provision can mean different things to different judges.

Frequently the Court speaks as if its duty is to ascertain the specific intent of those who framed and adopted the particular provision at issue. But this is often little more than pursuit of a phantasma. In most cases it is probable that nobody in 1787 or 1791 contemplated or could have contemplated the specific issue which the Court in the twentieth century is called upon to decide. How, for example, could the constitutional fathers have had any intent as to whether the government should or should not be allowed to prohibit the use of sound trucks by religious or political missionaries? Moreover, so many different individuals participated in the framing and adoption of a particular constitutional provision or amendment that the discovery of any universal intent with respect to it is close to impossible. The "no establishment" or "due process" clause may have meant one thing to Madison who drafted it, another thing to the majority of Congress which approved it, and something else again to the majority of the members of the State legislatures which adopted it as an amendment to the Constitution. Whose intent is to control?

Nor do previous decisions of the Supreme Court constitute as substantial a restriction upon its freedom of action in a given case as might be expected. In the first place, so many diverse precedents have been accumulated during the Court's history that the Court rarely has difficulty in finding adequate precedent for a particular decision it wishes to arrive at. In the second place, so long as words remain a less than perfect means of communicating meaning, Supreme Court decisions, like a constitutional provision, are subject to varying interpretations. It is by no means uncommon for a single decision to be cited as authoritative precedent in both the majority and minority opinions in a particular case. Moreover, no two cases are ever exactly alike, and astute lawyers and Supreme Court justices have little difficulty in finding differences that call for different determinations. Finally, nothing prevents the Court from expressly overruling or silently ignoring a previous decision that it does not now wish to follow. Since there is no appeal from the Supreme Court, the Court can never be wrong in any case before it.

This large measure of freedom of decision of the Supreme Court is the reason for the survival of the Constitution. Were the Court bound by the wording of the Constitution, or the intent of the constitutional fathers, or even its own prior decisions, an instrument written to govern the generation of 1787 could never effectively govern the generation of the atom age. It is because the Court, like a tree surgeon, has been able to prune off dead and diseased branches and to graft on needed new branches that the tree has lived and remains alive and blooming.

Let us consider a few examples. First, of pruning. In 1791 the right of citizens to bear arms was deemed an important liberty and was written into the Bill of Rights. Today practically no one would consider the right to carry a gun a liberty of an American. Indeed, it is almost unthinkable that the government should not have the right to prohibit it except in special cases. As we have seen, the Supreme Court has so held, in effect pruning the Second Amendment off the constitutional tree.

And some examples of grafting. In 1948, in the McCollum case, the Court held that a secular public-education system is among the liberties of Americans. But in 1791 education was neither public nor secular, at least as we understand those terms today. Or the right of silence. No such right is expressed in the Constitution except as to self-incriminating statements. Yet this did not prevent the Court in the Barnette case in 1943 from finding that such a right, at least in a limited sense, exists and is encompassed, of all things, in freedom of speech. The same is probably true of the right not to listen. The secret ballot, to take one last example, was unknown in the eighteenth century; all voting was open. Nevertheless, it is probable that the Court would today recognize the secrecy of the polling place as a constitutionally protected liberty of Americans.

Moreover, not only the language of the Constitution, but the decisions of the Supreme Court interpreting the Constitution, are dynamic and evolutionary in their meaning. The holding of the Court in a specific case may be quite narrow, but in later cases the Court may cite it as authority to justify broader holdings. The original decision thus in time acquires a new and expanded meaning and enables the Court at a later date to cite decisional authority for an interpretation of the Constitution not yet ripe when the original decision was handed down.

This freedom of decision insures a dynamic rather than a static Constitution and Bill of Rights. It is the most important of the Court's powers. Without it neither the Court nor the Constitution nor our liberties could long survive.

THE WEIGHING OF COMPETING VALUES

If the Court's decision in a particular civil-liberties case is not predetermined by either the text of the Constitution, the framers' intent, or the Court's own previous decisions, then what standard does the Court use to decide such a case? The answer is that it weighs the competing claims and decides the issue in accordance with its own judgment of values — or rather the judgment of a majority of its members at the time the issue is brought to it for decision. The Court's function in these cases is often said to be to reconcile the liberties of Americans with the well-being and security of the community. The Court must consider both the claim of the citizen to the free development and expression of his individuality and the claim of the government to restrain that development and expression in the interests of the common good.

In most cases there is no conflict between the demands of the individual and the demands of the community. Our republic was founded on the assumption that by and large the individual pursuit of happiness by the citizens is the surest way of achieving the happiness of the group. Perhaps the assumption is romantic and unreal; but it is an assumption fundamental to a constitutional democracy. Only when the individual's method of pursuing his happiness may be said to be unhealthy or abnormal — so that it presents a real threat to the well-being of the community — is communal restriction upon the individual's liberty justified, in the same way as a medical quarantine is justified.

Consider a simple illustration. Is a law restricting freedom of speech during wartime unconstitutional? If the issue were posed simply as a conflict between an individual's desire to express his feelings and the need to protect the country against its enemies the answer would be simple; obviously the individual's selfish desire to achieve his own happiness must yield to the safety and security of the commonwealth. But the issue cannot be posed so simply; for it is quite possible that if the individual were permitted to express his beliefs he would convince his fellow citizens that the course being taken by the government is wrong and inimical to the safety and security of the commonwealth. In such a situation the citizen's pursuit of his individual happiness would be consistent with rather than opposed to the common good. (It may be noted, parenthetically, that because of this great public interest in freedom of expression the Court has spoken of the freedoms secured by the First Amendment as occupying a preferred position in our constitutional scheme of things, entitled to more stringent judicial protection from legislative or executive impairment than other constitutional freedoms, particularly the freedom to do business and possess property.)

Or take another illustration. Should the government be allowed to compel a person to testify against himself? If the competing demand were simply a criminal's desire to avoid just punishment and the communal need to prevent crimes by punishing the guilty, there would be no problem. But when it is considered that compulsory self-incrimination has been found frequently to result in convicting the innocent, the issue is far from clear. Perhaps even a criminal's desire to avoid just punishment may promote the common welfare.

When, therefore, the Court considers a civil-liberties case it does not weigh merely the competing claims of the individual and the community; if that were all that was involved the decision would be obvious and predetermined. What the Court must also weigh is the competing demands of the community itself, and what it must decide is which way is best for the community. Is the commonwealth more likely to suffer seriously if the individual's freedom to speak is restricted than if it is not? Is the commonwealth more likely to suffer seriously if a defendant is compelled to incriminate himself than if he is not?

This would not seem to be the type of judgment that a court of law is ordinarily called upon to exercise. And it is not. The simple truth is that when the Supreme Court passes upon a civil-liberties case it is not sitting as a court of law. Although it employs the traditional forms and terminology of private litigation, its function is not law but statesmanship. The simple truth is also that the Court has no easy means or objective criteria to aid it in the exercise of its judgment; indeed the judgment is largely intuition and informed guess. If the guess is wrong, the consequences may be disastrous, as with the wrong guess made in *Scott* v. *Sandford*. History, fortunately, has shown that in most cases the Court has guessed right — that is, has accurately reflected the enlightened conscience of the people. And that, after all, is really its role as the guardian of our liberties, and that is why it has succeeded for so long in maintaining this role.

Chapter 2. *Liberty of Belief and Disbelief*

A REVOLUTIONARY EXPERIMENT

Of all our liberties, perhaps the most important is religious liberty. A government that will coerce its citizens in the domain of the spiritual will hardly hesitate to coerce them in the domain of the temporal. If it will direct how they shall worship it will certainly direct how they shall vote. Certain it is that religious liberty is the progenitor of most other civil liberties. Out of victory in the struggle for freedom to worship as one's conscience dictates came victory in the struggle for freedom to speak as one's reason dictates. Freedom of the press came from the struggle for freedom to print religious tracts, and freedom to assemble politically can be traced to the successful struggle for freedom to assemble religiously. Even procedural liberties incident to our concept of a fair trial grew largely out of the struggle for procedural fairness in heresy and other religious trials.

Another indication of the importance of religious freedom is the following. Exact statistics are not available, but it is a reasonable probability that in the course of human history more innocent blood has been shed in the name of God and the gods than for any other cause. This was certainly true up to 1791 when the Bill of Rights became part of our Constitution. Nationalism, the closest rival for this unenviable record of violence, did not achieve this status until the nineteenth and twentieth centuries. The disappearance of religious wars is in no small measure due to the result of the experiment articulated in the opening words of the Bill of Rights: "Congress shall make no law respecting an establishment of religion, or prohibiting the free exercise thereof." For this experiment has been emulated throughout the world. There is hardly a nation in the world whose constitution today does not pay at least lip service to the principle of religious freedom.

A great American jurist, David Dudley Field, once expressed the opinion that the "greatest achievement ever made in the cause of human progress is the total and final separation of church and state." Whether this is hyperbole or a defensible estimation, this writer, at least, believes that the greatest single contribution made by America to contemporary civilization is the evolution and successful launching of the uniquely American experiment of religious freedom and the separation of church and state.

Experiment, indeed, it was; and revolutionary. Revolutionary not only because of its radical departure from the tradition of ages that the relationship between man and God was a matter of legitimate concern of political government, but also in the speed with which the experiment was launched.

At the outbreak of the Revolutionary War it was illegal to celebrate the mass in any of the colonies other than Pennsylvania. In two-thirds of the colonies a particular church was established as the official state religion, toward the support of which all were obligated to contribute. In Virginia a Christian who denied the Trinity was punishable with imprisonment for three years and could be adjudged an unfit custodian of his own children. Baptists were frequently whipped, beaten, arrested, fined, and imprisoned, sometimes on bread and water. Madison, complaining to a friend about "that diabolical, hell-conceived persecution that rages," wrote in 1774 that "there are at this time five or six well meaning men in close jail for publishing their statements, which in the main are very orthodox," but which varied somewhat from the accepted doctrines of the established Anglican Church. In one Massachusetts town alone, eighteen dissenters were in jail for refusing to pay ministerial rates in support of the established worship.

In Philadelphia the Continental Congress began its operations in 1775 by adopting a resolution calling for prayer at the beginning of each session and designating an Episcopalian clergyman to act as its chaplain. This proclamation and other state papers not only were replete with references to religion, but expressed an unabashed adherence to Protestantism. The Congress legislated upon such subjects as morality, sin, repentance, penance, divine service, fasting, prayer, reformation, mourning, public worship, funerals, chaplains, true religion, and Thanksgiving.

Barely a decade later, Virginia in 1786 defeated a bill that would have required all to contribute to the support of some religion, and instead enacted Jefferson's great Statute for Religious Liberty, which sought forever to secure the "natural right" that "no man shall be compelled to frequent or support any religious worship, place or ministry whatever." The Constitutional Convention met for four months without the recitation of a single prayer. After the Convention had been in session for a month, the octogenarian Franklin, who in earlier years had been a Deist, moved "that hereforth prayers imploring the assistance of Heaven, and its blessings on our deliberations, be held in this Assembly every morning before we proceed to business, and that one or more of the Clergy of this City be requested to officiate in that service." The motion was received politely though not without embarrassment. "After several unsuccessful attempts for silently postponing the matter by adjourning," the adjournment was at length carried without any vote on the motion.

What perhaps most clearly expresses the change that occurred in less than a dozen years is the treatment of God in the Declaration of Independence and in the Constitution. The former short document contains no less than four references to the Deity; the latter, many times longer, contains not a single one. Indeed, the only reference to religion in the Constitution is the negative one prohibiting religious tests for public office.

This change in the conception of the relationship of religion and state was so rapid it can fairly be called revolutionary. The revolution culminated in 1791 with the adoption of the First Amendment ban on laws respecting an establishment of religion or prohibiting its free exercise. This Amendment embodied an experiment, unique in the history of civilization. The experiment rested upon the principle that government has no power to legislate in the field of religion, either by restricting its free exercise or providing for its support.

The launching of the American experiment cannot be attributed to any single event or cause. Practical considerations were undoubtedly of great significance. These included the enactment in 1689 of the English Act of Toleration, which conferred freedom of worship upon dissenting Protestants and which influenced colonial policy in America; the rise of commerce; the exigencies of the Revolutionary War, which required the cooperation of dissenters and Catholics; the expanding frontier; and, above all, the large variety of sects that settled along the Atlantic seacoast. Voltaire stated:

" If there were one religion in England, its despotism would be terrible; if there were only two, they would destroy each other; but there are thirty, and therefore they live in peace and happiness." Madison added: " Security for civil rights must be the same as that for religious rights; it consists in the one case in a multiplicity of interests and the other in a multiplicity of sects."

Important as these practical considerations were, it would be a complete misreading of American history if they were to be considered the sole reason for the separation of religion and government. Ideological considerations were at least equally important. The American experiment rests as much on the social contract as it does upon the mutual suspicions and rivalries of Anglicans, Congregationalists, and Presbyterians. With the exception of a relatively small minority who vainly sought to preserve their particular moribund established church — Congregationalist in New England, Anglican in the South — the generation that adopted the Constitution and the First Amendment was committed to the proposition that any power over religion was excluded from the powers delegated to the political state. The elevation of this concept into a constitutional principle was the achievement chiefly of two disparate and almost antagonistic forces that vied for the mind and soul of the new republic — a deeply religious, evangelical, and pietist force led by such devout Christians as Jonathan Edwards, George Whitefield, and Isaac Backus, and a skeptical anti-clerical force led by Jefferson and Tom Paine.

These religionists and rationalists were both motivated by an uncompromising enmity to established religion, Anglican or Congregationalist; but their ideological meeting place was the principle that religion was beyond the delegated jurisdiction of political society. They arrived at this meeting place from different directions. To the religionists, the source of all temporal power was Christ, and he had seen fit not to delegate power over religion to temporal governments. To these men, the relationship of state and church was governed by the text: " Render unto Caesar the things which are Caesar's and unto God the things that are God's." To the rationalists, the source of temporal power was the " people in nature," who had not seen fit to delegate power over religion to the governments instituted among men. The text of these men was the social contract.

It is not too much to say that when the men of Philadelphia met in 1787 to frame a constitution, the overwhelming majority of Americans accepted the proposition that religion was a personal, non-political matter, and concurred in Paine's statement in *Common Sense*: "As to religion, I hold it to be the indispensable duty of government to protect all conscientious professors thereof; and I know of no other business which government hath to do therewith." The concept that it is the duty of government to protect conscientious observers of religion is expressed in the First Amendment ban on laws prohibiting the free exercise of religion; the concept that government has no other business with religion is expressed in the ban on laws respecting an establishment of religion.

THE MEANING OF SEPARATION

Insistence upon the ideological basis of the "no establishment" clause is not merely a matter of academic history; it has real consequence in arriving at the true meaning of the clause. If the conceptual basis of the Amendment was the inherent lack of power in government to intervene in religious affairs, then the Amendment, as Jefferson said, erects "a wall of separation between church and state." It means that neither a State nor the Federal government can set up a church. Neither can pass laws which aid one religion, aid all religions, or prefer one religion over another. Neither can force or influence a person to go to or remain away from church against his will, or force him to profess a belief or disbelief in any religion. It means that no person can constitutionally be punished for entertaining or professing religious beliefs or disbeliefs, for church attendance or non-attendance. It means that no tax in any amount, large or small, may be levied to support any religious activities or institutions, whatever they may be called, or whatever form they may adopt to teach or practice religion. It means that neither a State nor the Federal government may, openly or secretly, participate in the affairs of any religious organizations or groups, and vice versa. It means, in short, not only that government must be neutral as among competing religious sects, but that it must be neutral as between religious belief and disbelief.

That, said the Supreme Court in the Everson case and again in the McCollum case, is what the First Amendment means. This in-

terpretation of the Amendment, however, has in the past several years been severely criticized by a large number of writers, both lawyers and non-lawyers. These writers deny that the Amendment was based on any ideological concept, or at least on an ideological concept that government is without inherent capacity to concern itself with religious affairs. According to these writers the Amendment was no more than a practical solution to a practical problem.

There were, these writers say, a large number of religious sects in 1791. These sects had no objection to an established church if their own church were the favored one. But each feared that, if establishment of religion by the new government were permitted, some religion or church other than its own might be established and might become the official religion of the government. So, like the woman who would rather have Solomon slay the babe than give it to her rival, they agreed that no church should have the greatly desired treasure, and therefore incorporated into the Bill of Rights a prohibition against the establishment of any particular religion.

That, according to the advocates of this view, is what the fathers of the First Amendment intended; that and no more. They intended that no church or religion should be preferred over other religions; but they did not intend that the government should completely separate itself from religion, or be godless or secular. Since the only evil they sought to avoid was the evil of favoritism, then it follows that if the government extends its favor impartially and equally among all religions it is violating neither the word nor the spirit — neither the text nor the purpose — of the First Amendment.

The practical consequences of this divergence of views on the meaning of the "no establishment" clause are great, as will shortly become apparent in the discussion of religion in public education and governmental aid to religious education. Much has been written by both sides of this controversy, and it would serve little purpose to extend the argument to these pages. For our purposes it is sufficient to indicate that, notwithstanding some ambiguous language in the majority opinion in the Zorach case, it is probable that the Court still adheres to the broad interpretation of the Amendment announced in its Everson and McCollum decisions.

One point, however, should be added. In the first chapter it was pointed out that the omission of a bill of rights from the original Constitution was defended by Hamilton on the ground, among others, that the impossibility of articulating an absolute absence of power would result in an incomplete prohibition giving rise to a false implication of an intent to confer some power. The controversy around the " no establishment " clause illustrates this vividly. If there were no such clause it would be difficult to argue that the government could aid all religions non-preferentially, since it is generally conceded that no power was delegated to the Federal government to intervene at all in religious affairs. Since, however, the ban of the First Amendment was directed against " an establishment of religion," it is argued that it was merely intended to bar the establishment of a particular sect — allowing the Government to intervene in religious affairs and grant financial and other aid to churches so long as it does not " establish " one particular church. Hamilton might well echo Hamlet's " O my prophetic soul! "

SEPARATION AND FREEDOM

The First Amendment provides that " Congress shall make no law respecting an establishment of religion, or prohibiting the free exercise thereof." What is the relationship between these two provisions? Here, too, there has been a good deal of difference among constitutional students and spokesmen for religious groups. One view, generally propounded by those who interpret the Amendment as barring only preferential aid to religion, is that the " no establishment " clause is the means and the " free exercise " clause is the end. According to this view the fathers of the Bill of Rights were concerned with ensuring freedom of worship. To ensure this they prohibited established churches because experience had shown that the establishment of a particular religion is likely to result in impairing the freedom of worship of other religions. According to this view a strict separation of church and state may occasionally if not frequently result in an impairment of freedom of religion. In such a situation the means must yield to the end, and separation must be compromised to keep freedom intact.

An example frequently given of this claimed conflict between separation and freedom is the ban on use of tax-raised funds to support parochial schools. Many Catholic parents, it is argued, are required by their religious convictions to send their children to parochial schools. These schools, receiving no support from the state, cannot operate without charging tuition, which many Catholic parents are unable to pay. The result is that, even if separation of church and state requires that tax-raised funds not be used to support religious education (which these advocates deny where the support is non-preferential), still adherence to the principle results in impairment of the religious freedom of many Catholic parents. Therefore, it is urged, separation (the means) should yield to freedom (the end), and public funds should be used to support parochial schools.

The opposing view finds no basic conflict between separation and freedom. On the contrary, it sees them as two sides of a single coin. Freedom requires separation, and separation ensures freedom. In the case of public funds for parochial schools, this view argues that to compel a Protestant to support Catholic religious teaching or a Catholic to support Jewish religious teaching may violate his religious convictions; and therefore the ban on such use of tax-raised funds promotes rather than impairs freedom of religion. Moreover, this view finds nothing in the First Amendment to indicate that the " free exercise " clause was intended to be superior to the " no establishment " clause, any more than there is anything in the Amendment to indicate an intent that the latter should be superior to the former.

While the Supreme Court has not expressly said so, the tenor of its opinions indicates that it does not recognize a conflict between freedom and separation but considers them as two aspects of a unitary principle. The first decision of the Supreme Court to consider the meaning of the First Amendment in the field of religion was *Reynolds* v. *United States,* a decision in 1878 that held that polygamy could constitutionally be outlawed even though Mormons practiced it from religious conviction. Although this was clearly a " free exercise " case, the Court asserted that the purpose of the Amendment was to erect a wall of separation between church and state, thus clearly indicating its acceptance of the " no establishment " and " free exercise " provisions as two parts of the same principle. In one of the most recent cases, *Kedroff* v. *St. Nicholas Cathedral,* which will be discussed shortly, the majority of the Court again used separation and freedom as interchangeable concepts. In between these two cases, the Everson and McCollum decisions likewise reflect a oneness of separation and freedom.

THE CONSEQUENCES OF SEPARATION

Despite the basic oneness of separation and freedom, it is convenient to discuss them separately here. In what arenas of American life does the principle of separation of church and state play a significant role? What are the practical implications and consequences of the separation of church and state?

The answer to the first question is fairly easy. The major arenas wherein the separation principle has substantial consequences and implications are: (1) state involvement in church affairs; (2) religion in public education; and (3) state aid to religious institutions and religious education.

The answer to the second question is much more difficult. It depends on how separation is interpreted. If the First Amendment is construed to ban no more than a preferential establishment of one particular church, the implications and consequences will obviously be much more limited than if the broader interpretation is accorded to the Amendment. Indeed, since it is far beyond the realm of probability that the Federal government or even any State would today establish a particular church as the official church to the exclusion of all others, it would seem that under the narrow interpretation there are no practical consequences of separation. This, of course, is not so — because the Court has refused to accord the First Amendment that narrow interpretation. On the contrary, the Court has given it the broad and liberal interpretation reflecting the ideological considerations on which the Amendment was founded.

STATE INVOLVEMENT IN CHURCH AFFAIRS

Neither a State nor the Federal government, said the Supreme Court, may, under the First Amendment, openly or secretly participate in the affairs of any religious organization or group. The fathers of the Bill of Rights were fully familiar with the long history of governmental involvement in church affairs, and they wanted none of it. They knew that the inevitable effect of such involvement was to corrupt and degrade the church and to restrict its religious freedom. In the very year that the First Amendment was adopted, John Leland,

Baptist leader in Virginia, wrote a tract entitled *Rights of Conscience and therefore Religious Opinions not cognizable by law,* in which he stated that " government has no more to do with religious opinions than it has with the principles of mathematics."

This analogy epitomizes the distinction between a totalitarian and a democratic state. A totalitarian state has no hesitation in entering the field of science and legislating on what is truth and what is falsehood. The Soviet government found no difficulty in decreeing that Lysenko's theories are truth and that acquired traits are hereditable. The Nazi government had no hesitation in decreeing as truth doctrines of racial superiority and inferiority. Neither would presumably hesitate to decree what is true and what is false in mathematics. And, were both not committed to the eradication of religion, neither would hesitate to decree which faith is true and which faith is false.

In a constitutional democracy such as the United States, the state acknowledges its lack of competence to pass judgment upon conflicting scientific theories. It cannot decree that acquired traits are hereditable or that they are not hereditable. It cannot even decree that two and two are four. It cannot decree that one faith is true and another false; or even that God exists or does not exist.

The incapacity of government to intervene in church affairs and particularly to adjudicate between conflicting claims to religious truth permeates the Supreme Court decisions in this area. For example, during the Civil War there was a deep schism in the Presbyterian Church following a declaration by its General Assembly that slavery was sinful. The Southern synods separated themselves from the General Assembly, asserting that its declaration was erroneous and heretical. In the border States the schism was re-enacted in individual congregations, each group claiming that it represented true Presbyterianism and was therefore legally entitled to possession of church property and the assets of the particular congregation. When one of these disputes reached the Supreme Court, it held in the landmark case of *Watson* v. *Jones* that under the " no establishment " clause the Federal courts had no competency to adjudicate which of the two contesting factions represented the true Presbyterian Church. The courts' inquiry could go no further than to determine what is the highest ecclesiastical tribunal of the particular denomination. Having identified that tribunal, the courts are bound by its decision as to which faction represents the true faith and will award the temporal assets to that faction.

Watson v. *Jones* concerned attempted intervention by a lower Federal court in the internal affairs of a church. The Russian Orthodox Church case, *Kedroff* v. *St. Nicholas Cathedral*, which also grew out of a civil war, concerned attempted intervention by a State legislature in the internal affairs of a church. After the Bolshevik Revolution in Russia, most of the Russian Orthodox churchmen in the United States, asserting that the Moscow patriarchate was under the domination of the Soviet state, declared themselves independent of the patriarchate in respect to the administration of church affairs in America. They established the "Russian Church in America" to care for the faithful until such time as the patriarchate should regain full freedom of action and thus resume its rightful status as supreme authority of the Russian Orthodox religion.

A minority of churchmen in the United States retained their allegiance to the patriarchate, and the dispute between the two factions gave rise to more than a quarter-century of court litigation, which is still going on. In New York the State legislature sought to resolve the controversy by enacting a statute that the Russian Church in America was the true Russian Orthodox Church and therefore entitled to obtain possession of St. Nicholas Cathedral, the seat of the Church in New York City, from the Metropolitan Benjamin, who had been designated by the Moscow patriarchate as Archbishop of North America.

When the case reached the United States Supreme Court, the Court held the statute unconstitutional. A State, no less than the Federal government, may not enact a law impairing the separation of church and state or infringing upon religious freedom. Separation of church and state and religious freedom mean that government has no capacity to intervene in ecclesiastical controversies or to determine which faith is true and which is false or which faction in a church schism represents the true faith and which is heretical. Under the Constitution such determinations can be made only by ecclesiastical tribunals, and the determination of the highest ecclesiastical authority of the particular religion (in this case the Moscow patriarchate) must be accepted by secular government.

The extent to which the Supreme Court has gone in holding that neither the Federal nor a State government or any of their agencies can decide what is true and what is false in religion is illustrated by *Ballard* v. *United States.* The Ballards, organizers of the "I Am" movement, were indicted for using the mails to defraud. The indictment charged that the Ballards had represented that they had been in personal communication with Jesus Christ, who had shaken hands with them, dictated to them the teachings of the "I Am" movement from heaven, and appointed them as divine messengers to spread the new faith. The indictment charged further that these representations were false and were made solely to extract dollars from the credulous.

The Ballards were convicted of fraud by a Federal court jury. When they appealed to the Supreme Court, that Court held that under the constitutional principles of the separation of church and state and religious freedom, neither a jury nor any other organ of government has the power or competence to pass on whether certain alleged religious experiences actually occurred. The jury could no more constitutionally determine that the Ballards did not shake hands with Jesus than they could determine the truth or falsity of any of the miracles of the New Testament, or the divinity of Christ, or life after death, or the efficacy of prayer. The fact that the religious views expressed by the Ballards might seem incredible if not preposterous to most persons is of no moment. To the non-believer, the miracles of the Bible are no less incredible or preposterous, and under our Constitution the law cannot decide between the credible and incredible in the field of religion. Our law knows no heresy and is committed to the support of no dogma, credible or incredible.

RELIGION AND PUBLIC EDUCATION

In probably no area has the principle of separation of church and state been subject to a more severe test than in the area of public education. Our public schools are organs of our government, controlled by the government (Federal, State, or municipal), and financed by it out of funds raised through the compulsory taxation of all. Does this mean, therefore, that our public schools must be godless? Does separation of church and state mean that the public schools may not teach children that there is a God who should be worshiped and who rewards good and punishes evil?

One thing would appear fairly clear and is generally not controverted. If our government knows no heresy and is committed to the support of no dogma, it is clear that our public or government schools may not constitutionally select one faith or dogma and teach it to the children as the true faith or dogma. They may not, for example, teach the children that immersion at adulthood is the only true method of baptism; or that Jesus decreed only two sacraments; or that the bread and wine in the eucharist is (or is not) the body and blood of Christ. Constitutional authorities would go even further and would probably agree that the public schools may not teach as a historical truth that Jesus was divine and the son of God, even if it should be shown that the majority of Americans believe that to be so, for government may not support even orthodox religious dogma.

If the public schools must be Christless, must they also be godless? Are there not some fundamental principles acceptable to all faiths — such as the existence of God and the divine origin and truth of the Scriptures — that may be taught in the schools? Or, to take another variant, may not the schools open their doors to all faiths, teaching Protestantism to Protestant children, Catholicism to Catholic children, and Judaism to Jewish children?

The answer depends on how we interpret the First Amendment. If we interpret the Amendment as ensuring merely that no one sect shall receive favored treatment or be preferred over other sects, then a system of religious instruction in the public schools that favors no sect but accords equal treatment to all is perfectly acceptable. If, on the other hand, the Amendment is interpreted to require not merely neutrality among beliefs but also neutrality between belief and disbelief, it is unconstitutional for the public schools to indoctrinate children even in the faiths of their fathers.

And that is what, in 1948, the Supreme Court held in *People ex rel. McCollum* v. *Board of Education,* the famous McCollum case. For, as we have seen, the Court is committed to the broad interpretation of the Amendment. The Court, therefore, had no choice (unless it were to abandon the broad interpretation) when Mrs. Vashti McCollum, rationalist, humanist, and non-believer, brought suit to declare invalid the Champaign, Illinois, system of religious instruction under which Protestant, Catholic, and Jewish religious teachers entered the public schools to teach their respective faiths to the children. The public-school system, said the Court, is an agency of the state and as such may not involve itself in church affairs, including religious instruction, even if it claims to treat all faiths equally.

What happened after the McCollum decision illustrates vividly what was indicated in the previous chapter — that the Court's civil-liberties decisions cannot be far in advance of the articulate opinion of the community. The McCollum decision was announced when the nation was on the threshold or in the early stages of a period of religious revival. Periods of great fear drive men toward religion, and the steadily advancing threat of atomic destruction made the mid-century a period of great fear. Religion, moreover, had become a staunch ally of nationalism, for in the eyes of many the major difference between Americanism and Communism was acceptance or rejection of God.

It was thus scarcely surprising that the McCollum decision, which in effect held that the public schools must be not only non-sectarian but secular or godless, should evoke a storm of acrimonious criticism. Even the nation's highest law-enforcement officer, the Attorney General, publicly criticized the decision as a distortion of the meaning of the First Amendment. While there were many who hailed the decision for throwing the mantle of constitutional protection over the secularity of our public educational system, their voices were drowned in the strident chorus of disapproval.

When, four years later, the involvement of the public-school system in religious instruction again came before the Supreme Court in *Zorach* v. *Clauson,* it was almost inevitable that the logic of the McCollum decision would not be extended to outlaw the New York City system of released time for religious education which was in issue in the Zorach case. The difference between the Champaign and New York systems was that in the former the public-school authorities were deeply involved in the religious-education program; not only was the instruction given within the public-school buildings during school hours, but the school authorities undertook a general supervision of the program. In New York, on the other hand, public-school involvement was minimal. All the school authorities did, according to the Court, was to release from their regular secular studies, for one hour a week, those children who without urging or pressure by the school authorities wished to partake of religious instruction in churches or church schools off the public-school premises. The school authorities assumed no further responsibility in respect to the program.

This, said the majority of the Court, is distinguishable from the Champaign program. Here all that is involved is no more than an adjustment of the public-school schedule to accommodate the religious needs of the children. While the principle of the McCollum case — that government may not finance religious groups or undertake religious instruction or blend secular and sectarian education — was reaffirmed, it was not to be extended to the present situation.

The upshot of the McCollum and Zorach decisions is that under our Constitution public education must be secular education. Within a secular public-school system, however, adjustments may be made to provide time for religious education for those children who desire it, provided that the school authorities take a neutral position as to attendance or non-attendance, not only refraining from seeking to influence the children to enroll for the religious instruction, but assuming no responsibility for the manner in which the program is carried on.

STATE AID TO RELIGIOUS TRAINING

Government, said the Supreme Court in the Zorach case, may not finance religious education; public funds, like public schools, must be secular. Under the broad interpretation of the First Amendment it is immaterial whether all religious education is aided with tax-raised funds or one or more particular faiths are selected to be the exclusive beneficiaries of the taxing power. In either event the Constitution forbids state aid.

While the state may not furnish direct financial aid to churches or for religious education, churches or church schools may be the indirect beneficiaries of legislation enacted for the benefit of children. In *Cochran* v. *Louisiana State Board,* the Supreme Court ruled in 1930 that a State program for furnishing secular textbooks for schoolchildren could constitutionally include children attending parochial or church schools even if the church authorities would otherwise have to purchase the books themselves. The intended beneficiaries of the program, the Court held, were the children, and the fact that the churches were incidentally or indirectly benefited by being relieved of the duty of themselves paying for the books did not make the program unconstitutional. The program would, of course, have been unconstitutional if the State had paid for *religious* textbooks for parochial-school children, since a State may finance only secular and not religious education.

The reasoning of this case was followed in 1947 in *People ex rel. Everson* v. *Board of Education,* the famous parochial-school bus case. There the Court, in a 5-to-4 decision, held that a State could constitutionally finance bus transportation of children to parochial as well as public schools. The purpose of the program, said the Court, was to protect children from traffic hazards and the dangers of the road. Such a program is constitutional; it does not become unconstitutional merely because an incidental benefit is conferred upon churches by reason of the fact that if the State did not pay for the transportation the churches might have to (or lose some of their children to the public schools).

The Everson case illustrates the Court's responsibility of arbitrating between competing values in a democratic society. On one side was the value of separation of church and state; on the other was the value of child welfare. In our society preservation of the health and welfare of children is, as we shall shortly see, one of the highest of communal values and, the majority of the Court held, will not be judicially restrained even if the consequence is some impairment of the principle of the separation of church and state through incidental benefits to churches out of tax-raised funds.

THE FREE EXERCISE OF RELIGION

The importance attributed to religious freedom in the minds of the fathers of our Bill of Rights is manifested by its position as the first of the rights, preceding speech, press, assembly, petition, and all the other rights. The Supreme Court has been faithful to the fathers' estimation of the importance of religious liberty. It has given a broad and liberal interpretation to the " free exercise " clause of the First Amendment, just as it has given a broad and liberal interpretation to the " no establishment " clause. The " free exercise " of religion means far more than freedom of worship. In the Russian

Orthodox Church case the Court held that the right of a church to select its own clergy and to administer its internal affairs is protected by the " free exercise " clause even when there is no governmental interference with the form or content of the worship. In other decisions the Court has held that the " free exercise " of religion encompasses, among others, freedom to distribute and even sell religious literature, to hold religious meetings in streets and parks, to raise one's children in one's own faith, and to abstain from saluting or pledging allegiance to the nation's flag.

But freedom of religion, high as it is in the democratic scale of values, is not — nor can it be — absolute. Free belief, perhaps, but not the free exercise of religion. A man may constitutionally believe that God demands human sacrifice, but he does not have a constitutional right to exercise his belief, i.e., put it into practice. The state may step in to prevent human sacrifice — but not because God really does not want human sacrifice; under the principle of separation of church and state, as we have seen, the state has no competence to make such a determination. Nor is the state's power to intervene based on the ground that one has no right to exercise his religion at the expense of another; the result would be the same if the sacrificial victim were the believer himself. There can be no doubt, the Supreme Court said in the Reynolds case, that if a wife religiously believed it was her duty to burn herself upon the funeral pyre of her dead husband, it would be within the power of civil government to prevent her putting this belief into practice.

The question is one of weighing competing values. Our democratic society undoubtedly deems it important that a citizen should be free to exercise his religion in the manner his conscience dictates. But our society deems it more important that human life be preserved, even against the will of the possessor. This is the basic problem in religious-freedom cases, as indeed it is in all civil-liberties cases: is it more important to our society to restrain the particular civil liberty or to permit its free exercise?

This is not stated in the Bill of Rights. The First Amendment ban on laws prohibiting the free exercise of religion contains no exception; it does not exempt laws necessary to preserve human life or to safeguard some other social interest deemed more important than the free exercise of religion. Yet there can be no doubt that this is implicit in the Amendment and was intended by its framers; else we would have not society but anarchy. Social living means that individual desires, regardless of their motivation, will be curbed in the interests of the community, and society under law means that government has the power to compel such curbing.

This does not mean that the state may outlaw any religious action it considers a threat to a more important social interest. The fact that the Constitution does not prohibit the state from forbidding human sacrifice does not mean that the state may forbid the reading of Genesis because some suggestible reader might be impelled to emulate Abraham in offering his son upon an altar of fire. The threat to the paramount social interest must be probable and imminent in order to warrant state intervention. This is the well-known "clear and present danger" test which will be discussed in more detail in our next chapter. Here it is sufficient to note that while the "clear and present danger" has lost (perhaps only temporarily) much of its significance in political-liberty cases, its vitality remains substantially unimpaired in religious-liberty cases. The basic issue in the religious-liberty cases considered in the remainder of this chapter is whether the interest the government seeks to protect by restraint on the free exercise of religion is more important to democratic society than the free exercise of religion; and, if so, whether the threat to that paramount interest is sufficiently clear and immediate to justify the restraint.

NATIONAL DEFENSE AND SECURITY

Few interests of government are deemed to be of equal importance — and probably none of greater importance — than defense against foreign enemies. The supremacy of national defense over the free exercise of religion has been recognized in numerous Supreme Court decisions. This supremacy is not required by any express language in the Constitution. The Preamble lists provision for the common defense as the fourth of the six purposes for which the Constitution was established; there is no indication of its intended primacy, nor of its superiority over the purpose of securing the blessings of liberty. The powers to declare war and maintain armed forces are placed well down in the long list of powers conferred upon Congress in Article I of the Constitution. The First Amendment expresses no limitation upon the ban on laws prohibiting the free exercise of religion. It is, therefore, not illogical to suggest that the power to raise armies and wage war must be effectuated within the limitations of the "free exercise" provision. At least, there is nothing to show that the fathers of the Bill of Rights intended the free exercise of religion to be sacrificed in the interests of the nation's defense, any more than they intended the national defense to be sacrificed for the free exercise of religion.

The discussion is academic. No nation will allow individual liberties to stand in the way of the successful prosecution of a war. If the Constitution had expressly made exercise of the nation's war power subject to the free exercise of religion, the nation would undoubtedly disregard the limitation — just as Lincoln disregarded Chief Justice Taney's order to deliver a prisoner pursuant to a writ of habeas corpus to which the Chief Justice held the prisoner constitutionally entitled. Lincoln justified his action on the ground that although "life and limb must be protected, yet often a limb must be amputated to save a life; but a life is never wisely given to save a limb."

The Supreme Court has not repeated Taney's improvidence. It has prudently construed religious liberty to be an expendable limb where the survival of the life of the nation depends upon the successful prosecution of war. It has championed religious liberty (indeed all liberties) against the war power only where assertion of the liberty did not embarrass the effective exercise of the war power; where there is a real conflict between the war powers and religious liberty, the latter must yield to the former.

The most obvious illustration is compulsory military service in wartime. The number of persons of military age whose religious convictions preclude participation in armed conflict is relatively small. It would not seriously embarrass the nation's ability to wage war if these persons were not compelled to serve against their religious beliefs. This is not speculation; Congress has exempted conscientious objectors from military service in two world wars, and has not found the consequences sufficiently detrimental to justify elimination or even modification of the exemption. But the decision must be made by Congress, not by the Supreme Court. If in a future war Congress should find that national safety would be jeopardized by exempting religious objectors, the Court would not interfere with its judgment. The Court has often held that the exemption from military service accorded to religious objectors is a matter of Congressional grace, subject to withdrawal or modification by Congress at its will, and not of constitutional right.

The Court has given great weight — perhaps too great weight — to the opinion of government on whether the effective prosecution of war really necessitates a particular infringement of religious liberty. The Court has held that compulsory military service, notwithstanding religious objection, is constitutionally permissible in peace as well as in war. In 1945 it held, in the case of *In re Summers,* that the power to compel military service even by religious objectors is possessed not only by Congress but also by the States, which have only secondary responsibility for national defense. About a decade earlier, in *Hamilton* v. *Regents of the University of California,* the Court held that a number of young members of the Epsworth League could constitutionally be expelled from a State college for refusing to enroll in the required military-training course, even though, according to the students, the discipline and tenets of the Methodist Church to which they belonged forbade participation in military training. In the Summers case the Court held that the State of Illinois could refuse to license as a lawyer a conscientious objector who was otherwise fully qualified to practice law.

Where considerations of national loyalty and unity have motivated restraints upon the free exercise of religion, the Court has been less willing to yield to the judgment of the government than where direct military considerations are involved. The several flag-salute cases of the late 1930's and early 1940's illustrate dramatically that the Court will not always accept the opinion of a governmental agency that national security requires a certain restriction upon individual liberty. They illustrate also how the Court's decisions reflect the enlightened conscience of the community.

The cases arose out of the refusal of Jehovah's Witnesses children in the public schools to participate in the usual assembly ceremony of saluting the flag and pledging allegiance to it. Their refusal was based upon the belief that saluting the flag would constitute an act of idolatry in violation of the Second Commandment. In most schools sensible authorities worked out some practical solution of the difficulty; but in a number the authorities insisted that the children comply, and upon their refusal expelled them from the school system.

The Jehovah's Witnesses organization brought many legal suits to prevent expulsion or to compel readmittance of the children. Beginning in 1937, they appealed to the Supreme Court from unsuccessful suits in lower courts. In each case the Court dismissed their appeal on the basis of the University of California military-training decision. In 1940 the Court finally agreed to consider their appeal but then handed down a decision — from which only Justice (later Chief Justice) Stone dissented — rejecting their claims. The Court held that " national unity is the basis of national security " and that the States have the constitutional power to take such measures as they deem appropriate to achieve national unity. If State authorities decide that the way to achieve national unity is to have all children participate in a symbolic act of unity, such as saluting or pledging allegiance to the flag, then the Court will not interfere with their judgment even if it disagrees with them as to the effectiveness of the means chosen by them to accomplish their purpose.

The announcement of this decision, *Minersville School District* v. *Gobitis,* loosed upon the Jehovah's Witnesses throughout the country a torrent of abuse, physical as well as verbal. In a period of only one week hundreds of physical attacks upon Jehovah's Witnesses were reported to the Federal Department of Justice, and hundreds more probably went unreported. Their meeting places were burned, their meetings dispersed, and their leaders driven out of town. In one town the chief of police and the deputy sheriff forced a group of Jehovah's Witnesses to drink large doses of castor oil and then paraded them through the streets tied together with police-department rope. In another, a local judge warned a group of Witnesses that unless they compelled their children to salute the flag he would take the children away from them and place them in an institution where they would be taught to understand what Americanism really is.

These incidents shocked the American conscience. The Court's decision that had evoked them was subjected to almost unanimous adverse criticism among enlightened leaders of community opinion. The dissatisfaction of responsible Americans with the Court's decision was evidenced by the fact that one of the most nationalistic of all organizations, the American Legion, sponsored a bill enacted by

Congress in 1942 providing that "civilians will show full respect to the flag when the pledge is given by merely standing at attention, men removing the headdress" — conduct which Jehovah's Witnesses always expressed their willingness to perform. When the controversy again came before the Supreme Court in 1943 in a suit by Witness Walter Barnette to restrain the West Virginia State Board of Education from enforcing a compulsory flag-salute regulation, the outcome was foreordained.

In the Barnette case the Court expressly overruled the Gobitis decision and held that the First Amendment prohibited governmental agencies from using compulsion to achieve national unity through participation in a symbolic ceremony. The Bill of Rights permits public officials to foster national unity only by persuasion and example. "If there is any fixed star in our constitutional constellation," the Court's eloquent opinion concluded, "it is that no official, high or petty, can prescribe what shall be orthodox in politics, nationalism, religion, or other matters of opinion, or force citizens to confess by word or act their faith therein."

PUBLIC MORALS AND PUBLIC PEACE

It is rare that the courts are called upon to weigh the competing claims of religious freedom and preservation of the public morals. The problem did reach the Supreme Court several times during the last quarter of the nineteenth century as a result of the clash between the American moral standards, which view polygamous marital relations with revulsion, and the then dogmas of the Mormon Church, which considered such marriages not only permissible but obligatory. In these cases — the Reynolds case, *Davis* v. *Beason,* and others — the Court upheld as constitutional measures taken by the Federal government to eliminate polygamy among Mormons.

Bigamy and polygamy, said the Court, are crimes by the laws of all civilized and Christian countries. They tend to destroy the purity of the marriage relations, to disturb the peace of families, to degrade women and to debase men; few crimes are more pernicious to the best interests of society and receive more general or more deserved punishment. It was never intended or supposed, continued the Court, that the First Amendment could be evoked against legislation to punish acts inimical to the morals of society. Hence there can be no doubt, the Court held, that the practice or advocacy of plural marriages can constitutionally be punished notwithstanding the claim of religious freedom.

The clash of the competing claims of religious freedom and the preservation of the public peace has reached the Court much more frequently. Most, though not all, of such cases involved Jehovah's Witnesses and arose out of the aggressiveness of their missionary activities and the violence of their verbal attacks upon other religions, particularly Catholicism. Their refusal to salute the flag or to serve in the armed forces also contributed substantially to their unpopularity.

When the Witnesses swept down upon a community in a mass-conversion campaign, acrimonious and violent reactions were almost inevitable. In many instances the outraged citizenry took the law into their own hands and resorted to force. In others, the Witnesses were met by the legal arm of the community and were arrested for disturbing the peace, or for violating anti-peddling ordinances or laws against the use of sound trucks or traffic regulations or revenue laws. Often these cases reached the Supreme Court, and out of its decisions came much of the American constitutional law of religious liberty.

One case, *Cantwell* v. *Connecticut* (1940), arose out of the action of a Witness, Jesse Cantwell, who accosted two pedestrians upon the streets of New Haven, and with their permission played for them a record on a portable phonograph he carried with him. The record contained an attack upon organized religions generally and upon the Catholic religion in particular; the latter was stated to be an instrument of Satan that for fifteen hundred years had brought untold sorrow and suffering upon mankind by means of fraud and deception. No violence occurred, but Cantwell was arrested and convicted of inciting a breach of the peace.

Cantwell appealed all the way to the United States Supreme Court which reversed the conviction as an unconstitutional violation of his right to the free exercise of religion. While there can be no doubt, the Court said, that the state has the right to prevent breaches of the peace and to punish those who incite such breaches even out of religious considerations, the fact that a person resorts to exaggeration or vilification in his missionary endeavors and thereby arouses public animosity may not render him subject to punishment in the absence of a clear and present menace to public peace. In the case at issue there was no assault or threat of bodily harm, no truculent bearing, no intentional discourtesy, no personal abuse — and therefore no clear and present menace to the public peace.

In another case, *Kunz* v. *New York*, the Court held in 1951 that the City of New York could not deny a Baptist missionary, Carl Kunz, the right to preach in the public streets even though he engaged in scurrilous attacks on Catholics and Jews, charging that "the Catholic Church makes merchandise out of souls," that Catholicism is "a religion of the devil" and the Pope "the anti-Christ," and denouncing the Jews as "Christ-killers" who "should have been burnt in incinerators" as garbage. If such preachings actually incite to violence, the Court held, Kunz could be criminally prosecuted, but he could not in advance be denied the right to preach in the public streets.

While the right to preach upon the public streets is guaranteed by the First Amendment, it can hardly be disputed that the use of the streets as a thoroughfare is of primary importance and that the government's interest in preserving that purpose must be balanced against individuals' interest in using the streets as preaching places. In balancing these competing claims, the Supreme Court has reached the conclusion that, although all the streets in a municipality may not be closed to use for preaching, such use may be regulated in the interest of their primary purpose. Thus it is constitutional for a town to restrict religious meetings to particular streets or particular times, and to require religious groups to obtain permits for such use, so long as the municipality acts reasonably and the permits are not withheld because of disapproval of the content of the preachings or the reputation of the religious groups seeking them. And, as the Court held in *Fowler* v. *Rhode Island* (1953), if a municipality allows one group to use a particular street or park for a religious meeting it may not refuse to allow other groups to use it for the same purpose.

A municipality has an interest in keeping its streets clean and free of litter. It may not, however, said the Court in 1939 in the case of *Schneider* v. *Irvington*, protect this interest by preventing the distribution of religious handbills or other religious literature to pedestrians, even though they are likely to throw the handbills into the streets. (The fact that three years later the Court held in *Valen-*

tine v. *Chrestensen* that a municipality may forbid such distribution of *commercial* handbills indicates clearly the high esteem held by religious freedom.) Similarly a municipality's interest in protecting its residents from unwanted canvassers does not, the Court held in *Martin* v. *City of Struthers,* empower it to make it unlawful to ring doorbells for the purpose of distributing religious literature.

THE PUBLIC HEALTH AND THE PUBLIC WELFARE

Since the preservation of human life is obviously one of the most important interests of society — perhaps the most important — it is certain that religious convictions cannot be permitted to stand in the way. It is for this reason that religiously motivated suicide as well as homicide may constitutionally be restrained. It is for the same reason, the Court held in *Jacobson* v. *Massachusetts,* that all persons, regardless of religious objections, may be compelled to undergo vaccination in order to prevent the spread of serious communicable diseases. For the same reason, a State, the Court held in *Bunn* v. *North Carolina,* may prohibit snake-handling, even if it is part of a religious exercise, as it is in some Southern communities in the United States.

Where the lives of children are at stake, the state's interest is even greater. Adults might have the right to make martyrs of themselves, but the government will not allow them to make martyrs of little children too young to decide their own fate. For example, it is a dogma of Jehovah's Witnesses that blood transfusion is prohibited by the Biblical command against eating or drinking blood, and Witnesses have refused to allow transfusions for their children even when, according to medical opinion, the children's lives required it. In such cases, the courts have not hesitated to direct the medical authorities to give the transfusion notwithstanding the parents' refusal to consent; and in 1952 the Supreme Court, in *People ex rel. Wallace* v. *Labrenz,* refused to interfere with the State's judgment.

The state has an important interest not only in the people's survival but also in the people's health. While it probably may not compel a Christian Scientist to undergo medical treatment for an illness that is neither probably fatal nor communicable, it may fluoridate the public water supply to prevent or minimize tooth decay, even though the drinking of such water is forbidden by the teachings of Christian Science. So, too, the state may compel all persons to rest one day in seven, and may select the day upon which all shall rest. It is on this theory that compulsory Sunday observance or "blue laws" were upheld in *Soon Hing* v. *Crowley*, *Hennington* v. *Georgia*, and *Petit* v. *Minnesota*. According to the Court in *Friedman* v. *New York*, the fact that the origin of these laws was religious, and that the day chosen for uniform abstinence from labor is a day held sacred by Christians, does not alter the fact that the purpose of the laws today is not to promote religion but to preserve health.

The people's welfare is likewise an important interest which government may promote even though religious considerations occasionally interfere. For example, many communities have come to the conclusion that the people's welfare requires that no communal, business, or industrial buildings be permitted in areas where the people have their residences. Accordingly, it has been held by the Supreme Court in *Corporation of Presiding Bishop* v. *City of Porterville* that a municipality may constitutionally exclude churches along with other non-residential structures from areas zoned exclusively for residential purposes.

For the same reason, the church buildings and other assets of religious groups and the income of clergymen may be taxed to raise the income necessary to provide for the general welfare. As is well known, the Federal government and all the States by statute exempt churches and church property from taxation, but they do this as a matter of grace or privilege, not because of any constitutional restraint; there is nothing in the First Amendment that prevents Congress or State legislatures from subjecting religious property or income to the same taxes imposed on commercial property or income. What the Amendment does prohibit is the imposition of a tax on the practice of religion. A State may impose a license tax on the privilege of practicing law or medicine or plumbing, but (the Supreme Court held in *Murdock* v. *Pennsylvania*) it may not license preachers of religion or impose a tax on the right to preach religion, for that would be a law prohibiting the *free* exercise of religion.

When the welfare of children is at stake, the government's power is even broader. In 1944 the Supreme Court held in *Prince* v. *Massachusetts* that a State may enact child-labor laws and may enforce them against parents whose religious convictions impel them to permit their young children to engage in labor or even to sell religious publications on the public streets. The same considerations, the Court held in *Donner* v. *New York* (1951), permit a State to compel all parents to see to it that their children receive a basic secular education, even if their religious convictions preclude participation in secular education. A State may not, however, require all children to receive such secular education in public schools. Parents, said the Court in *Pierce* v. *Society of Sisters* in 1925, have a right to send their children to church or parochial schools so long as such schools provide the same basic secular education that is available in public schools.

CHAPTER 3. *Liberty of Speech and Silence*

THE FIRST AMENDMENT AND SEDITION

Man graduated from the animal kingdom when he learned to speak. Since then he has been speaking of many things and most of them have got him into all kinds of trouble, particularly with the authorities.

Man has spoken of God and/or the gods and his relationship to him and/or them, and this has got him in trouble with the authorities. Socrates spoke about the gods in a manner unpleasing to the Athenian authorities, and he drank hemlock. Anne Hutchinson spoke about salvation by grace, and she was banished to her death. Michael Servetus and Hugh Latimer and scores of others were burned at the stake because they spoke about God and his ways in a manner not approved by the authorities. William Thomas was hanged and quartered because he spoke about the failings of the Italian clergy in a way which offended Bloody Queen Mary.

Man has spoken about the physical world and his relation to it, and this too has got him into trouble with the authorities. Galileo spoke the " damnable heresy " that the earth revolved around the sun, and he got into trouble. He got off comparatively lightly (being required only to recite the seven penitential psalms once a week for three years) because he spoke words of recantation in a loud voice — adding the obstinate heresy, " Nevertheless it does move," in a murmur too low for the Holy Inquisitors to hear. Tom Scopes got into trouble with the authorities because he spoke about man being descended from monkeys or some similar heretical nonsense; but he too got off lightly because what he said had long ceased to be heretical or nonsense in the eyes of his jury — twentieth-century America.

Man has also spoken of love and poetry and art, and this too has got him into trouble with the authorities. Ovid was exiled from

Rome because he wrote some poems about the Art of Love in a manner deemed immoral by the Emperor Augustus. Ben Jonson was thrown into jail for writing a play that was derogatory to the Scots. Dmitri Shostakovich got into trouble with the Soviet authorities for speaking music heretically.

And man has spoken of the authorities and his relationship to them — and this threatens to get him into the most trouble of all. For today one can say pretty much what he wants in the field of religion or science or art without serious consequences. But one can still get into serious trouble for criticism of the political order. For practical purposes, the issue of freedom of speech today is largely the issue of freedom of political speech. The struggle for religious freedom has been won. So too has the struggle for freedom of artistic expression and freedom of scientific inquiry. It cannot, however, be said that the struggle for freedom of political expression has been successfully concluded. Of all our liberties, the liberty of political dissent is in the most precarious position. Full freedom of political expression yet remains to be won.

When the fathers of the Bill of Rights proclaimed in the First Amendment that "Congress shall make no law . . . abridging the freedom of speech or of the press" they were thinking primarily in terms of political speech. This guarantee of freedom of speech grew out of the struggle against the severities of the English law of sedition and seditious libel. Originally sedition was the equivalent of treason and was punishable by death. In the fifteenth century one could incur the death penalty for calling the king a fool or for making astrological predictions of the time of his death. By the seventeenth century seditious libel had achieved a distinct and lesser status as a crime, and it was no longer punishable as treason to say of King Charles I that he was unwise and no more fit to be king than was a simple shepherd. By the time the First Amendment was written into our Constitution the crime of seditious libel was clearly recognized in English law as "the intentional publication, without lawful excuse or justification, of written blame of any public man, or of the law, or of any institution established by law."

Contemporaneously with the struggle against the severities of punishment for sedition was the struggle against censorship of books and the press. This will be discussed in further detail in a later chapter. Here it is sufficient to note that by 1791 it was generally accepted in England that the press could not be censored in advance of publication, although the publisher could thereafter be punished for seditious libel. The status of the law of England as stated by Blackstone (an authority well known in the United States in 1791) was somewhat as follows:

Liberty of the press, essential as it is to the nature of a free state, consists in laying no previous restraints upon publications, but not in freedom from punishment for publishing what is criminal. Every person has an undoubted right to express publicly whatever sentiments he pleases, but if he publishes what is improper, mischievous, or illegal he must take the consequences. The punishment of dangerous and offensive writings, which, when published, are found by a fair and impartial jury to be of a pernicious tendency, is necessary for the preservation of peace and good order.

HAMILTONIAN AND JEFFERSONIAN VIEWS OF FREE SPEECH

This was the state of the English law at the time the Constitution was amended to prohibit laws abridging the freedom of speech. The First Amendment does not spell out what is intended by the term "freedom of speech." The Amendment speaks in terms of the absolute; it prohibits any law abridging freedom of speech. Yet the fathers of the Bill of Rights could not have intended that the right to speak should be absolute and subject to no punishment irrespective of the nature of the speech and its consequences. They could not have intended that a person who during wartime discloses to the enemy the positions, strengths, and planned movements of our armed forces should be immune from punishment.

If, then, the Amendment is not to be construed literally as conferring an absolute right to say anything, anywhere, anytime, how is it to be construed? There are some who contend that the fathers of the Bill of Rights meant to do no more than crystallize and formalize the English law as expressed by Blackstone. According to this view, the basic purpose of the Amendment was to guarantee the right not to be prevented in advance from saying whatever one wants to say — but this does not guarantee him any right to immunity from punishment after he has had his say. This does not mean that the government may make a crime of any utterance whatsoever; it may not, for example, make it a crime to campaign against a member of Congress running for re-election. Nevertheless, the government's discretion in what utterances should be made punishable is quite broad. If it reasonably finds that a particular type of speech may have, to use Blackstone's phrase, a "pernicious tendency," the government may make it punishable — although the government may not in advance prevent its publication.

This was the view of a number of the Federalist judges appointed by Washington upon the establishment of the republic. They held that the English common-law crime of seditious libel was part of the Federal law even though no statute by Congress made it a crime. They interpreted the freedom-of-speech guarantee of the First Amendment to mean only that Congress might not penalize utterances which were not then seditious under the English common law. Since common-law sedition then included criticism of the government even without any incitement to illegal action, it is clear that under this view the Amendment granted an extremely limited protection to free speech.

This was also the view taken by the Federalist Congress in 1798 when it sought to destroy the Republican opposition by enacting the Alien and Sedition Acts. The Alien Act empowered President Adams to imprison or deport aliens if he deemed such action necessary for public safety. The Sedition Act, which concerns us here, made it a criminal act, punishable by fines and imprisonment, to utter or publish false, scandalous, and malicious sentiments tending to bring the government of the United States or its officers into disrepute or to excite the hatred of the people. The Act, applied with vigor by the Federalist judges, resulted in fines and prison sentences not only for editors of anti-Federalist newspapers but even for bystanders at political meetings who were overheard to make contemptuous remarks against President Adams or others in the government.

The underlying philosophy of this approach to freedom of speech is simple. It is that people are inherently evil and must be restrained by their rulers, who by nature are and ought to be their superiors. The people, Hamilton said, is a beast, and it were better for him if he behaved as a beast, or as close to a beast as he could. Man can keep out of trouble if he does not speak at all. Unfortunately, the evolutionary process cannot be retraced and there is no practicable way to stop man from speaking at all. But if he must speak, he should speak as little as possible and limit his speech to beastly matters, i.e., food, drink, shelter, etc. He should avoid speaking of the government and other public matters, but if he speaks at all concerning his rulers he must make sure that he speaks nothing but good of them. Since the purpose of government is to protect the wealthy and wise from the predatory instincts of the people, it would be disastrous if the people were permitted to speak ill of the government.

This was the underlying philosophy of the English common law of sedition and of the Sedition Act of 1798. Hamilton and John Marshall, who concurred in this philosophy, were nevertheless too astute politically not to realize that its implementation through rigorous enforcement of the Sedition Act would not be accepted by a people who had only a short time before waged a bloody and successful revolution against a government that sought to implement that philosophy even less harshly than the Federalist judges. Accordingly they cautioned restraint; but in vain. The Federalist judges would not be restrained. The resentment against them, the Act, and the Federalist Party intensified to a degree bordering upon revolutionary fervor. It was probably the fortunate intervention of the election of 1800, enabling the people to throw the Federalists out of office, repeal the Alien and Sedition Acts, and destroy the Federalist Party through peaceful means, that prevented forceful defiance and armed resistance.

It is not surprising that such a philosophy should be abhorrent to the generation nurtured on the social contract and the romanticism of Rousseau. The Declaration of Independence had sprung from a diametrically opposite philosophy: from the philosophy that man was born good not evil; that government was established by the people in order to secure the people's inalienable rights; that government was therefore the servant, not the master, of the people; that government had to be watched carefully lest it usurp powers not conferred upon it by the social contract and thus become a tyranny and a despotism. Under such a philosophy, public discussion of public issues is not merely a right but a duty, and criticism of government and its officials is desirable so that they will keep within the bounds of their conferred powers.

These conflicting philosophies lead to conflicting approaches to political speech. Significantly, the classic expression of each approach was made by the leading advocate of each philosophy, Hamilton for the one and Jefferson for the other. Under the common-law-sedition or Federalist approach, political speech is looked upon with suspicion, and political speech critical of the government is *prima facie* wrong and can escape merited punishment only if it be justified. According to Hamilton, liberty of political expression "is the right to publish with impunity, truth with good motives, for justifiable ends though reflecting on government, magistracy, or individuals." In other words, to justify saying anything critical of the government and its officials, one must be able to prove that he has spoken only the truth, that his motives were good, and that his aims were acceptable. In effect this means little more than that constitutional liberty to speak means that one may say what one would most likely not be prevented or punished for saying were there no First Amendment.

The opposite approach assumes full liberty of expression as the norm and scrutinizes with suspicion any governmental restriction upon that liberty. It is governmental restriction upon speech, not speech critical of government, that is *prima facie* wrong and must be justified. This approach was expressed by Jefferson in his Virginia Statute for Religious Liberty, which, though addressed primarily to religious expression, articulates a philosophy intended to encompass discussion of all public issues. Said Jefferson:

> To suffer the civil magistrate to intrude his powers into the field of opinion, and to restrain the profession or propagation of principles on supposition of their ill tendency is a dangerous fallacy, which at once destroys all religious liberty, because he being of course judge of that tendency will make his opinions the rule of judgment, and approve or condemn the sentiments of others only as they shall square with or differ from his own; *it is time enough for the rightful purposes of civil government for its officers to interfere when principles break out into overt acts against peace and good order;* truth is great and will prevail if left to herself; she is the proper and sufficient antagonist to error and has nothing to fear from the conflict unless by human interposition disarmed of her natural weapons, free argument and debate. [Italics added.]

This approach is thus based upon the romantic faith in the inherent goodness and wisdom of the people. If truth and error are permitted to struggle without the interposition of force on one side or the other, truth will win out. The people, in short, can be trusted. It may be an oversimplification, yet it is not far from the truth to suggest that the extent to which the expression of political opinion has been allowed or restricted by the courts reflects the extent to which the courts have judged that the people can or cannot be trusted.

WHAT IS MEANT BY SPEECH?

Both the Hamiltonian and Jeffersonian approaches recognize the social interest in free speech. The Hamiltonian approach, by exempting from punishment truthful speech published with good motives for justifiable ends, implicitly recognizes that such speech serves a useful and beneficial social purpose. The Jeffersonian approach goes further and finds a useful and beneficial purpose in all speech since only by competition in the free and open market of ideas can truth be distinguished from falsehood and error. While the Jeffersonian view also considers speech as an inherent right of human beings, the exercise of which is essential to the individual's happiness, nevertheless it agrees that if such exercise were detrimental rather than beneficial to the public welfare, the state would have a right to restrain or suppress it.

Since the key to the issue of free speech is the communal interest in what is said, it follows that the First Amendment is concerned primarily not with the articulation of sound but with the expression of ideas or the communication of thoughts. The degree to which speech is protected by the Amendment is directly proportionate to the degree to which it constitutes communication of ideas. Not everything which is said is " speech " within the purview of the Amendment.

This is well illustrated by the 1942 case of *Chaplinsky* v. *New Hampshire*. A man named Chaplinsky, one of the Jehovah's Witnesses, while being brought to a police station in the town of Rochester, New Hampshire, after complaints about his tactics in distributing the sect's literature, was met by a city police official at whom Chaplinsky shouted: " You are a God-damned racketeer and a damned Fascist, and the whole government of Rochester are Fascists or agents of Fascists." Chaplinsky was prosecuted and convicted under a statute making it a crime to address " any offensive, derisive or annoying word " to any other person in a public place.

The conviction was sustained by the Supreme Court. It was not the purpose of the First Amendment, said the Court, to protect insulting or "fighting" words. Such utterances are no essential part of any exposition of ideas, and are of such slight social value in the quest for truth that any benefit that might be derived from them is clearly outweighed by the social interest in order and morality.

"Fighting words" are not "speech" as contemplated by the Amendment; or at best they are such a low grade of speech as to be easily expendable. Their motive is not to communicate ideas but to give vent to the emotions. Their purpose is not to convince the listener but to hurt him. They may properly be described as verbal blows.

In the same category is the lewd, the obscene, or the profane. To call someone by a dirty name in public is hardly an essential part of any exposition of ideas, and the social benefit from such a verbal act is negligible. In a similar, though not identical, category is the fraudulent and the libelous. In the "I Am" case, mentioned in the preceding chapter, the Court held that while the jury could not constitutionally determine whether or not the Ballards actually spoke with Jesus, the Ballards could constitutionally be convicted of fraud if the jury found that they themselves did not believe that they had spoken with Jesus but made the misrepresentation solely to defraud the gullible out of their money. The social interest in fraudulent misrepresentations made for a venal purpose is so slight that it is clearly outweighed by the social interest in preventing fraud and protecting the fool and his money.

The same is true of defamatory statements. These are frequently made in anger, and like insulting or fighting words their purpose is not primarily to communicate ideas but to hurt the person defamed. They may therefore be classified as verbal blows (aimed, of course, not at the listener, but at the subject of the defamation). If I fall out with my neighbor and go around telling everybody he is a thief or a rapist, little social purpose is served by my statements, and the spirit of the First Amendment is not offended if I am held legally accountable for the injury I thus cause my neighbor.

The case is not so clear where my neighbor happens to be running for public office. Here there is a clear social interest served by allowing free discussion of his character. This fact is generally recognized by the courts, which usually will allow fairly severe attacks upon the character of candidates for public office, provided the speaker is not motivated by a special malice against the individual defamed. But this is a matter of general libel law and not of the constitutional law of free speech. It is doubtful that the Supreme Court would interfere if a State should make defamers of candidates for public office liable to the same extent as defamers of private citizens.

Nor is the case clear where the defamation is aimed not at a single person but at a large group, particularly a racial or religious group, such as Negroes or Jews or Catholics. At common law and today in most States the concept of group libel is not recognized. To write in a newspaper that a particular person is a rapist or a Communist may subject the writer to civil and criminal liability, but there is no penalty for writing that all Negroes are rapists and all Jews Communists.

In a few States, however, statutes have been enacted changing the common law and subjecting to criminal penalties those who defame racial or religious groups. Such a statute was enacted in Illinois, and under it Joseph Beauharnais was indicted in 1950. Beauharnais was a racist rabble-rouser, the leader of an organization called the White Circle League of America, Inc. Serious tension arose when a Negro purchased a house in a Chicago residential district previously closed to Negroes by so-called "gentlemen's agreements." Beauharnais rushed to the scene of the trouble and passed out leaflets setting forth a petition calling upon the mayor and city council "to halt the further encroachment, harassment and invasion of white people, their property, neighborhoods and persons, by the Negro." The leaflet also called for "one million self respecting white people in Chicago to unite," adding: "If persuasion and the need to prevent the white race from becoming mongolized by the Negro will not unite us, then the oppression, rapes, robberies, knives, guns and marijuana of the Negro surely will." The leaflet concluded by urging the reader to become a member of the White Circle League of America, Inc.

Beauharnais was convicted. He appealed to the United States Supreme Court, claiming that his constitutional freedom of speech had been infringed. In *Beauharnais* v. *Illinois*, the majority of the Court, in a sharply divided decision, overruled his contention and upheld the conviction on the ground that there was no basic distinction between the libel of an individual and the libel of an ethnic group; and since the former, like obscene or fighting words, is not deemed "speech" within the protection of the First Amendment, so too is the latter excluded. Hence, it is immaterial that distribution of the leaflet may not have given rise to any "clear and present danger" of a public disturbance, since that test (to be considered shortly) is applicable only to the type of speech protected by the First Amendment and its purpose is to measure the extent of the protection; it is inapplicable to expressions deemed to be verbal blows rather than communication of ideas.

While, therefore, not all verbal articulations constitute speech within the protection of the freedom-of-speech guarantee, conversely the term "speech" may encompass expression completely unrelated to the vocal organs or even to silent reading. In *Stromberg* v. *California* the Supreme Court, in 1931, upset a conviction of the operator of a children's camp who each day raised a camp-made reproduction of the red flag of Soviet Russia, which was also the flag of the Communist Party of the United States. The defendant had been indicted under a State statute making it a felony to display a red flag "as a sign, symbol or emblem of opposition to organized government." The Court held that exhibition of the flag is a part of political discussion within the guarantee of freedom of speech. The display of a symbol may communicate ideas no less than the articulation of words.

Moreover, the term "speech" in the First Amendment may include silence, and freedom of speech may encompass freedom not to speak. This will be discussed in fuller detail later.

Finally, freedom of speech may include freedom not to listen. This was suggested in 1952 in *Public Utilities Commission* v. *Pollak*, a case in which the Supreme Court refused to invalidate an order of the Public Utilities Commission of the District of Columbia permitting the broadcasting of music and commercial advertisements on public buses and trolley cars. Since no political or similar propaganda was broadcast, the Court did not find it necessary to pass upon the issue. Nevertheless, it would seem that the liberties of Americans include the liberty not to be compelled to listen to political speeches or read political literature. Captive audiences, so familiar in totalitarian societies, are offensive to American democratic concepts.

The exclusion of fighting words, obscenities, commercial frauds, and libels, individual or group, from the mantle of constitutionally protected speech is based upon the judgment that these types of utterances constitute so minor a medium for the communication of ideas that their social value is practically negligible and the government therefore has almost unrestrained discretion to prohibit or restrict them. The judgment is made by the Supreme Court in the exercise of its function as the interpreter and guardian of our civil liberties. And the judgment relates not to the particular utterance for which the defendant is accused, but to the type of utterance.

A legislature, for example, may declare that obscenities uttered in the presence of women or children shall be punishable, but not those uttered in the presence of adult males. The Supreme Court, however, may not make such a distinction; it may not declare that obscenities in the presence of men are constitutionally protected as free speech if the legislature decides that these too shall be punishable. Similarly the legislature, if it wishes, may make untruthful group libels punishable and permit truthful libels; but if it does not make the distinction the Court may not declare that truthful defamation of an ethnic group enjoys constitutional protection.

So the Court held in the Beauharnais case, and the holding was based upon the assumption that even truthful libels of *racial* or *religious* groups are of minimal social benefit. (This is a questionable assumption; for if Negroes were potential rapists and Jews potential traitors it would surely be socially valuable that these facts become known so that appropriate protective measures might be taken.) On the other hand, there is a strong social interest in the free discussion of political issues and of the failings and evils of political parties. Therefore, the legislature could probably not outlaw libels on *political* groups. It probably could not, for instance, constitutionally make it criminal to charge that the Democratic Party is a party of treason or follows the Communist Party line or is a front for the Communist Party. And the legislature could probably not constitutionally penalize such libels even if they were false, since it is the *type* of utterance (discussion of political issues and parties), rather than the particular utterance, that is the beneficiary of constitutional protection.

CAN SPEECH BE ABSOLUTELY FREE?

If particular verbal articulation is found to be truly a communication of ideas on a matter of public concern, the unqualified language of the First Amendment would seem to guarantee its complete freedom no matter what consequences might flow from the communicated thoughts. The Amendment would appear to secure the right to say anything on a matter of public interest, at least so long as no obscenities or fighting words are used and no person or ethnic group is defamed.

This broad and even unrestricted view of the right of speech represents the thinking of the Jeffersonians. To them government could legitimately concern itself with deeds, not words. The rightful purposes of civil government can be served if its officers interfere only when principles break out into overt acts against peace and good order. It is the overt acts against peace and good order that are the proper subject of governmental action, not the articulated principles that bring them about. "We have," Jefferson said, "nothing to fear from the demoralizing reasonings of some, if others are left free to demonstrate their errors and especially when the law stands ready to punish the first criminal act produced by the false reasonings; these are safer corrections than the conscience of the judge."

It requires a courageous, perhaps even a foolhardy government — one with an unbounding faith in the good judgment of people — to accept and practice fully the Jeffersonian principle of free speech. Brutus, it will be remembered, tried it and would not allow Mark Antony's freedom of speech to be interfered with; the result was mischief afoot which could not be restrained. When presented with the Jeffersonian principle that the government can rightfully punish only the unlawful act and not the speech that evoked it, Lincoln asked bitterly: "Must I shoot a simple soldier boy who deserts, while I must not touch a hair of a wily agitator who induces him to desert?"

Our government, obviously, will not go to this extreme; nor can it realistically be expected to. Words which directly incite riot or the desertion of soldiers during war will be punished, and it would be quixotic to expect the Supreme Court to interpret the freedom-of-speech guarantee as precluding such punishment.

EVIL MIND AND EVIL TENDENCY

If, then, the Constitution does not exempt from punishment all communication of ideas, what does the principle of free speech protect? According to the Hamiltonians, it protects the communication of truthful ideas which have no evil tendency and which are uttered for a good motive. It does not exempt from punishment the utterance with evil intent of words having an evil tendency. This was the English common law as interpreted by Blackstone, and the First Amendment, say the Hamiltonians, was not intended to change this rule. To the Jeffersonian argument that the rulers will judge evil tendency and evil intent according to their own opinions, the Hamiltonians reply that the only safeguard is the right to a jury trial. If the Jeffersonians argue that this means that speech is only so free as a cross-section of the people, reflected in a jury, will allow it to be, the Hamiltonians will answer, along with Madison, that it is unrealistic to expect a " parchment barrier " to protect the people from themselves and that it is inevitable that expression will be only as free as the people will allow it to be.

There are a number of decisions of the Supreme Court reflecting this approach in greater or lesser degree. Under the old common law it was punishable to speak evil of the king regardless of whether or not any harmful consequence could conceivably result therefrom. The reason was simply that it was wrong even to think evil of the ruler; although unexpressed evil thoughts could not be punished since the Devil himself knows not the mind of man, the thinking was nonetheless culpable and if articulated rendered the thinker subject to dire punishment. A number of Supreme Court decisions too reflect an emphasis on the evil in the speaker's mind. True, reference is also made, as in the late common-law decisions, to the evil *tendency* of the spoken words; but this is of little meaning, since the Court assumes in these cases that, if the legislature declares that certain language is by its nature evil or possesses an evil tendency, the Court may not question whether there is a probability of evil consequences from the words. It is bound by the legislature's declaration and must find the defendant guilty if he uttered the language with evil mind. In any event, evil tendency is not easily susceptible of proof, and a jury will almost invariably find an evil tendency in any language with which it strongly disagrees.

Consider, for example, some of the cases during and shortly after World War I. After the United States entered the war, Congress adopted an Espionage Act, one section of which was aimed not at espionage but at sedition. It provided for the imposition of imprisonment up to twenty years against any person who willfully made false statements with intent to interfere with the Government's military operations or to promote the success of its enemies or to attempt to cause insubordination or disloyalty or obstruct the Government's recruiting program.

In one case, Eugene V. Debs, ofttime Socialist candidate for the Presidency, was convicted under the statute for attempting to cause insubordination in the armed forces and to obstruct recruiting. The conviction was based on a speech Debs had made at a Socialist convention in which he denounced capitalism and pointed to the war as one of its evils. During the course of the speech he praised a number of individuals who had been convicted of resisting the draft or causing insubordination. Perhaps his most extreme statement was: "You need to know that you are fit for something better than slavery and cannon fodder." The trial judge instructed the jury that they could convict Debs if they believed that his intent (i.e., his mind) was evil (that is, his intent was to encourage resistance to the draft) and that the speech had an evil tendency (that is, had a tendency to bring about such resistance). The Supreme Court, in *Debs* v. *United States*, affirmed the conviction. Debs began his ten-year sentence when he was sixty-three years old, and the following year polled almost a million votes for the Presidency. His sentence was commuted in 1921 by President Harding.

In *Schaefer* v. *United States*, the editors of a German-language newspaper were convicted of making false statements with the intent to interfere with the government's military operations and to promote the success of its enemies. Their offense consisted in the publication of an editorial entitled "Yankee Bluff" which derided American war efforts. The Supreme Court affirmed the conviction, finding that the derision of American efforts could have had evil influence in that it might have chilled the ardency of patriotism of some readers and caused them to relax their efforts. That, said the Court, must have been the (evil) intent of the defendants, and although it could not be shown that the article actually had that effect, it was enough to show that such might be its tendency.

In *Pierce* v. *United States*, the Court upheld the conviction of three Socialists who had distributed a pacifist pamphlet written by a prominent Episcopal clergyman. The defendants were charged with making false statements, in violation of the Espionage Act, in that the pamphlet asserted: "Our entry into it [the war] was determined by the certainty that if the allies did not win, J. P. Morgan's loans to the allies will be repudiated, and those American investors who bet on his promises would be hooked." The Court held that the untruth of this statement was a matter of common knowledge; that proof of untruth was unnecessary since the untruth was within the knowledge of the jury as of all loyal Americans. Moreover, the statement was so obviously false that it could not be doubted that the defendants knew it was false and therefore acted with an evil mind in circulating it. As for the evil effect of the publication, the Court held that the jury's finding that it would have a natural tendency to cause insubordination, disloyalty, and refusal to enlist was conclusive, and it was not necessary to prove that any particular person was in fact influenced by the pamphlet to act disloyally or resist the draft.

In *Abrams* v. *United States*, the defendants, five young men and a young woman, were indicted under the second Espionage Act (substantially more Draconic than the first) for publishing abusive language about the government and intending to bring it into contempt, for encouraging resistance to the United States in the war, and for urging curtailment of the production of arms for prosecution of the war. The indictment was based upon two sets of poorly printed leaflets, one in English and the other in Yiddish, which the defendants threw out of the window of a loft building on Houston Street in lower New York City. The leaflets, denouncing President Wilson for sending American troops into Russia, stated: "Workers in the ammunition factories, you are producing bullets, bayonets, cannon, to murder not only the Germans, but also your dearest, best, who are in Russia and are fighting for freedom." One of the pamphlets, signed "Revolutionists," ended with the call: "Awake! Awake! You Workers of the World!" It added: "P.S. It is absurd to call us pro-German. We hate and despise German militarism more than do your hypocritical tyrants. We have more reason for denouncing German militarism than has the coward in the White House."

The Supreme Court affirmed the conviction on the ground that the plain purpose of the leaflets was to excite disaffection, sedition, riots, and revolution for the purpose of embarrassing the government's military efforts in Europe. Of course, if that was their purpose it was evil enough; and, under the decisions previously discussed, it mattered little that there was nary a chance that their purpose would be achieved by the quixotic act of throwing a handful of hand-printed leaflets into the air. Recognizing that under those decisions the test of guilt was evil intent, counsel for the misguided young would-be revolutionaries contended that it was not their purpose to hinder the war against Germany. They were, he claimed, as opposed to the German government as was the Federal court (which was to convict them) and the Supreme Court (which was to affirm the conviction). Their sole purpose was to create disaffection with the government's policy of sending the armed forces to suppress the revolution in Russia, a country with which we were not at war but presumably on friendly terms.

Of this argument the Court made short shrift. A worker in a munitions factory, it said, could not possibly know whether the particular shell he was making would go to Germany or to Russia, and if he refused to make it because he believed it would go to Russia, he was obstructing the war effort if actually the shell was intended for Germany. The defendants must have known this, and therefore they had an evil purpose and an evil mind and were rightfully convicted.

Justice Holmes, in an eloquent dissent in which Justice Brandeis concurred, vainly invoked the "clear and present danger" rule (of which more shortly). "In this case," he said, "sentences of 20 years imprisonment have been imposed for the publishing of two leaflets that I believe the defendants had as much right to publish as the Government has to publish the Constitution of the United States now vainly invoked by them."

The case of *Gitlow* v. *New York* arose not under the Espionage Acts but under a New York statute punishing the advocacy of criminal anarchy. Gitlow was one of the leaders of the "Left Wing" which in 1919 broke away from the Socialist Party to become the Communist Party. Like the revolutionaries of 1776, Gitlow and his associates felt it necessary to declare the causes that impelled them to the separation. There, however, the similarity ended; the *Left Wing Manifesto* consisted of thirty-four closely printed pages whose effect was far more likely to induce sleep than revolutionary activity. There were the usual calls to "mass strikes," "expropriation of the bourgeoisie" and establishment of a "dictatorship of the proletariat." In a 7-to-2 decision (Holmes and Brandeis dissenting) the Supreme Court affirmed the conviction on the ground that the legislature of New York was not forbidden by the Constitution to make it a crime to utter words it deemed dangerous, whether or not there was any real likelihood that in a particular case the utterance would in fact provoke revolution, anarchy, or other unlawful acts.

"CLEAR AND PRESENT DANGER"

These decisions show an emphasis, not on the consequences of the spoken words, but on the evil mind of the speaker. Under this approach speech is free only to the pure in heart; others must pay dearly for it; the price may be ten or twenty years' imprisonment. And since a jury of patriotic citizens will not often find anything but evil in the mind of a radical who sows disaffection with the government in time of war, prosecutions under the Espionage Acts of World War I rarely resulted in acquittal.

This, according to the Hamiltonians, is as it should be. Speech should be as free as a cross-section of the community, reflected in a jury, will allow it to be. If this seems to afford little protection for the expression of unpopular views, the solution lies in educating the community — and thus juries — to the importance of tolerating the expression of unpopular views.

This approach worked fairly well during the first century of our republic's existence — a period that included a bitter and bloody civil war. The expanding frontier, the spirit of American individualism, the tradition of suspicion of government inherited from Locke, Rousseau, and the anti-Federalists — all combined to assure among the people generally and juries particularly a robust tolerance for heretical views and a decent respect for freedom of speech.

However, with the industrialization of America, the disappearance of the frontier, the intensification of nationalism, the rise of international Marxism with its threat to a wealthy capitalist society growing ever wealthier, the tolerance of juries could no longer be relied upon. The Hamiltonian approach proved wanting in the eyes of the enlightened conscience of the community. Such an approach makes of the Constitution little more than a parchment barrier, and of the First Amendment an almost meaningless exhortation to be tolerant. It makes the Judiciary merely the referee in an uneven battle between an enraged and fear-ridden majority and a weak, defenseless, and detested minority (rather than the protector of that minority, as Madison believed its role would be).

This was not what Justices Holmes and Brandeis, and later Justices Stone, Murphy, Rutledge, Black, and Douglas, envisaged as the true function either of the Constitution or of the Court. Out of their disaffection with the Hamiltonian philosophy came the "clear and present danger" approach, an approach that seeks a satisfactory reconciliation of the competing demands of national security and personal liberty. Briefly, the following is the "clear and present danger" theory.

As in all constitutional problems concerning the liberties of Americans, the question is the proper weighing of competing interests. On the one hand is the interest the community has in communication of thoughts so that in the free market place of ideas truth will prevail and the community benefit thereby. On the other hand is the need to prevent internal violence and external aggression. The fulfillment of this need may sometimes require the restriction of the free communication of ideas, as when the idea communicated is that the government should be overthrown by force or violence or that able-bodied men should not volunteer for military service.

The ultimate responsibility of reconciling these competing claims and of marking the boundary between the areas properly belonging to each rests upon the Federal Judiciary. Its members serve for life and presumably have relinquished all further political desires. They are therefore most likely to be free of the ambition that may corrupt the conscience of the legislators, who make the initial evaluation in enacting the particular sedition statute under which the defendants are being tried; and most likely to be free of the passion that may blind the judgment of the jury, which makes the second evaluation in determining the guilt or innocence of the defendants under that statute.

In evaluating the claims of freedom of expression as against the other social interests whose promotion is asserted to justify a particular restriction on freedom of expression, the Court must consider the high estate held in our democratic scheme of things by the rights secured in the First Amendment. Hence, the competing interest must be of great concern to justify the restriction. The rights secured by the First Amendment stand in a preferred position, and any claim to restrict one of these rights will be scrutinized suspiciously by the Supreme Court. Only if the Court is convinced that the interest threatened by the speech sought to be restricted is truly superior in importance will it uphold the restriction.

For example, a municipality has an interest in keeping its streets clean and unlittered. Because people who are handed leaflets in the street frequently throw them away immediately and thus litter the streets, the municipality passes a law prohibiting the distribution of leaflets in the public streets. Is this law constitutional? The answer, as we have seen, is yes, if it is limited to commercial leaflets; no, if it extends to political (or religious) leaflets. The community's interest in clean streets is sufficiently important to justify the restriction on commercial activities but not on freedom of speech, which stands in a preferred position.

Moreover, even if the threatened interest is of sufficient importance to warrant restriction on speech for its protection, it will not be upheld if an alternative practicable method exists to protect that interest without restricting freedom of speech. Suppose a municipality finds that if Republicans and Democrats hold political rallies on the streets at the same time in close proximity to each other, fist fights frequently break out between them, particularly if the meetings are held in the heat of a political campaign. To avoid this, the municipality simply prohibits all political speeches or rallies on the streets. This prohibition is clearly unconstitutional. While the municipality's interest in the avoidance of violence is undoubtedly sufficiently important to justify a restriction on speech if there were no other way to avoid street violence, here there obviously is another way. The municipality can simply require that political speeches in the streets be made at a distance from each other, or perhaps at different times. Perhaps it might be simpler and more convenient to outlaw all public political meetings, but the First Amendment was adopted to prevent such short cuts with democratic processes.

Finally, the threat to the superior interest must be immediate and certain, not remote and speculative. It is not sufficient that the words used may have a tendency to bring on evil consequences at some time in the remote future. In other words, the danger must be *clear and present.* A passionate pacifist valedictory address delivered in wartime to a class graduating from West Point may constitutionally subject the speaker to criminal penalties; the same address delivered in peacetime to a class graduating from elementary school would not. No danger flowing from speech can be deemed clear and present unless the evil feared (here, hindrance of the prosecution of war through discouraging service in the armed forces) is so imminent that it may occur before there is opportunity for full discussion. If there is time to expose the falsehoods and fallacies through discussion, to avert the evil by the processes of education, the remedy to be applied is not enforced silence but more speech.

This, then, is the "clear and present danger" approach. Two things should be noted about it. In the first place, while it does not go so far as the all-out Jeffersonian formula, which would punish only unlawful overt acts and not the speech that provoked them, it is close to that formula in demanding that the danger of the outbreak of unlawful overt acts be immediate. This means that, under the "clear and present danger" test, speech is constitutionally protected until it has virtually become action. In the second place, the emphasis is not on the evil mind or evil intent of the speaker, or even on the evil nature of the spoken words; the emphasis is on the overt act immediately consequent upon the spoken word.

THE HISTORY OF "CLEAR AND PRESENT DANGER"

The "clear and present danger" test was first expressed by Justice Holmes in *Schenck* v. *United States*. In that case, decided by a unanimous Court in 1919, a conviction under the first Espionage Act was upheld on evidence that the defendants (Socialists) had printed and circulated among men who already had been drafted and were awaiting induction into the armed forces a leaflet which argued that the draft was unconstitutional and that the government had no power to send American citizens to shoot up the people of other lands. It contained a good deal of similar language regarding the cold-blooded ruthlessness of mercenary capitalist Wall Street and urged the recipients to "assert your rights" and not to be subject to intimidation. There was nothing in the leaflet urging the recipient to resist conscription, nor was any evidence presented to show that anyone who had received the leaflet had actually resisted conscription.

Justice Holmes, nevertheless, rejected the defendants' claim that the conviction violated their constitutional right of free speech. The most stringent protection of free speech, said Holmes, would not protect a man from the penal consequences of falsely shouting " Fire! " in a theater and thus causing a panic. The question in every case is whether the words used are used in such circumstances and are of such a nature as to create a clear and present danger that they will bring about the substantive evils that Congress has a right to prevent. It is a question of proximity and degree. Here there was a clear and present danger that some of the recipients of the leaflet would in fact be induced by it to resist induction into the armed forces.

Thus was the " clear and present danger " test born. And having been born it fell into almost twenty years of desuetude. The later decisions under the Espionage Acts (discussed in the previous section) ignored both the " clear and present danger " test and the eloquent dissents of Holmes and Brandeis, and relied on evil mind and evil tendency. So too did the decisions under State sedition and syndicalism laws, such as *Gitlow* v. *New York.* Even where, as in *Fiske* v. *Kansas,* the Supreme Court upset the conviction of an IWW organizer under a State anti-syndicalism law, it did so on the ground that there was no evidence that the defendant or the IWW had the evil intent of effecting abolition of the wage system by violent or otherwise unlawful means, and not on the ground that there was no clear and present danger that such an intent would have been efficacious. It remained for the New Deal or Roosevelt Court to rediscover and reactivate the " clear and present danger " doctrine.

This it did in 1937. In *Herndon* v. *Lowry,* a 5-to-4 decision, the Court set aside the conviction under a Georgia anti-insurrection statute of a Negro organizer for the Communist Party who was shown to have had in his room Communist literature calling on whites and Negroes to overthrow class rule in the Black Belt by violent revolution, had addressed three public meetings, and had possessed a Communist Party membership book. The Georgia courts had upheld the conviction on the ground that under the statute the test was the defendant's evil intent and that it was not necessary to show that his intent was likely to be carried out at any time in the immediate or even foreseeable future. In reversing the conviction, the Supreme Court held that speech could not be penalized merely because of the speaker's evil intent; there must be a reasonable apprehension of danger to organized government. Nor was evil tendency sufficient, nor the possibility that in the distant future the speaker's words might lead to violence and revolution; there must be a clear and present danger of unlawful force and violence.

For a decade or so after *Herndon* v. *Lowry,* the Roosevelt Court was in full swing, and " clear and present danger " was invoked in case after case to strike down governmental restrictions on rights secured by the First Amendment. In *Thornhill* v. *Alabama* the Court invalidated a State anti-picketing law because peaceful picketing presents no clear and present danger of destruction of life or property or breach of the peace. In *Cantwell* v. *Connecticut,* as we have seen, the Court reversed the conviction of a Jehovah's Witness for inciting a breach of the peace in playing an anti-Catholic phonograph record on a public street. The Court held that, although the contents of the record naturally aroused animosity, the defendant's conduct raised no clear and present menace to public peace and order sufficient to justify his conviction.

In *Terminiello* v. *Chicago* (1949) the Court reversed the conviction of an unfrocked Catholic priest who had delivered a passionate anti-Semitic speech to a packed private hall in the presence of some eight hundred persons. Terminiello was convicted under an ordinance that included in its definition of breach of the peace any speech that " stirs the people to anger, invites disputes or brings about a condition of unrest." This, the Supreme Court said, violates the free-speech guarantee. Words that arouse anger, disputes, or unrest may not be made criminal in the absence of a clear and present danger of a serious substantive evil.

Even where the Court upheld a conviction for unlawful speech it did so on the basis of " clear and present danger." In *Feiner* v. *New York,* Feiner, a young university student, made a street-corner speech in Syracuse for the purpose of publicizing a meeting of the Young Progressives of America to be held that evening at a local hotel. Speaking to a mixed group of some seventy-five Negroes and whites in a predominantly Negro section of the city, he stood on a large box and used loudspeakers mounted on a car. During the course of the speech he called the local mayor, the mayor of New York City, and President Truman each a " bum," charged the American Legion with being a Nazi Gestapo, and asserted that Negroes did not have equal rights and should rise up in arms and fight for their rights. The meeting was well policed and there was no disorder; but after some twenty minutes of this harangue a man said to the police officers, " If you don't get that son of a bitch off, I will go over and get him off there myself." Thereupon the police ordered Feiner to stop speaking and, when he refused, arrested him for disorderly conduct.

The Supreme Court, in a 6-to-3 decision, upheld the conviction on the ground that the New York courts, after a full and fair trial, had found that there had been clear and present danger of disorder when Feiner was ordered to desist. Justices Black and Douglas, who by this time (1951) were already playing the role in the post-World War II civil-liberties cases that Holmes and Brandeis had played in the post-World War I cases, dissented along with Justice Minton. Their dissent was based on the ground that the evidence did not show a clear and present danger that disorder would break out and that, even if it had, the police should have used constitutional means to avert it — i.e., protecting the speaker from hostile members of the audience — and not the unconstitutional means of seeking to silence the speaker.

COMMUNISM AND " CLEAR AND PRESENT DANGER "

Thus " clear and present danger " stood until the outbreak of the Cold War after the hot World War II. Up to then restrictions on freedom of political expression had not been focused on a single target, but had been generally directed against radicals of all shades, anarchists, syndicalists, pacifists, left-wing Socialists, right-wing Socialists, IWW's, etc. Toward the turn of the midcentury, Communism and Communists became the focus of fear and hate. New terms, such as " un-American," " subversive," " disloyal," became current, but all were identified in some way with Communism and Communists, avowed Communists, Communist sympathizers, Communist dupes, Communist fronts, Communist party-line followers, etc.

This developing concentration on a single target is perhaps best indicated by a comparison of two statutes enacted ten years apart. The Smith Act, adopted in 1940, was modeled after the many State criminal anarchy laws that sprang up after the assassination of President McKinley. Specifically it followed closely the wording of the New York Criminal Anarchy Act which had been upheld in *Gitlow* v. *New York.* The Smith Act made no mention of Communism or Communists, but was aimed generally at any person or group seeking to overthrow the government by force or violence. On the other hand, the Internal Security Act (popularly known as the McCarran Act), enacted ten years later, was frankly and expressly aimed at Communism and Communists. The whole Act is predicated upon the identification of subversive activities with Communist activities, and of internal security with the effective control of Communist activities.

Therein lies the critical civil-liberties problem of today: To what extent are constitutional principles and precedents developed in the century-and-a-half struggle to preserve liberties of unpopular Americans — radicals, revolutionaries, anarchists, pacifists, Socialists, and malcontents of every hue — applicable to Communists and Communist organizations. That is the problem which has so divided the Supreme Court. At the one extreme was the late Justice Jackson, who found Communism so dissimilar to any other movement or ideology in American history as to render all those principles and precedents practically irrelevant. At the other are Justices Black and Douglas, who find American (not foreign) Communism and American Communists not basically different from any other of the many feared and hated ideologies and radicals in American history and who, therefore, find those principles and precedents as applicable to Communists as to any other individuals or groups in America. In between are found most of the members of the Court, who are not prepared to scrap all the old concepts of civil liberties just because the claimant is a Communist or a Communist organization, yet feel that the traditional principles and precedents require re-evaluation and probably substantial modification where Communists and Communist organizations are involved.

This problem pervades the entire area of political liberties today. It will crop up again and again throughout much of the balance of this book. It will be discussed in greatest detail in the next chapter, which deals with liberty of association; for therein perhaps lies the heart of the problem — to what extent does liberty of association entitle Americans to associate in the Communist Party? Here we will concern ourselves only with the aspect of the problem that affects freedom of speech, and specifically the " clear and present danger " test. In other words, how, if at all, is the " clear and present danger " test to be applied to the advocacy of Communism?

This question was faced by the Court in 1951 in *Dennis* v. *United States.* Eleven top Communist leaders in the United States were indicted for violation of the Smith Act in that they conspired (a) to organize the Communist Party, and (b) to advocate and teach the necessity of overthrowing the government of the United States by force and violence. Only the second count concerns us here; the first will be discussed in the next chapter. The trial took place in New York City; it extended over a period of nine months, and was front-page news for most of the period. It was as thrilling as a television drama, with the forces of good arrayed against the forces of evil. As in all acceptable television dramas, in the end the good triumphed over the evil; those on the side of evil received their just deserts, and those on the side of the good were handsomely rewarded. The defendants were convicted and received long-term prison sentences. Their lawyers were imprisoned for contempt of court and disbarred. On the other side, the judge who presided over the trial and sentenced the defendants and their attorneys was elevated to a higher court, and the prosecuting attorney received a judgeship.

The evidence showed that the defendants taught and advocated the Marxist-Leninist doctrine contained chiefly in four books: Stalin's *Foundation of Leninism, The Communist Manifesto* of Marx and Engels, Lenin's *State and Revolution,* and *History of the Communist Party of the Soviet Union.* These works preached the necessity of overthrowing government by force and violence, and the trial judge instructed the jury that, if the defendants advocated these doctrines with the intent to overthrow the government by force and violence as speedily as circumstances would permit, they should be found guilty.

The Supreme Court affirmed the conviction by a vote of 6 to 2. Justice Clark did not participate in the case, since he had been Attorney General when the prosecution was commenced. Justices Black and Douglas dissented in separate opinions. Justices Frankfurter and Jackson concurred in the result but wrote separate opinions. Hence, the opinion of Chief Justice Vinson actually reflected the expressed views of only a minority of the Court, consisting of himself and Justices Reed, Burton, and Minton. Since the decision was handed down, Chief Justice Vinson and Justice Jackson have both died; they have been succeeded by Chief Justice Warren and Justice Harlan, neither of whom has at this writing indicated his view as to the meaning and applicability of "clear and present danger." Hence, it cannot be said definitely that the Dennis opinion represents the present thinking of a majority of the Court, much less how long it will continue to do so if it does. Nevertheless, it is the latest authoritative consideration by the Court of the "clear and present danger" test and therefore warrants careful study.

For convenience the dissenting and concurring opinions will be considered first. Justices Black and Douglas, in separate opinions, dissented on the ground that the "clear and present danger" test was applicable to Communists as to anyone else, that that test should not be impaired, qualified, or compromised, and that under that test the indictment should have been dismissed since there was no substantial danger that the handful of known, discredited, and detested Communists in the country could successfully overthrow the government by force or violence. Justice Douglas, in addition, argued that the effect of the decision was to re-establish the common law of sedition under which the test of criminality in speech was the evil mind of the speaker. For all agree, said Justice Douglas, that the teaching of the doctrines of the four books upon which the indictment was based would not have been a crime and would not have been punishable if it had been done in a college or university as an intellectual exercise. It was a punishable crime only because it was done with the intent that these doctrines should be accepted as true and acted upon. Therefore, it was not the spoken words that were punishable but the evil mind of the speaker. This was the common law of sedition which it was the intent of the First Amendment to abrogate in the United States.

Justice Jackson concurred in the conviction on a ground he had previously expressed — that the "clear and present danger" test was devised for the American type of individualistic, native radicalism and was totally inapplicable to the government's efforts to meet the threat of the international Communist conspiracy. The "clear and present danger" test grew out of cases all of which arose before the era of World War II had revealed the subtlety and efficacy of modernized techniques used by totalitarian parties. It is completely unrealistic to expect a court to be able to prophesy when the Communist conspiracy is likely to break out in a revolutionary assault upon the government. The Communist *coup d'état* in Czechoslovakia vividly shows the danger in according to Communists the usual protection of freedom of speech, press, and assembly. Jackson's approach is epitomized perhaps best in the four word title of Sidney Hook's book: *Heresy, Yes — Conspiracy, No.*

Justice Frankfurter's concurrence was based on his oft-expressed dissatisfaction with the "clear and present danger" test and with the premise upon which it was based — that the rights secured in the First Amendment stand in a preferred position and are entitled to greater judicial protection than other constitutional rights. To Frankfurter a statute restricting speech was not constitutionally different from a statute restricting business activity, and like all statutes was entitled to the benefit of a presumption of constitutionality. For a century and a half the Court had expressed adherence to Marshall's doctrine that an act of Congress should not be invalidated by the Court unless there is patently no reasonable basis for it. The responsibility for balancing and reconciling the competing demands of national security and individual freedom to speak rests with the democratically elected Congress and not with judges appointed by the President to serve for life without political responsibility and not subject to recall or retirement. Hence, the fact that the members of the Court would themselves have acted differently if they had been Congressmen and would have voted against the Smith bill does not justify their setting aside the act of Congress unless it is clearly outside the pale of fair judgment and can only be characterized as arbitrary and unreasonable. In the present case, the universally known facts of the ends and methods of Communism establish that the judgment of Congress was far from unreasonable, and therefore should not be disturbed.

Chief Justice Vinson's opinion was, as we have seen, concurred in by three other members of the Court and thus represented the views of four of the eight justices who participated in the decision. The Chief Justice first considered the contention that the effect of the Smith Act was to make the criminality of speech depend upon the mind of the speaker and that the same words might or might not subject the speaker to a long-term prison sentence depending on the intent of the speaker.

The Chief Justice found nothing unusual or unprecedented in this; intent is a common determinative element in criminal law. Let us take a homely example which, though not suggested in his opinion, may clarify his point. If I walk off with somebody else's umbrella in a restaurant I may or may not be guilty of a crime, depending upon the state of my mind. If I walk off with the umbrella because I mistakenly believe it is my own, nothing happens to me except that I have to return the umbrella. If, however, I take the umbrella because I covet it and know it is not my own, I am guilty of a crime. Thus, whether I go to jail or not depends exclusively on the state of my mind. If, then, the act of walking off with an umbrella may be innocent or criminal depending on the walker's intent, there is no reason why the defendants' innocence or criminality may not depend on whether they taught the doctrines of Communism as theoretic problems to be examined objectively and philosophically, or, conversely, they taught them with the intent that they be accepted as true and be acted upon as soon as circumstances permitted.

It is true that the First Amendment guarantees freedom to speak and does not guarantee freedom to walk off with other persons' umbrellas. But everybody admits (everybody, that is, with the possible exception of a few extreme Jeffersonians) that not all speech is protected by the First Amendment and that some speech — either because of its evil tendency or because it presents a clear and present danger or because of some other reason — is not within the protection of the Amendment. If that is so, there is no reason why Congress cannot decree that one who utters such unprotected speech shall be thrown into a Federal penitentiary or be awarded a doctorate in philosophy, depending on his intent.

The constitutional issue then, according to Chief Justice Vinson, is not the state of the defendants' mind, but whether or not the words spoken by them (or, more accurately, which they conspired to speak) are within or without the area of First Amendment protection.

In deciding this issue the Court might have repudiated the "clear and present danger" test and returned to the rule of *Gitlow* v. *New York*, that when the legislature itself declares that a certain kind of speech is by its nature evil and harmful and makes utterance of such speech illegal, the Court must abide by the legislative judgment if it is reasonable (which a statute designed to protect the state from violent overthrow undeniably is). The Chief Justice, however, did not do this. He accepted the "clear and present danger" test, but asserted that it must be properly understood and applied.

In the first place, he said, the evil that the government has a right to avert under the " clear and present danger " test is not limited to the *successful* overthrow of the government by force and violence. That is not the only evil the Constitution empowers the government to prevent, even at the cost of restricting speech. Admittedly, the evil must be grave; littered streets do not constitute a sufficiently grave evil to justify declaring criminal the handing out of leaflets discussing matters of public concern. But an attempt to overthrow the government by force or violence, even if *unsuccessful* or doomed to failure from the start, is a grave evil which the government has the right and duty to seek to prevent. Hence, the fact that the present strength of the Communist Party in America makes it highly unlikely that an attempted revolution instigated by it would succeed does not mean that the government may not constitutionally punish its leaders for instigating the attempt.

In the second place, " clear and present danger " is not an absolute standard that can be applied like a yardstick equally in all circumstances. It is a relative concept to be applied in the light of the particular circumstances in which it is invoked. A danger that is clear in one set of circumstances may not be clear in another set, and what is present in one instance may not be in another. In any case in which the " clear and present danger " test is invoked the courts must decide *whether the gravity of the evil, discounted by its improbability, justifies such invasion of free speech as is necessary to avoid the danger.*

What this means is that, in determining whether the requisite clarity and immediacy is present to justify a restriction on speech, due consideration must be given to the degree of gravity of the evil sought to be prevented. If it is a comparatively minor evil, such as littered streets, the evil must be extremely clear and extremely close to justify the restriction on speech. If, however, the evil is a serious one, such as the loss of life and property attendant even upon an unsuccessful attempt to overthrow the government by force or violence, much wider scope must be given to the discretion of the government in seeking to avert the evil, and the courts must accept a much lower standard of clarity and immediacy. The " clear and present danger " test, properly understood, does not require the government to wait until the *putsch* is about to be executed, the plans have been laid, and the signal is awaited. In view of the nature of the Communist conspiracy, highly organized with rigidly disciplined members subject to the immediate and unquestioned call of their leaders, and in view of the inflammable nature of world conditions, the Chief Justice held that the danger was sufficiently clear and present to justify punishing the defendants for conspiracy to advocate the overthrow of the government by force and violence.

That is where " clear and present danger " stands today. It would be idle to suggest that it is the same test that was first announced by Holmes and amplified by Brandeis and the Roosevelt Court. On the other hand, the Dennis case offered the Court an opportunity to repudiate " clear and present danger " and return to the principle of *Gitlow* v. *New York*, which accorded practically complete power to the legislature to restrict speech deemed by it to have an evil tendency. Realistically, the " clear and present danger " test as qualified and applied in the Dennis case is of little practical difference from the Gitlow test of legislative supremacy. It is probable that where Communism and Communists are concerned it is of little more than academic or semantic significance as to which test is applied. To whichever the Court expresses adherence, the practical result is the same; except in an extreme case the Court will not interfere with the government's judgment as to how to meet the threat of the Communist conspiracy. However, it is significant that the Court passed by the invitation to overrule " clear and present danger " and return to the Gitlow rule. In non-political expression, and particularly religious expression, " clear and present danger " still retains its original vitality; and even in political expression other than Communist expression, it is probable that much of this vitality still remains.

FREEDOM OF SILENCE

Neither the Bill of Rights nor any part of the Constitution itself expressly recognizes any general right of silence. The Fifth Amendment secures a specific right to be silent where what is said may incriminate the speaker. The Fourth Amendment secures a restricted right of privacy in its prohibition of unreasonable searches and seizures. But nowhere in the Constitution is there an express general guarantee of freedom not to speak, as there is of freedom to speak.

Yet the right of privacy, the right of silence, the right to be left alone has accurately been described as the most fundamental of all liberties. Life would hardly be worth living if man could not keep quiet when he wanted to keep quiet. Certainly man would not be free if he did not have the right of silence; forced speech no less than forced labor is slavery.

Perhaps it was because the founding fathers assumed universal acceptance of the right of silence that they did not include it in their bill of liberties. In view of the general acceptance of the social contract, with its underlying premise that powers not specifically conferred upon government were retained by the people (a premise made explicit in the Ninth Amendment's warning that rights not specifically expressed in the Bill of Rights shall not thereby be prejudiced or disparaged), the omission of express reference to a right of silence may not be of particular significance. Whether expressly spelled out or not, the liberty not to speak is unquestionably one of the liberties of an American. It is most closely allied to the liberties set forth in the First Amendment, and it has been treated by the Supreme Court as a First Amendment right. In any event, convenience and logic as well dictate that it be considered in our discussion of freedom of speech, even though it might appear paradoxical to interpret a prohibition of laws abridging freedom of speech as including laws abridging freedom of non-speech.

Although freedom of non-speech is guaranteed by the Constitution, government may nevertheless occasionally compel speech. Like freedom of speech, freedom of non-speech must occasionally yield to a higher societal interest. Where an important need of society can be satisfied only by coercing speech, the Constitution, as interpreted by the Supreme Court, allows government to coerce speech, just as in a similar situation it allows government to coerce silence. The problem in both instances is to weigh the competing interests and, if the societal interest is found superior, to judge whether protection of that interest clearly and immediately requires abridgment of the right.

In discussing the competing values of coerced speech and the right of silence, it may be convenient to consider three kinds of silence: first, the right not to say what one does not believe; second, the right not to say what one does believe; and third, the right not to say what one knows. The social interest in overriding each of these rights will vary in importance, and the degree of constitutional protection accorded each of these rights will vary in inverse proportion.

It is fairly clear that society, at least a democratic society, has a minimal interest — if any at all — in compelling persons to say what they do not believe. Historically, freedom of such silence has been primarily an aspect of freedom of religion, for it has largely been the expression of religious beliefs that has been coerced, such as the coercion upon the early Christian martyrs to express a belief (which they did not hold) in the divinity of the Roman emperor, or the coercion upon Galileo to express a belief (which he did not hold) in the centrality of the earth in the universe. It was in connection with the religion clause of the First Amendment that the Supreme Court said (in the Everson and McCollum cases) that under the Amendment neither a State nor the Federal government may force a person to profess a belief or disbelief.

Freedom of such silence, however, is not exclusively freedom of religious silence. In *West Virginia Board of Education* v. *Barnette,* Justice Jackson's opinion made it clear that the basis of the decision invalidating the compulsory flag salute and pledge of allegiance was not the fact that the religious convictions of Jehovah's Witnesses precluded participation in such a ceremony. Freedom of speech (i.e., non-speech) rather than freedom of religion was the issue, and the result would have been the same if the motivation of the children's parents had been philosophic rather than religious. (It should be noted that the pledge of allegiance to the flag did not then, as it does now, contain the phrase "under God.") The issue was whether the social interest sought to be furthered (the inculcation of loyalty and national unity) was sufficiently important and the method chosen clearly necessary to justify coercion of expressing what one does not believe. The community's interest in having little children recite a pledge in which they do not believe, the Court held, does not constitutionally justify compulsion in achieving that end.

In view of the negligible interest society has in having people profess what they do not believe, freedom of such silence may be said to be as nearly absolute as any freedom can be under the Constitution. Freedom not to say what one does believe, i.e., freedom not to disclose one's beliefs, may be less absolute. That the First Amendment protects the right generally not to disclose one's beliefs is hardly open to doubt. Beliefs, the Supreme Court has said, are inviolate, and the freedom not to disclose such beliefs is likewise inviolate in the absence of a clear necessity of a disclosure to protect an important social interest. Unquestionably, the government may not compel a person to disclose whether or not he believes in God or in the Christian or any other religion. Nor for that matter may the government compel a person to disclose whether he believes in the principles of the Democratic or Republican Party, in a high or low tariff, in capitalism or socialism, or ordinarily even in the violent overthrow of the government.

There are, nevertheless, instances in which the community has a legitimate and important interest in having its citizens disclose what they believe. Our system of justice depends upon the power of the state to round up twelve citizens, confine them to a jury box when they would much rather be taking care of their business or playing golf, compel them to listen to a complaint in which they have no interest recited by a person whom they have never met before and would be happy never to meet again, and then disclose their belief as to whether the complaint is or is not justified. A juror who, at the end of a trial, refused to disclose to the court his belief regarding the issues of the trial would be summarily punished for contempt of court, and it is highly unlikely that a plea of the First Amendment would get him very far.

Other instances might be cited. The community has a legitimate interest in knowing whether an applicant for citizenship believes in our system of government, and may require him to disclose his belief and deny him citizenship if he refuses to do so. Our community has a similar interest in knowing whether our public officials believe in the violent overthrow of our government and may make disclosure of their belief a prerequisite of public employment.

In *American Communications Association* v. *Douds*, decided in 1950, the Supreme Court upheld the constitutionality of the so-called "non-Communist oath" requirement of the Taft-Hartley Act. This disqualified from the benefits of the Labor Relations Act any union whose officers failed to sign an affidavit stating (1) that they were not members of or affiliated with the Communist Party or of any other organization advocating the forcible overthrow of the government and (2) that they did not themselves believe in the forcible overthrow of the government. The part of the decision that concerns disavowal of membership or affiliation will be considered in the section of the next chapter dealing with freedom of association; here our concern is with the requirement of a disavowal of belief in the forcible overthrow of the government.

Three of the nine justices did not participate in the case at all. Of the remaining six, two believed the provision requiring disavowal of belief to be unconstitutional. Only four, or less than a majority of the whole Court, upheld the validity of the requirement. Since, however, the four did constitute a majority of the participating justices, their opinion constituted the decision of the Court.

These four justices refused to accept the contention that one may under no circumstances be required to state his belief or suffer the loss of any right or privilege because of his belief or his refusal to disclose it. To accept this proposition, they said, would convert the Bill of Rights into a suicide pact, for it would bar the government from questioning applicants for positions in the Secret Service, assigned to protect the President, whether or not they believe in the assassination of the President. The reason the question is permissible is because it is necessary for the security of an important public interest, the protection of the President's life; and the restriction on the right of silence extends no further than is necessary to secure that interest. In other words, if the applicant refuses to answer he simply will not be employed, but he may not in any other way be punished for his refusal.

The same is true with respect to the Taft-Hartley oath. Congress found that persons believing in the forcible overthrow of the government are likely to employ their strategic positions as union officers to further their revolutionary aims. To prevent this, such persons must not be allowed to serve as union officers, and to discourage their selection as officers the Government may withhold the benefits of the Labor Relations Act from unions that select them as officers. Beyond that, no penalty is imposed upon the union or its officials. Such a minor restriction upon freedom of silence as to one's belief, when weighed against the public interest in preventing use of labor unions for revolutionary ends, may not be held unconstitutional.

The third right of silence — the right not to say what one knows — is the one most subject to constitutional restriction. There are countless instances in which the government has a right to be informed of matters within the knowledge of its citizens and may therefore compel disclosure of such knowledge. The administration of justice requires that witnesses tell what they know of the controversy in a case before the court, and if they refuse to do so they may be punished for contempt of court. In order to raise revenue the government must know the amount and details of citizens' income, and their refusal to disclose this information in tax returns may land them in the penitentiary. Refusal to speak to the draft board, the census taker, the bureau of motor vehicles, or a score of other governmental agencies may be made punishable by the government.

Our Anglo-American law has recognized some instances where society would be better served if disclosure of knowledge were not coerced than if it were. A wife may not be compelled to disclose what her husband tells her over the breakfast table; nor a lawyer what his client tells him in his office; nor a priest what a penitent tells him in the confession box. But these exceptions or privileges are not constitutionally protected, and there is little reason to believe that the Supreme Court would upset the judgment of a legislature that decided to abolish any or all of them.

CONGRESSIONAL INVESTIGATIONS AND THE RIGHT OF SILENCE

The foregoing would seem to be more or less obvious. Few persons are likely to urge seriously that the First Amendment protects their right not to speak to police officers regarding a crime or accident that they have witnessed. It is primarily with respect to legislative investigating committees, and principally Congressional committees investigating Communism and subversion, that the plea of the First Amendment has chiefly been used. It is here that the difficult constitutional problem arises: To what extent may a Congressional committee compel a witness to reveal his private affairs and particularly his political affiliations? A witness queried by a Congressional committee as to whether he is or ever was a member of the Communist Party may plead the Fifth Amendment privilege against self-incrimination; but may he with impunity assert that under the First Amendment he has a right of silence whether or not the answer might tend to incriminate him?

This question has not yet been conclusively answered by the Supreme Court, and it is probable that there is no single answer applicable to all cases. Undoubtedly there are instances in which the query may validly be put to the witness, and a refusal to reply (without pleading the Fifth Amendment) may be punished as an act of contempt of Congress. But it is equally probable that in other instances the witness might effectively plead a right of silence.

The first time the Supreme Court was faced with the issue of the power of a Congressional committee to question witnesses arose out of the failure, during the 1873 financial crisis, of the banking firm of Jay Cooke in which Federal funds were deposited. A House committee, investigating Cooke's financial dealings, subpoenaed one of Cooke's associates, Hallet Kilbourn, who refused to answer questions on the ground that the House had no authority "to investigate private business in which nobody but me and my customers have any concern." The House ordered Kilbourn imprisoned for contempt of Congress, and Kilbourn retaliated by suing the Sergeant at Arms of the House for false imprisonment.

In *Kilbourn* v. *Thompson* the Supreme Court upheld Kilbourn's claim that he had been unconstitutionally imprisoned. The issue was whether Congress had the power to compel Kilbourn to disclose the operations of a private real-estate pool in which the Federal government had an indirect interest by virtue of the fact that a depository of Federal funds, the Jay Cooke company, had been a participant in the pool. The Court held that the investigation was not related to any valid legislation Congress might enact and therefore was an unauthorized inquiry into the personal affairs of individual citizens.

The issue again came before the Supreme Court in connection with Senatorial investigations of mismanagement and corruption during the Harding administration. The specific subject of investigation was the Justice Department, and the person subpoenaed was Mally S. Daugherty, brother of the Attorney General. Daugherty disregarded the subpoena, and the lower court upheld his refusal to testify on the ground that the investigation was not in connection with a legitimate legislative purpose but was intended as a trial of the Attorney General. The lower court relied for its decision on *Kilbourn* v. *Thompson,* but the Supreme Court, in *McGrain* v. *Daugherty,* reversed the lower court and held that the investigation of the administration of an Executive department, such as the Department of Justice, was a legitimate legislative function. This ruling was reaffirmed in *Sinclair* v. *United States,* where the Supreme Court upheld the contempt conviction of an oil magnate, Harry Sinclair, who refused to answer questions in connection with a Senatorial investigation of the Teapot Dome transactions.

Quite a number of constitutional authorities have viewed the Kilbourn case as overruled by the Daugherty and Sinclair decisions. These writers have expressed the opinion that the investigatory powers of Congress are practically unlimited and that a witness called before a Congressional committee has no right of silence or privacy other than the right under the Fifth Amendment to remain silent where his answer might tend to incriminate him. One writer has suggested, perhaps somewhat hyperbolically, that Congress has "the right to investigate everything below the earth, on top of it, and in the heavens beyond," since the Constitution has granted to Congress "all legislative power," and there can thus be no constitutional limit on the exercise of any investigative activity incident to the use of that power.

That this view is erroneous was made clear by the opinion of the Supreme Court in *Quinn* v. *United States,* decided in 1955. Quinn, an official of the United Electrical Workers Union, was subpoenaed to testify before the House Committee on Un-American Activities, which was investigating Communist infiltration into the union. Quinn was asked whether he was a member of the Communist Party and based his refusal to answer (as did other officers of the union) on "the First Amendment to the Constitution, supplemented by the Fifth Amendment." The Supreme Court held that this constituted an adequate assertion of the privilege against self-incrimination secured by the Fifth Amendment, and therefore did not find it necessary to decide whether Quinn also had a constitutional right of silence under the First Amendment. But in so holding the Court went out of its way to reaffirm the ruling of the Kilbourn case.

The power to investigate, the Court said, broad as it may be, is subject to recognized limitations. It may not be used to inquire into private affairs unrelated to a valid legislative purpose. Nor does it extend to an area in which Congress is forbidden to legislate. Similarly, the power to investigate must not be confused with any powers of law enforcement; those powers are assigned under our Constitution to the Executive and the Judiciary.

On the basis of the Kilbourn, Daugherty, Sinclair, and Quinn cases a pattern of constitutional law in respect to Congressional investigations and the right of silence emerges with a reasonable degree of clarity. The basic responsibility of the Court here as elsewhere is the accommodation and arbitration of competing interests. On the one hand is the social interest in the efficient and effective carrying out by Congress of its constitutional responsibilities; on the other is the individual's interest in his own right of privacy and silence and the social interest in a democracy that the right of privacy and silence be preserved.

In weighing the competing interests, it is important to recognize what legitimate constitutional function the investigation is incident to. Of all the functions of Congress by far the most important is its lawmaking function. Hence, when its powers of investigation are exercised as part of the lawmaking function, they are likely to be held broadest by the Supreme Court and least subject to judicial restriction. To legislate intelligently, Congress must know the relevant facts, and the Court is not likely to interfere with its efforts to obtain those facts if the bona-fide purpose of a particular investigation is the acquisition of facts necessary for intelligent lawmaking.

Broad as is the power to investigate as an incident of lawmaking, it cannot be broader than the lawmaking power itself. The power to investigate legislatively does not extend to an area in which Congress is forbidden to legislate. The First Amendment forbids Congress to make any law respecting an establishment of religion. Congress, therefore, may not investigate to ascertain facts relevant only to legislation respecting an establishment of religion. Congress may investigate direct or face-to-face lobbying but, as we shall see in the next chapter, it probably may not investigate so-called indirect lobbying, i.e., appeals to the public to exert pressure upon Congressmen; for the power of Congress validly to legislate in that area is denied by the First Amendment guarantee of freedom of the press and freedom of petition.

Besides making laws, Congress has a direct concern in knowing how they are being enforced and administered. Hence, as the Daugherty and Sinclair decisions make clear, it may investigate the operations of the Executive and Judicial departments of the government and may (subject, of course, to the privilege against self-incrimination) compel disclosure of relevant information, not merely from the Federal officials themselves but from private persons who are not connected with the government but who possess the relevant information. This too, it should be noted, is clearly related to the lawmaking function of Congress; for if Congress finds that a particular law is being poorly administered by the department charged with its administration, Congress may change the law to prescribe more closely how it should be administered or may transfer its administration to a different department, or, in an extreme case, may impeach the officials under the constitutionally conferred legislative power of impeachment.

Congress, however, has power to impeach only government officials; it has no power to try, convict, or punish private individuals who may have violated any of the laws enacted by Congress. The responsibility for prosecuting, trying, and punishing law violators has been conferred by the Constitution upon the other departments of our government, and indeed, under the provision forbidding bills of attainder, has been expressly denied to Congress. It would appear, therefore, that, only if in the course of a legitimate investigation for a valid legislative purpose a Congressional committee should uncover evidence of wrongdoing on the part of private individuals, may it validly turn over this evidence to the Department of Justice or to any other law-enforcement official for appropriate action; it may not validly engage in an investigation for the specific purpose of uncovering such evidence and initiating the process of prosecution, trial, and punishment.

Perhaps the most difficult problems in the area of Congressional investigations arise out of the exercise by Congress of its so-called " informing function." Woodrow Wilson and a host of other scholars have argued that, besides making laws, Congress has the power and responsibility of educating the American public on matters affecting the public interest. This has been the principal justification for much of the Congressional and State legislative investigation into Communism and other subversive activities. The House Committee on Un-American Activities, for example, has been operating since 1938 and during this entire period has made almost no recommendations for legislation. It has conceived its function primarily as exposing subversive activities and educating the American public to the dangers of Communism. To what extent Congress may infringe upon a private citizen's right of silence in order to carry out its " informing function " remains yet to be definitively decided by the Supreme Court.

Chapter 4. *Liberty of Petition, Assembly, and Association*

THE RIGHT TO PETITION

Every American who at some time has (and what American has not?) sent a letter to the President commending or criticizing his position on the farm problem or civil liberties, or to the head of the local sanitation department deploring the littered condition of the streets, or to his alderman urging him to vote for an appropriation to purchase new equipment for the school gymnasium, has thereby exercised his constitutional right of petition. If, unable to obtain a satisfactory reply from the President, the sanitation commission, or the alderman, he attends a meeting of like-minded indignant citizens in the school auditorium or in somebody's living room, he has exercised his right of assembly. And if, at the meeting, it is decided to form a Committee for More Trash Cans on Street Corners, or a Committee For (or Against) the United Nations (or the Public Schools), or a Committee for a Higher (or Lower) Tariff, and he joins the Committee, he has exercised his right of association.

The First Amendment does not mention the right of association; it speaks only of "the right of the people peaceably to assemble, and to petition the Government for a redress of grievances." Moreover, the right of assembly was historically conceived merely as an incident or aid to the right of petition, as if the Amendment had read "the right of the people peaceably to assemble *in order to* petition the Government for a redress of grievances." Today, however, it is universally recognized and accepted that the right of peaceable assembly for a lawful purpose is an independent right, as fundamental as free speech and a free press to a democratic society and equally protected from Federal restriction by the First Amendment and from State restriction by the Fourteenth. Association is nothing more than continuing assembly, and, therefore, though not expressly mentioned in the Bill of Rights, is equally a constitutionally protected, basic liberty of Americans.

The citizen who sent a letter to the local sanitation department demanding more trash cans so that the streets may be cleaner is obviously petitioning for the redress of a specific grievance; but this is not so obvious in the case of the citizen who writes an indignant letter to the President on his lack of concern for civil liberties. It is even less obvious if the letter is commendatory rather than critical, for in such case the citizen has no grievance to be redressed. Nevertheless, there is no question that today the right of petition is as broad as the right of speech, and encompasses any communication to the government or a government official on any matter within the area of governmental concern.

It might seem surprising that the right to send a letter to a Congressman needs to be constitutionally guaranteed. Every American takes it for granted that, although there is no assurance that the Congressman will do what he is asked or even read the letter, still "there is no harm in asking." Perhaps this is true today; but if it is, it was not always so; there was a time when there could be much harm in asking. Alice, it will be remembered, had read in a book somewhere that "a cat may look at a king," but the book had not said that it could with impunity address the king. According to the Book of Esther, it was the law of the Persian Empire, known to all from India even unto Ethiopia, that whoever came into the presence of the king without prior invitation was punishable with death, and this law included the queen coming to petition for her own life and the lives of her people. In 1641 the Long Parliament tried a group of Anglican bishops for treason because they presented a petition to the king charging that they had been unlawfully excluded from sessions of the House of Lords. In 1650 the same Parliament banished John Lilburne for petitioning it in behalf of his uncle whose property had been confiscated.

When, in 1767 and 1768, the citizens of Massachusetts petitioned the king in protest against imposts on tea, Parliament and the king severely rebuked them and directed the governor of the colony to transmit to London full information "touching all treasons" so that the offenders might be tried and punished. It was for that reason that when the First Continental Congress met in Philadelphia in 1774 and recited the colonists' grievances against the king and their rights as

Englishmen, it asserted: "That they have a right peaceably to assemble, consider of their grievances, and petition the King; and that all prosecutions, prohibitory proclamations, and commitments for the same are illegal."

It should not be assumed that all this is ancient history and that the right of petition has always been recognized and accepted in the United States. When, in the 1830's, petitions against slavery began pouring into Congress, the House of Representatives adopted a standing rule, in force from 1840 to 1845, that "no petition, memorial, resolution or other paper praying the abolition of slavery shall be received by this House, or entertained in any way whatever." During the depression of 1893–94, J. S. Coxey of Ohio led his "army" of some thousand persons into Washington to petition for the establishment of a nation-wide public-works program to end the depression. The demonstration fizzled out when its leaders were arrested for walking on the grass of the Capitol grounds. The Bonus Army march in 1932 to petition the government for immediate payment of a bonus culminated in a less humorous denouement; the marchers were expelled from Washington and their camps burned by Federal troops and tanks under command of General Douglas MacArthur. In the World War I period petitions for repeal of the sedition laws and against recruitment measures resulted in imprisonment for the petitioners.

In our own day persons who signed the Stockholm peace petition, or a petition for clemency for the Rosenbergs, or a Communist Party or even Progressive Party nominating petition are very likely to have that fact count against them in applying for or seeking to retain government employment or employment in private industry working on defense contracts, or in resisting deportation, or in a variety of other situations where their loyalty is called into question. The fact that the American public does not uniformly believe that "there is no harm in asking" and that exercise of the right of petition does not entail punitive consequences is indicated by the difficulties encountered not long ago by a reporter of a Midwestern newspaper who vainly sought to obtain signatures from street passers-by to a petition incorporating part of the Declaration of Independence.

The First Amendment guarantee of the right of petition stems from the Magna Carta, one section of which provided that if the king or any of his officers "shall in any circumstances have failed in the performance of them [his obligations] toward any person or shall have broken through any of these articles of peace and security," then a committee of four barons should present the grievance to the king and "petition to have it redressed without delay." The importance of the right of petition in a representative democracy is evidenced by the fact that the development of Parliament itself is traceable to this provision. By the eighteenth century the right of petition was well recognized as a liberty of Englishmen, and its denial to the citizens of Massachusetts and the other colonies was one of the grievances that gave rise to the Revolutionary War. The incorporation of the right of petition in the First Amendment as a liberty of Americans was therefore a natural and inevitable development.

Like all constitutional rights, the right of petition may find itself competing with another and in a particular instance superior societal interest. In such case the right of petition must yield to the extent necessary for the protection of the superior interest. It is rare that exercise of the right of petition would seriously threaten any other societal interest; yet it is by no means inconceivable.

This, the State of California claimed, was the situation in *Bridges v. California*. That case arose out of a labor dispute between A. F. of L. and CIO unions struggling for control of the Pacific waterfront. After a California judge issued a decision in favor of the A. F. of L. union, and while a motion for a new trial was being considered by him, Harry Bridges, leader of the CIO union (who had divided his career in the United States between militant unionism and defending himself from unceasing and multifarious prosecutions and legal proceedings), sent a telegram to the U. S. Secretary of Labor in which he referred to the judge's decision as "outrageous." The telegram stated further than any attempt to enforce the decision would tie up the port of Los Angeles and involve the entire Pacific Coast, and concluded with the announcement that the CIO union, representing 12,000 members, did "not intend to allow State courts to override the majority vote of members in choosing its officers and representatives and to override the National Labor Relations Board."

Bridges was brought before the judge and convicted of contempt of court on the ground that the telegram tended to obstruct justice, since its effect might be to intimidate the judge and thus influence his decision on the motion for a new trial. The Supreme Court reversed the conviction on the ground that the sending of the telegram to the Secretary of Labor was an exercise of the First Amendment right of petition and under the circumstances of the case did not present any clear and present danger to the obstruction of justice, since there was nothing in it that would have affected a mind of reasonable fortitude, which it was to be presumed the judge possessed.

The Court did not find that Bridges' exercise of the right of petition presented a clear and present danger to the fair and uncoerced administration of justice. But it is clear that, if it had, the result would have been different. Suppose petitions in large numbers are presented to members of a jury sitting in a particular case. It is probable that those responsible could constitutionally be punished for obstructing justice. There is a strong societal interest that a jury should decide a person's innocence or guilt exclusively on the basis of the evidence presented to it in open court and not on the basis of petitions from outsiders. Since a jury is not likely to have the same fortitude and objectivity that a judge has, the submission of the petitions may well constitute a clear and present threat to that societal interest, and the government therefore has the constitutional power to avert the danger even if to do so it must restrict somewhat the right of petition.

While petitions to juries are extremely rare, petitions of clemency to judges are by no means uncommon, if indeed not usual. Generally, the petition is in the form of individual letters, frequently by the minister, priest, or rabbi of the defendant's family. Where the case is well publicized such letters may be sent by hundreds of strangers whose knowledge of the case comes exclusively from newspaper accounts. If the case has political elements the letters of petitions may come in the thousands, and may be the result of intense organizing activity by a " Committee for Justice to " or " Committee for Clemency for." The Sacco-Vanzetti case and, more recently, the Rosenberg espionage case are illustrations.

Even the Supreme Court has been subjected to the exercise of the right of petition. Anglo-American law has developed the brief *amicus curiae* or " friend of the court." The purpose of such a brief, submitted by one who is not a party to the litigation before the court, is to supply the court with legal enlightenment from a more or less disinterested source on an issue not adequately argued by the parties' attorneys. With the advent of the Roosevelt Court and its liberal approach towards civil rights and welfare legislation, briefs *amicus curiae* descended upon the Court in great number. The overwhelming majority of the briefs were from organizations interested in the particular political issue before the Court, and often their real purpose was not to shed light on a particular constitutional or legal question, but to reveal to the Court the feelings of the organizations and their members on how they should like the case to be decided. In other words, the brief *amicus curiae* became a petition for the redress of grievances. This might not all be improper in view of the great political power of the Court, exercised though it may be through judicial forms and patterns. Nevertheless, the ever-mounting number of petitions in the form of briefs filed with the Court threatened the supposition that the Court was after all a legal tribunal for the legal adjudication of claims between individual litigants and not a senate for the determination of political issues. The Court, accordingly, found it necessary to revise its rules and place severe restrictions on the filing of briefs *amicus curiae*.

It is the legislative branch of government that is most subjected to the exercise of the right of petition. The exertion of "pressure" upon legislators, through letters and postcards, petitions, personal visits, telephone calls, and so on, organized or spontaneous, is an important part of the legislative process under the American democratic system. The fact that the exercise of these "pressures" was accorded constitutional protection in the First Amendment evidences the conviction of the fathers of our republic that the right of petition is essential to enlightened, democratic government.

Legislators are presumed to be mature, sophisticated, and responsible persons who are not likely to be panicked into doing some rash and disastrous act. Hence, it is not likely that there are many instances where a clear and present danger to a superior societal interest would justify restriction upon the right to petition the legislature for a redress of grievances. It is for these reasons that of all the liberties of Americans the liberty to petition the legislature for the redress of grievances has probably been subject to the least restriction.

Yet even the right to petition the legislature for the enactment of certain laws or the defeat of others may constitutionally be subject to some regulation. Professional lobbyists exercise the right of petition for themselves and for their clients, and the fact that they are paid for their services does not remove them from the protection of the First Amendment any more than it does paid newspaper editors, radio commentators, or clergymen. Nevertheless, the fact that they are paid may be relevant information which the legislators (and the people) are entitled to have and may need in order to legislate wisely.

Present-day legislative complexities, said the Supreme Court recently in *United States* v. *Harriss,* are such that individual members of Congress cannot be expected to explore the myriad pressures to which they are regularly subjected. Yet full realization of the American ideal of government by elected representatives depends to no small extent on their ability to properly evaluate such pressures. Otherwise the voice of the people may all too easily be drowned out by the voice of special interest groups seeking favored treatment as the public weal.

This is an evil which Congress has a right to prevent, even if the price is some slight restriction upon freedom of petition. Hence, the Court held, Congress may require the professional lobbyist to register and report the source of his income. A Congressional committee, the Court also held in 1953 (in *United States* v. *Rumely*), may likewise investigate lobbying and compel lobbyists to disclose the identity of their clients. Unquestionably this restricts the right of petition to some extent, for undoubtedly some organizations and associations will refrain from engaging a lobbyist if their identity will be revealed. Nevertheless, the restriction is comparatively minor and must yield to the superior need of Congress to obtain the information in order to legislate wisely. This is so, however, only with respect to lobbying in the commonly accepted meaning of that term, i.e., face-to-face influencing of Congressmen. Where it is sought to influence legislators by appealing not to the legislator but to the public generally, as through publications distributed to the public seeking to obtain its support for or against a proposed enactment and urging the readers to communicate their views to their Congressmen, it is probable that a similar requirement of registration and disclosure of subscribers to the publications would not withstand attack under the First Amendment.

ASSEMBLY, LAWFUL AND UNLAWFUL

Since man is a gregarious creature, the history of assembly is as ancient as the history of man. As long ago as history is recorded, men assembled together in worship to the gods. Assembly to discuss secular affairs is probably just as old. America particularly, with its town-meeting tradition, recognizes freedom of assembly as an indispensable element of its democratic system. The British king's interference with the right of the colonists to assemble peaceably was one of the grievances specified by the First Continental Congress in 1774. The very idea of a government republican in form, the Supreme Court said in 1875 in *United States* v. *Cruikshank*, implies a right on the part of its citizens to meet peaceably for consultation in respect to public affairs. The right of peaceable assembly is a right cognate to the rights of free speech and of free press, and is equally fundamental. Like these rights it is not subject to governmental prohibition or restriction in the absence of a clear and immediate threat to a superior societal interest.

It is for that reason that the Roosevelt Court, in *Thomas* v. *Collins*, invalidated a Texas statute requiring labor organizers to register with the secretary of state and obtain official organizers' cards before they could legally solicit union membership. The statute had been enforced against R. J. Thomas, then president of the United Auto Workers, who went to Texas to test the law and, giving the police adequate advance notice, addressed a union meeting at which he urged all non-union members present to join his union. The interest of the State in protecting its citizens through the regulation of vocations was deemed by the Supreme Court to be insufficient to sustain the statutory restriction upon the right of peaceable assembly to organize a labor union. On the other hand, the Court, in *International Auto Workers* v. *Wisconsin Board*, did later sustain the constitutionality of an order by a State Employment Relations Board forbidding work stoppages through the calling of special union meetings during working hours.

Of course, an assembly that develops into a riot or is clearly and immediately about to develop into a riot may constitutionally be dispersed by the police. The community's interest in preventing riots is necessarily paramount over the right of assembly. Nor is an assembly formed preparatory to an insurrection or other attempt to overthrow the government constitutionally immune from interference. Such assemblies are by their nature unlawful and the First Amendment does not make them lawful. What the Amendment does is to impose upon the government a standard of strict accountability, requiring it to establish the clarity and immediacy of the threat to the paramount interest.

Consider *De Jonge* v. *Oregon.* There Kirk De Jonge, a Communist Party organizer, was convicted under a State criminal-syndicalism law for helping to organize and for speaking at a public meeting in Portland held under the auspices of the Communist Party, which, the State charged, was an organization advocating criminal syndicalism, i.e., violent or unlawful change in government or industry. The evidence showed that some 150 to 200 persons were present at the meeting, which was open to the public without charge; that the meeting was peaceful and orderly; that the purpose of the meeting was to protest against illegal raids on workers' halls and houses and against the shooting of striking longshoremen by the police. The meeting was raided by the police and De Jonge was arrested, convicted, and sentenced to prison for seven years.

The Supreme Court set aside the conviction on the ground that an assembly otherwise lawful may not be made unlawful merely by reason of the auspices under which it is conducted. Under the First Amendment, peaceable assembly for lawful discussion cannot be proscribed and those who conduct it cannot be branded as criminals on that score. The test of the lawfulness of an assembly is not *who* conducts it, but *how* it is conducted and *for what purpose.* If it is conducted peaceably for a lawful purpose, it does not become unlawful merely because it is sponsored by the Communist Party.

De Jonge v. *Oregon* was decided in 1937, long before Congress found the Communist Party to be an unlawful, international conspiracy to overthrow the government of the United States by force and violence. Yet it is probable that the result would be the same today under the particular indictment involved in that case. De Jonge was not charged with advocating at the meeting the overthrow of the government by force or violence; nor with advocating membership in the Communist Party (although, in fact, he did that); nor was it charged in the indictment that the conducting of the meeting was part of a step in the conspiracy of the Communist Party to overthrow the government. De Jonge was charged only with actively participating in a meeting conducted by the Communist Party. The unlawfulness of the sponsor, said the Court, was personal and did not corrupt all that it touched.

The meeting participated in by De Jonge was conducted on private property, and since it was conducted peaceably and for a lawful purpose it could not be prohibited by government. But may the government prohibit peaceable assemblies on public property? May a municipality prohibit peaceable meetings on its streets and in its parks? The Supreme Judicial Court of Massachusetts, in an opinion by Justice Holmes shortly before he was elevated to the United States Supreme Court, answered that it could. The streets and parks, said Justice Holmes, belong to the municipality, which has the same proprietary rights over them that a private owner has over his property and which can forbid assemblies in the streets and parks to the same extent that a homeowner can forbid them in his parlor.

In *Davis* v. *Massachusetts,* the United States Supreme Court affirmed this decision, but in *Hague* v. *CIO* the Roosevelt Court in effect overruled it. Wherever the technical title to streets and parks may rest, the Court said, they have immemorially been held in trust for the use of the public and time out of mind have been used for purposes of assembly, communicating thoughts between citizens, and discussing public questions. Such use of the streets and public places has from ancient times been a part of the privileges and immunities, rights and liberties of citizens. While it may be regulated to ensure equality for all, it may not be prohibited.

Hague v. *CIO* represented the culmination of a long series of incidents involving public assemblies for political and industrial purposes in New Jersey. Meetings called to organize workers and induce them to join labor unions were frequently suppressed, as were meetings called to protest the suppressions. Roger Baldwin, director of the American Civil Liberties Union, was arrested when he started to read the Declaration of Independence in front of the city hall in Paterson and was convicted of conducting an unlawful assembly.

Restrictions on public assemblies were most severe in Jersey City, whose mayor, Frank Hague, achieved immortality with his proclamation, "I am the law." Hague resisted the unionization of Jersey City workers with all his energy and ingenuity. Speakers seeking to protest were promptly relieved of their literature, escorted to the wharf, placed on ferry boats, and "deported" to New York. The editor of the *Catholic Worker* was refused permission to explain the papal encyclicals at a public meeting. Even a United States Senator, William Borah, was not allowed to speak. Organizers for the

A. F. of L. and CIO were invariably denied permits to hold meetings in streets and parks.

The permits were denied under a city ordinance forbidding all public assemblies in the streets or parks without a permit, which might be refused by the Director of Public Safety "for the purpose of preventing riots, disturbances or disorderly assemblage." Counsel for the Jersey City officials contended before the Supreme Court that if the proposed meetings were held riots were likely to follow. They showed that protests against the meetings had been received from the Chamber of Commerce, two veterans' organizations, and the Ladies of the Grand Army of the Republic. A group of veterans had announced that if the CIO were allowed to hold an open-air meeting they would take matters in their own hands and see to it that the meeting was broken up. (It was also shown by opposing counsel that at least some of the protests were inspired by Mayor Hague and his associates. As the Federal Circuit Court remarked: "Reversing the usual procedure, Mayor Hague troubled the waters in order to fish in them.")

In *Hague* v. *CIO* the Supreme Court held the ordinance void on its face. Some two years later the Court was to hold in *Cox* v. *New Hampshire* that a municipality may constitutionally prohibit parades (in that case a religious parade by Jehovah's Witnesses) on the streets without a prior permit, if the permit is granted or refused only for " considerations of time, place and manner so as to conserve the public convenience." In other words, public assemblies can be regulated in the interest of all uses that properly may be made of the streets and parks. A permit could therefore be refused if a group sought to parade or hold a public meeting on a busy traffic-laden street or at a time and place previously pre-empted by another group.

Hence, if the ordinance in Jersey City had empowered the city officials to grant or withhold permits for the purpose of accommodating as equally as practicable all persons and groups, it would probably have been upheld as constitutional. But the ordinance did not make comfort or convenience in the use of streets or parks the standard of official action. It enabled the Director of Public Safety to refuse a permit on his mere opinion that such refusal would prevent " riots, disturbances or disorderly assemblage." Such an ordinance can be made the instrument of arbitrary suppressions of the free expression of views on public affairs, since the prohibition of all public assemblies would undoubtedly prevent riots, disturbances, and disorderly assemblage. But, the Court said, uncontrolled official suppression of the right of assembly cannot be justified on the basis of the duty of the government to maintain order in connection with the exercise of that right.

Mayor Hague and the city administration accepted the decision in full faith and made no further attempt to interfere with public meetings. It is at least possible that this change of heart came about in part from some spirited discussions between Hague and representatives of the Roosevelt administration; but the fact that it occurred immediately after the Court's decision was announced gives good ground for belief that the decision played a major part in the reversal of the city's policy and actions. This is another illustration of the Supreme Court's role in molding the conscience of the community.

As we have seen, the First Amendment does not protect unlawful assemblies, i.e., assemblies whose purpose or whose procedure is unlawful. This is well illustrated by a consideration of picketing, which, though usually spoken of in terms of freedom of speech, may also constitute an exercise of the right of assembly. Peaceful picketing for a lawful purpose may not be forbidden by court injunction, but where the purpose is illegal it may be prohibited. For example, in *Hughes* v. *Superior Court* the Supreme Court held that a group of persons could be enjoined from picketing a chain store which, the pickets claimed, refused to hire Negro clerks in proportion to the ratio of Negro customers. The California courts held that while the law of California, which had no Fair Employment Practices statute, did not forbid an employer voluntarily to adopt such a racial quota system for employees, it did forbid compulsion to effect that end. Since picketing constituted a form of compulsion, the United States Supreme Court held, it might constitutionally be forbidden by the State. Similarly, picketing to induce an employer to breach a valid contract with a rival union or to adopt a closed shop in a State which prohibits closed shops may be forbidden by the State, since the purpose of the picketing is unlawful.

On the other hand, even if the end sought to be achieved by picketing is lawful, the picketing may be restrained if its method is unlawful. Thus, if the pickets carry signs with statements that are factually untruthful, the picketing may be forbidden. And if the picketing is attended by violence or other disturbance of the peace, it may likewise be forbidden. As the Court held in *Milk Wagon Drivers Union* v. *Meadowmoor Co.*, utterance in a context of violence loses its significance as an appeal to reason and becomes part of an instrument of force. As such it is not sheltered by the Constitution.

We have also seen that the government is not required to wait until violence has actually broken out before it may restrict the right of assembly; it may act if a clear and present danger exists that violence will break out. This is clear if those conducting the assembly are responsible for the threatened outbreak of violence, as where they incite violence against others. Suppose, however, that those conducting the meeting are acting lawfully, inciting no violence to any person, but are expressing unpopular (though lawful) views that appear likely to arouse the audience or some of its members to violence against the speakers. May the police constitutionally disperse the assembly and direct the speakers to move on? May an assembly be declared unlawful even though those conducting the assembly have said or done nothing unlawful?

The decision in *Feiner* v. *New York,* discussed in the preceding chapter, indicates that the answer probably is yes. But only as a temporary emergency measure in extreme circumstances. The Bill of Rights protects the expression of unpopular views; no Constitution is needed to protect persons who tell the people what the people want to hear. The First Amendment imposes upon the government an affirmative obligation to take such measures as may be necessary to insure the safety of those expressing views that are unpopular and even hated and feared. Hence, the primary duty of the police is to protect the speaker and to arrest, not him, but those who would use force to prevent him from speaking. But if on a particular occasion there are not enough policemen present or available to restrain the crowd should the speaker be permitted to continue, and the danger of an outbreak of violence against the speaker is clear and immediate, it is probable that the Court would hold that the Constitution empowers the police to silence the speaker and disperse the assembly in order to protect the higher societal value of preserving the public peace.

FREEDOM OF ASSOCIATION

The Bill of Rights nowhere makes specific reference to freedom of association. The Constitution and Bill of Rights were written in a generation and a milieu that emphasized individualism and the rights of individuals. The experiences the fathers of our republic had with associations undoubtedly conditioned them toward a suspicious approach to associations, to the extent that they thought of associations at all. The associations they were familiar with were the religious associations constituting the established churches and the political associations constituting the British government and colonial agents. The political associations known as political parties were looked on with suspicion and mistrust by many of the founding fathers, and Washington in his Farewell Address warned against "factions" in the political life of the new nation. When, therefore, the Supreme Court in *Hague* v. *CIO* dismissed the companion action of the American Civil Liberties Union (which too had been denied a permit to hold a public meeting) on the ground that it was a corporation and that the constitutional liberty of freedom of assembly was secured only to individuals, it was reflecting truly the philosophy of the founding fathers.

The individualistic spirit of the fathers was a natural consequence of the expanding frontier and, at least in its pristine purity, was doomed to disappearance with the frontier. Even as Washington warned against "factions," political parties had crystallized and become a prominent and permanent aspect of the American political system. Madison inveighed against monopolies, but Hamilton more accurately predicted the inevitable development of the American economy in the form of commercial associations known as corporations. Inasmuch as most newspapers and other publications today are owned by corporations, freedom of the press would have little significance if the Supreme Court took the same position (which, of course, it has not done) in respect to that right as it took in respect to the right of assembly.

Today we are beginning to recognize that associations, even those competing in some degree with the state for loyalty and sovereignty of individuals, need not be inimical to democracy. Quite the contrary, with the ever-expanding scope of governmental activities and jurisdiction, and the magnitude and increasing complexity of modern social life, voluntary associations, political, religious, economic, cultural, fraternal, social, have become an indispensable ally in the struggle to preserve democracy against totalitarianism. To take one simple illustration: the industrial associations known as labor unions have probably been the most important single force in the struggle for industrial democracy.

While the Bill of Rights makes no mention of association, and the founding fathers looked with suspicion upon such associations as they were acquainted with, there can be little doubt that they recognized the right to associate as a liberty of Americans. When men band together for a single public demonstration of feeling or expression of a grievance they exercise their right of assembly; when they continue banding and acting together until the grievance is redressed they exercise their right of association. Freedom of indefinite or permanent association is as fundamental to democracy and as much a liberty of Americans as freedom of temporary assembly, and no less entitled to constitutional protection.

Like the other First Amendment rights, the right of association is subject to governmental restriction where necessary for the protection of an important societal interest. In 1947 it was so held in *United Public Workers of America* v. *Mitchell*, where the Supreme Court upheld the validity of a provision of the Hatch Act forbidding officials and employees of the Federal government to " take any active part in political management or political campaigns." The statute had been attacked as an unconstitutional restriction of various First Amendment rights, including the right of assembly (i.e., association).

The Hatch Act provision impinged upon several liberties — specifically, freedom of speech, freedom of the press, freedom of petition, freedom of association, and freedom of the elective franchise. All but the last (which will be considered in a later chapter) are First Amendment liberties, and the opinion of the Court in the Mitchell case did not spell out which particular liberty or liberties were at issue; it simply referred to " the right of a citizen to act as a party official or worker to further his own political views," and spoke of this as one of the " essential rights of the First Amendment."

However, what was really in issue, if not exclusively then predominantly, was the right of (political) association. This is particularly indicated by the provision in the Hatch Act permitting government employees "the right to vote as they choose" and to express their opinions on "all political subjects and candidates," but forbidding them only to "take any active part" in any campaign or cause "specifically identified with any National or State political party."

The validity of the provision was upheld by a majority of the Supreme Court because it felt that Congress acted reasonably in deciding that political activities by government employees menace the integrity and competency of the civil-service system and that legislation was necessary to forestall the danger. Political activity by Federal employees, moreover, tends toward a one-party system, and the social interest in maintaining a two-party political system and a non-partisan civil service is sufficiently important to justify the restriction upon the employees' right of association. Justices Black and Rutledge dissented because they deemed the Act an infringement of rights protected by the First Amendment.

UNLAWFUL ASSOCIATION AND THE COMMUNIST CONSPIRACY

Just as assembly for an unlawful purpose is not constitutionally protected, so too association for an unlawful purpose is not made immune from governmental interference by the First Amendment. Today unlawful associations in the context of civil liberties are generally taken to refer to political associations whose purpose is to overthrow the government; but surprisingly the constitutional law concerning unlawful associations goes back more than half a century and grew out of religious, not political, association.

Up until the end of the nineteenth century the practice of polygamy was an important part of the doctrine of the Church of Jesus Christ of Latter-Day Saints, popularly known as the Mormon Church, although it was unlawful in practically all States. The Territory of Idaho, to implement its laws against polygamy, had enacted a statute disenfranchising all persons who practiced or advocated polygamy or were members "of any order, organization or association" that taught or advocated polygamy. In *Davis* v. *Beason* the Supreme Court in 1890 upheld the constitutionality of this statute and the conviction of a member of the Mormon Church who, notwithstanding the statute, registered and voted in the Territory.

The defendant, it is important to note, was not himself charged either with practicing or with teaching polygamy; he was charged only with being a member of the Mormon Church which, he knew, advocated polygamy. The statute was aimed not merely at the individual Mormons who practiced or preached polygamy, but at those who associated through common membership in the Church with the practitioners and preachers of polygamy. The Court's opinion considered only the question whether polygamy could be outlawed; it did not consider or even mention the difficult problem whether the statute could constitutionally penalize those who did no more than belong to the Mormon Church, even though they personally may have disagreed with that particular tenet of the Church.

Admittedly the practice of polygamy was not the only tenet of the Mormon Church. Important as it was, it was not an indispensable tenet; for, since 1890 and as a result of the Supreme Court's decisions, the Church has given up polygamy, yet the Church survives and flourishes. The effect of the decision, therefore, would seem to be that if one purpose of an association is unlawful the association itself may be declared unlawful and membership in it penalized. That this was the effect of the decision was made clear a few months later when, in *Church of Jesus Christ of Latter Day Saints* v. *United States,* the Supreme Court upheld the constitutionality of an act of Congress that voided the charter of the Mormon Church and declared its property forfeited to the government. Congress, said the Court, has the power to dissolve this unlawful association and to prevent its funds from being used for the unlawful purpose of promoting polygamy.

The issue of freedom of association was implicit in both of these cases, but it was neither asserted in argument nor considered in decision. The extent, therefore, to which they may now be deemed by the Supreme Court to be persuasive precedent in cases involving claimed infringement upon the right of association is uncertain. Today the arena of contest between the power of the legislature and the right of association lies in the field of political association, and the major issue is the degree to which associations may be outlawed because of the unlawfulness of their ultimate goal to overthrow the government by force and violence.

An understanding of the problem of unlawful political associations requires some understanding of the concept of conspiracy, developed in the criminal law and borrowed from the criminal law by the protectors of internal security. The purpose of the criminal law is to prevent the commission of crimes, and punishment is inflicted on the assumption that others will thereby be deterred from committing the particular crime. If two persons hold up a bank and escape with the loot, the law, if it catches up with them, will punish them for having committed the crime of *robbery*. It does so not (we hope) out of vindictiveness, but to deter other would-be holdup men. Suppose the holdup men are apprehended after they have drawn their weapons but before the bank teller hands the money over to them. They will be punished for *attempted robbery;* for the community has an interest in deterring not only successful holdups, but also unsuccessful holdup attempts, and therefore punishes as crimes unsuccessful attempts to hold up banks. Suppose one of the two persons urges the other to hold up the bank. The urging too may be declared a crime (*incitement to robbery*) and may be punished as such. And suppose the two persons agree to hold up the bank, decide upon a plan of procedure, purchase weapons and a getaway car, and set a date for the holdup, but are apprehended by the police before that day arrives. They may be punished for *conspiracy to commit* the crime of *robbery*. Finally, suppose that they agree to urge a third person to rob the bank but are apprehended before they meet that person. Since incitement to robbery is a crime of itself, they may be punished for *conspiracy to commit* the crime of *incitement to robbery*.

Our present concern is with conspiracy. A number of points should be noted here. In the first place, the state designates conspiracy as a crime and punishes it as such irrespective of the probability or improbability of success. It is not a valid defense to a prosecution for conspiracy to rob a bank that the defendants' plans were so poor and impracticable that any attempt to carry them out would almost certainly have failed.

Secondly, unlike robbery, attempt, or incitement, conspiracy requires two or more guilty participants; there can be no conspiracy by a single individual.

Third, although there must be two or more participants, all the participants are considered by the law to be a single unit and each participant is legally responsible for any act in furtherance of the conspiracy committed by any other participant, whether or not he knew or approved of it.

Fourth, unlike robbery or attempted robbery (but like incitement to robbery) conspiracy necessarily involves the exercise of speech.

Finally, unlike attempt to commit robbery, whose time relationship to the robbery itself is that of immediacy, conspiracy may be remote in time from the robbery itself. Persons may conspire in January to rob a bank in June or in the following January, or even five years hence.

The anti-Communist laws of today are predicated, sometimes expressly and sometimes implicitly, upon the premise that the Communist Party is not really a political party but a criminal conspiracy — a conspiracy to rob the American people of their democratic government by force and violence, in no whit different from the conspiracy of the holdup men to rob the bank's stockholders of their assets by force and violence. In the Communist Control Act of 1954, for example, Congress declares that the Communist Party, " although purportedly a political party, is in fact *an instrumentality of a conspiracy* to overthrow the Government of the United States." The Act lists the differences between the Communist Party and the generally accepted political parties in the United States: the policies of the Communist Party are dictated by foreign leaders; its members are subject to slavish discipline imposed by its chiefs; the Party recognizes no constitutional or statutory limitations upon either its conduct or that of its members; and, finally, it is dedicated, as the agent of a hostile foreign power, to the violent overthrow of the United States government.

If the Communist Party is deemed a conspiracy to rob the American people of their democratic heritage analogous to a conspiracy to rob a bank, serious civil-liberties problems are avoided. The probability or improbability of success in capturing the government becomes as irrelevant as the probability or improbability of success in capturing the bank deposits. The fact that a particular member of the Communist Party may not approve or even know of any specific action taken by the Party leaders is immaterial, since every member of a conspiracy is guilty by association with every other member and is responsible for the acts of every other member. The fact that speech is involved in the activities of the Communist Party no more entitles that Party to the benefits of the freedom-of-speech guarantee than it does the bank robbers. And there need be no concern about any " clear and present danger " concept since a conspiracy to rob a bank is equally criminal whether it calls for immediate or future action.

Moreover, it need not even be shown that the Communist Party leaders themselves actually intend to overthrow the government by force or violence. It is criminal to incite or advocate the forcible overthrow of the government by others, as it is criminal to incite or advocate bank robberies by others, and a conspiracy to incite or advocate either is equally a crime. This, it will be remembered, was the basis of the prosecution in *Dennis* v. *United States;* the Communist Party leaders were convicted not of *conspiracy to overthrow* the government, but of *conspiracy to advocate* its overthrow. As the late Justice Jackson said in his concurring opinion in the Dennis case: " The law of conspiracy has been the chief means at the Government's disposal to deal with the growing problems created by such organizations (as the Communist Party). . . . I find no constitutional authority for taking this weapon from the Government. There is no constitutional right to ' gang up ' on the Government."

The Smith Act, under which the Dennis case arose, was not based on the premise that the Communist Party is an illegal conspiracy. Indeed, it did not even mention the Communist Party. Dennis and his co-defendants were indicted (1) for *conspiracy to advocate* the forcible overthrow of the government and (2) for *conspiracy to organize* the Communist Party whose purpose, the prosecution charged, was to advocate the forcible overthrow of the government. The first count of the indictment — conspiracy to advocate — relates to freedom of speech and has been considered in the preceding chapter. The second count — conspiracy to organize the Communist Party — relates to freedom of association, for it sought to declare criminal the formation of an association of persons for political purposes.

The difficulty with the theory of the indictment was that for years the Communist Party had been considered to be not a criminal conspiracy but a legal political party not fundamentally different from other political parties. It had been on the ballot in many States and had presented to the electorate its candidates for public office. Indeed, one of the defendants in *Dennis* v. *United States* had himself been elected to the city council of New York on the Communist Party ticket.

The prosecution overcame this difficulty by asserting and presenting evidence to show that in April 1945 a change took place in the character of the Communist Party. At that time, on orders from Moscow, the leaders of the Communist Party abandoned their previous goal of peaceful coexistence and of working within the framework of democracy to achieve peace and prosperity in the postwar period, and instead reorganized the Party and established as its goal the initiation of a violent revolution to capture the government of the United States. The Communist Party then exhibited its true character as a highly disciplined conspiratorial organization, adept at infiltration into strategic positions, use of aliases and of Aesopian or double-meaning language, rigidly controlled and tolerating no dissent.

The jury accepted this evidence and the Supreme Court refused to upset the jury's finding. Acceptance of the jury's finding removes all disturbing difficulties about freedom of association. The right of association secured by the First Amendment certainly does not encompass the right to associate in a conspiracy to commit the crime of advocating the violent overthrow of the government any more than it encompasses the right to associate in a conspiracy to commit the crime of advocating bank robberies. If the Communist Party is an illegal association not protected by the First Amendment, then mere membership in it may constitutionally subject the members to penalties and disqualifications, just as mere membership in the illegal association which was the nineteenth-century Mormon Church subjected the members to the penalty of being barred from running or voting for public office, and just as mere membership in a conspiracy to rob a bank subjects the members to prison penalties.

The Smith Act, passed in 1940, had not adopted this logic. It did not mention the Communist Party by name, and did not make membership in the Party a crime, although the Act made it a crime knowingly to be a member of an association that advocates the forcible overthrow of the government. But the logic, if not the exact holding of the Dennis decision — that the Communist Party is an unlawful conspiracy to commit the crime of advocating the forcible overthrow of the government — requires the conclusion that mere membership in the Party, with knowledge of its purpose, constitutes a crime and may be made punishable by fine and imprisonment (even though the defendants in the Dennis case were charged with active participation rather than mere conscious membership). Congress never quite got itself to implement this logical conclusion, although it almost did so. The Communist Control Act of 1954, which declared the Communist Party to be an unlawful conspiracy, originally provided that mere membership in the Party, even if only dues-paying and card-holding, should be punishable as a crime. At the last moment this provision was deleted, and no Federal law today specifically declares it a crime merely to be a member of the Communist Party. A number of States have gone further than Congress, and there already have been several convictions under State statutes making mere membership in the Party a criminal offense. The constitutionality of these convictions has not yet, as of this writing, been passed upon by the Supreme Court.

While neither the Congress nor most State legislatures have carried the Dennis decision to its logical extreme, they have stopped barely short of it. Anti-subversion statutes enacted after the indictment was handed down in the Dennis case no longer content themselves with referring generally to organizations formed to advocate the violent overthrow of the government, but make specific mention of the Communist Party and Communist organizations. They impose severe disabilities and sanctions just short of imprisonment upon membership in the Party, and expressly designate it to be an organization whose purpose is to cause or advocate the overthrow of the government by force.

The best example is the Communist Control Act of 1954, which deprives the Party of all legal rights and bars it from access to the ballot. Another is the McCarran Internal Security Act of 1950, which bars members of Communist organizations from employment by the Federal government or in any defense plant and prohibits them from applying for or using a passport. The Taft-Hartley Act, as we have seen, deprives of the benefits of the National Labor Relations Act any union whose officers fail to file an affidavit swearing that they are not members of or affiliated with the Communist Party. Under another statute membership in or affiliation with the Party subjects an alien to deportation. A Federal statute (the so-called Gwinn Amendment) bars Party members from occupying apartments in housing projects financed in whole or in part with Federal funds.

The States have followed suit with reckless abandon. In some

States, Party members are ineligible for unemployment-compensation benefits, for admission to the bar, for teaching positions, for public employment, for election to public office, for tax exemption. In Pennsylvania, affiliation with the Party bars an indigent from public relief, unless (charitably) he is blind. In the District of Columbia, Party members may not engage in any business for which a license is required, and this ordinance has been enforced against a dealer in secondhand pianos.

The constitutionality of most of these and similar statutes has been challenged in the State and Federal courts. In the large majority of cases the challenges have been unsuccessful and the constitutionality of the statutes upheld. A number of these cases have reached the United States Supreme Court, and it is with these that we are concerned.

In *American Communications Association* v. *Douds,* which has been partly considered in the preceding chapter, the Supreme Court upheld the constitutionality of the non-Communist affidavit provision in the Taft-Hartley Act. The Court held that it was within the constitutional power of Congress to discourage labor unions from choosing as officers persons who were members of the Communist Party; Congress had acted on the basis of evidence that Communist leaders of labor unions had in the past and would continue in the future to subordinate legitimate trade-union objectives to obstructive strikes, often in support of a foreign government. There was considerable evidence concerning a strike at the Milwaukee plant of the Allis-Chalmers Manufacturing Company, which was producing vital materials for the national defense program. The strike, according to the testimony presented to Congress, had been called in 1941 (before the Nazi invasion of Russia changed the Communist Party line in respect to the nature of the war) solely in obedience to Party orders for the purpose of starting the "snowballing of strikes" in defense plants.

Justice Jackson's concurring opinion set forth for the first time the thesis on which he based his later concurrence in other cases involving anti-Communist statutes and which was to pervade most legislative and much judicial thinking — that behind its political-party façade the Communist Party is a conspiratorial and revolutionary junta, organized to reach ends and to use means incompatible with our constitutional system. He listed five ways in which the Communist Party is basically different from real political parties, including radical parties:

(1) The goal of the Communist Party is to seize powers of government by and for a minority rather than to acquire power through the vote of a free electorate.

(2) Alone among American parties, past and present, it is dominated by a foreign government.

(3) Violent and undemocratic methods are the calculated and indispensable means to attain its goal.

(4) It has sought to gain its leverage and hold on the American people by acquiring control of the labor movement.

(5) Every member of the Communist Party is an agent to execute the Communist program.

Since the Communist Party is not a political party in the traditionally understood sense, but a criminal conspiracy, constitutional concepts of freedom of speech and freedom of association are irrelevant, and membership in the Party may validly subject the member to such sanctions as disqualification from holding labor-union office.

Justice Black's dissent was based on the directly contrary thesis — that the Communist Party is not fundamentally different from the other hated, radical, and dangerous political groups for whose protection in the interest of democracy the constitutional guarantees of the First Amendment and the rest of the Bill of Rights have been developed.

In 1951, following the Douds case, the Supreme Court in *Gerende* v. *Board of Supervisors* upheld a Maryland statute that barred from a place on the ballot any person who refused to take an oath that he was not knowingly a member of an organization engaged in an attempt to overthrow the government by force or violence. During the same year, in *Garner* v. *Los Angeles Board,* the Supreme Court sustained an ordinance of the city of Los Angeles requiring all civil-service employees to file affidavits stating whether they were or ever had been members of the Communist Party. The Court (Justices Black and Douglas dissenting) upheld the requirement on the ground that past conduct may well relate to present fitness, and past loyalty may have a reasonable relationship to present and future trust. The Court also sustained a provision in the ordinance barring from public employment persons who now are, in the future become, or within the past five years have been members of any organization advocating the violent overthrow of the government.

The next year the Court, in *Adler* v. *Board of Education,* sustained a New York statute barring from employment as a public-school teacher any member of an organization advocating the overthrow of government by force, violence, or unlawful means. A teacher, said the Court (Black and Douglas dissenting) works in a sensitive area in the schoolroom, where he shapes the attitude of young minds toward the society in which they live. In this the state has a vital concern, for it must preserve the integrity of the schools, and school authorities therefore have the right and duty to screen teachers as to their fitness. To the claim that the effect of the statute is to infringe teachers' freedom of association, the Court replied that one's associates, past and present, may properly be considered in determining fitness and loyalty. From time immemorial one's reputation has been determined in part by the company he keeps. There is therefore, concluded the Court, no constitutional rule that prevents a State, in determining the fitness and loyalty of public-school teachers, from considering the organizations and persons with whom they associate.

In view of the consequences attendant upon membership in conspiratorial or subversive organizations — i.e., those advocating the violent overthrow of the government — serious questions arise as to how and by whom it is to be determined that a particular organization is subversive. The traditional American method would appear to be that employed in the Dennis case — that is, by a judge or jury in a court of law in accordance with the accepted rules of legal evidence. But this is a long and expensive method; it took nine months to complete the trial, and three years elapsed between the time the defendants were first indicted and the time their conviction was finally affirmed by the Supreme Court.

It is therefore hardly surprising that impatient legislatures should seek more expeditious and economical methods of determining whether a particular organization is subversive. In respect to the Communist Party, the legislatures, Federal and State, have now found a simple solution — a declaration in the statute that the Party is in fact such a conspiratorial or subversive organization. When it seeks to impose some sanction or disqualification upon an accused person, all the particular tribunal need do is determine whether the accused is or is not a member of the Communist Party; it need spend no time or effort in determining whether the Communist Party is or is not conspiratorial or subversive. This solution, simple as it appears to be, nevertheless raises the serious question whether such legislative condemnation of the Communist Party is not an unconstitutional bill of attainder. This question will be considered in a later chapter in which bills of attainder are discussed.

Even if legislative designation of a named organization as subversive or conspiratorial survives the constitutional test, its practicability is still limited. Only a relatively small fraction of potentially disloyal persons are actually dues-paying or card-carrying members of the Communist Party. Many more, it is believed, are members of scores of Communist-front or Communist-controlled or Communist-infiltrated organizations. What obviously is needed is a list of subversive organizations to which speedy reference can be made whenever anyone is accused of membership in a subversive organization.

The attractiveness of this solution is readily apparent, and it is quite natural that increasing use should be made by governmental authorities of lists of subversive organizations. For example, New York's Feinberg law, whose constitutionality was upheld in *Adler* v. *Board of Education,* after declaring that the Communist Party advocates the violent overthrow of the government, directs the State Board of Regents to prepare a list of other organizations that likewise advocate the violent overthrow of the government. In upholding the constitutionality of this procedure the Supreme Court pointed out that under the statute an organization must receive notice and hearing with a right to appeal to the courts before it may be listed as subversive. The Court also pointed out that under the statute membership does not automatically disqualify a teacher but constitutes only *prima facie* evidence of unfitness to teach, and that the teacher is entitled to a hearing at which he can present evidence to rebut the presumption of unfitness.

The progenitor of these lists was the so-called "Attorney General's list," first prepared in 1947 by Attorney General Biddle. The purpose of the list, which initially contained the names of 80-odd organizations, was to assist the Loyalty Review Board established by order of President Truman to determine the loyalty of Federal employees. Since then the list, which has more than tripled in size, has become an accepted standard for numerous Federal and State officials and bodies in passing on the loyalty of public employees.

Shortly after the list was initially promulgated, three listed organizations brought suit in the Federal courts to declare the listing illegal and unconstitutional. The suit culminated in a decision by the Supreme Court in the case of *Joint Anti-Fascist Refugee Committee* v. *McGrath*. The result was inconclusive inasmuch as there was no majority that concurred in any of the six opinions written by the eight Justices who heard the case. Nevertheless, it is clear that the Court held (1) that the Joint Anti-Fascist Refugee Committee was entitled to bring suit to protect its name, reputation, and ability to carry on its activities, and (2) that the Attorney General acted unlawfully in listing the organization without according it a hearing and without any factual basis for finding it subversive. What can reasonably be said of the decision is that it recognizes a constitutionally protected freedom of association possessed by an organization and its members, at least until such time as it is found by due process of law to be an unlawful conspiracy.

This conclusion is reinforced by the Supreme Court's decision in *Wieman* v. *Updegraff*. There the Court invalidated a loyalty oath prescribed by Oklahoma statute of all State officers and employees. The statute required all employees to swear that they were not affiliated with any organization on the Attorney General's list of Communist-front and subversive organizations. The Court held that, since a person might have joined an organization on the list innocently and without knowledge that it was a Communist front or otherwise subversive, and since the statute applied equally to such persons, it was an unconstitutional infringement of freedom of association. The fact of association alone may not constitutionally determine disloyalty and disqualification for public office or employment. It is not due process of law for a State to penalize *innocent* association; else freedom of association would no longer be a liberty of Americans.

Chapter 5. *Liberty of Knowledge and Learning*

THE INVENTION AND SUPPRESSION OF PRINTING

Almost since the day Gutenberg first reproduced the Bible by use of movable type the printed word has been the principal medium for the perpetuation and transmission of our culture. Many thoughtful educators have expressed concern that before long reading may become a lost art and be replaced by television as the chief molder and transmitter of our culture. Similar fears were expressed when motion pictures became popular and later when mass manufacture of low-priced radios was achieved. Similar fears may have been expressed when traveling troupes of actors performed Shakespeare's plays to enthusiastic audiences about the English countryside; if not, it was probably only because then printing was a comparative newcomer on the cultural scene whereas the drama had an honored tradition of many centuries, going back not merely to Everyman and the morality plays but almost two thousand years earlier to Aeschylus and Aristophanes.

It is likely that present fears for reading in competition with television will prove as groundless as those expressed on the advent of the cinema and the radio. Reading has exhibited a remarkable virility and longevity. The multiplication of book clubs and firms producing paper-backed and other low-priced volumes in mass quantities should reassure any who might fear that the art of reading is moribund. In any event, it can hardly be doubted that as of today the printed word is the chief repository of our knowledge and its transmitter from generation to generation and place to place.

Hard on the heels of the introduction of printing came the recognition by the ruling powers of its trouble-making potentialities. Perhaps movable type was not the invention of the Devil; the fact that the first book printed in the Christian world was the Bible would seem to indicate this — although, of course, if the cunning Devil can quote Scripture there would appear to be no reason why he could not print it. Certain it was that movable type was not the invention of angels. The best that could be said for it was that it was neutral in the eternal war between the forces of God and those of the Devil, serving with indifferent loyalty whichever employed its tremendous powers. The same press that printed Gutenberg's authorized Bible in Latin could also print Tyndale's heretical Bible in English.

Not that spoken and handwritten words could not be trouble-makers in their own right. The good people of Athens were forced in self-defense to request Socrates to drink hemlock even though, as far as history records, he never put stylus to tablet, and all that we know of his troublesome teachings is what was recorded reverently by Plato or irreverently by Aristophanes. Long before the invention of printing, the Preacher complained that of making many books there was no end, and many of these handwritten books proved dangerous to those whom the gods selected to rule lesser men. When, under Tiberius, one Aulus Cremutius Cordus wrote a seditious book that praised Brutus and Cassius, he was seized and avoided condemnation only by deliberately starving to death. The senators ordered his books burnt; but some copies were successfully concealed and later published, causing a Roman historian to "laugh at the stupidity of men who suppose that the despotism of the present can actually efface the remembrances of the next generation."

Nevertheless, the capacity of serious trouble-making through the spoken and handwritten word was greatly limited. Physical factors necessarily restricted a speaker's audience and thus potential discontent to an insignificant percentage of the total population. It was only in rare cases that the evil spoken by such supreme trouble-makers as Socrates and Jesus was not interred with their bones. And if, notwithstanding the Roman senate's diligent efforts, the evil that Cordus wrote lived after him, it must be remembered that so long as handwritten books had to be reproduced by laborious hand-copying the ability to read was pretty much restricted to the ruling classes and these were the least likely to be affected by trouble-makers and malcontents. (The English jury which, in 1792, tried Tom Paine *in absentia* for seditious libel in publishing his *Rights of Man* with its revolutionary proposals for a graduated income and steep inheritance taxes, was a "special" jury chosen from the upper classes which alone could be "entrusted" with judging the enormity of Paine's crime.)

All this changed with the development of a cheap and comparatively effortless method of reproducing writing in limitless quantities. The advent of printing inevitably brought with it the spread of literacy, and this was compounded by the rise of Protestantism with its revolutionary doctrine that God's word, translated into the popular tongue, was as available to parishioner as to priest, and that the ordinary person not only was competent to read and understand the Bible but was obligated to do so. Natural, therefore, it was that the real history of the widespread diffusion of knowledge began with the invention of printing and concomitantly began the history of governmental efforts to prevent by forcible means the diffusion of dangerous knowledge.

LICENSING AND CENSORSHIP IN ENGLAND

The earliest method of dealing with evil printed words was the ancient one of dealing with evil spoken or written words — punishing the utterer. Tyndale was condemned by Cardinal Wolsey for his heretical Bible and ultimately he was burned at the stake. Giordano Bruno suffered the same fate, as did Michael Servetus and many others. Thousands of others suffered lesser penalties. The punishment of the utterer was accompanied by attempts to destroy the utterances. Tyndale's Bible was suppressed by Cardinal Wolsey, and Servetus' book attacking the doctrine of the Trinity was burned with him at the stake. When, in 1632, the Star Chamber ordered William Prynne set in stocks with his ears cut off for publishing a book that castigated the immorality of the theater King Charles enjoyed attending, and for referring to "women actors" as "notorious whores" (the queen herself took part in a play), all copies of his book that could be found were burned close to the pillory.

These efforts to suppress printed words by repressing the author or destroying his books were even more surely destined to futility than similar efforts to suppress spoken and handwritten words. If the Roman magistrates could not prevent the concealment and preservation of some of Cordus' hand-copied books, it was foolish of Cardinal Wolsey to imagine that he could consign to the flames all copies of Tyndale's printed Bible or of the Star Chamber to expect to do the same with Prynne's *Scourge of Stage Players.*

A more effective method of dealing with trouble-making books had to be devised, and the ingenuity of the Anglo-Saxon mind could be counted on to devise it. The way to control what is printed is to control the printing. The sixteenth century saw the establishment of the High Commission as a sort of ecclesiastical adjunct of the Star Chamber. The Anglican equivalent of the Inquisition, its function was to deal with heresy, witchcraft, schism, and religious non-conformity (although its jurisdiction also included matrimonial offenses). Unlike the Inquisition, the High Commission could not impose the death sentence; its penal powers were limited to fines and imprisonment and such ecclesiastical penalties as excommunication.

A statute enacted in 1596 added to the High Commission's functions. To detect and extirpate printed heresy and non-conformity before they could spread, the High Commission was given control over printers, publishers, and booksellers. The law confined all printing to London and to the two university towns of Oxford and Cambridge, and empowered the High Commission to limit the number of printing presses to the number it deemed needful. This was done, no doubt, to ensure effective supervision, but perhaps also to discourage excessive printing, whose potentialities for evil were already well recognized; Marlowe's Faustus, it will be recalled, as his final attempt to save his soul from the Devil, offered to burn his books.

All books were required to be registered with the Stationers' Guild and to be licensed by the Archbishop of Canterbury and the Bishop of London, who had uncontrolled authority to refuse to license any book they did not like. The 1596 law, however, proved inadequate to suppress evil books, and in 1637, the High Commission under Archbishop Laud revived and expanded it. The number of authorized London printers was reduced to twenty, and a license was required for publication of new books and pamphlets as well as the republication of previously licensed books. Printers violating the decree were to be punished by being set in the pillory, whipped through London, and forever thereafter " disabled to use or exercise the Art or Mysterie of Printing."

The later measure proved no more effective than the earlier. Clandestine presses continued to pour forth pamphlets which were gobbled up by admiring and increasing crowds. Nevertheless, when the Star Chamber and the High Commission were abolished by the Long Parliament of 1641, censorship of printing continued, from then on under Parliament's rather than the King's control. In 1643 a law was enacted providing for the licensing of all printed books, pamphlets, and papers by Parliament-appointed licensers.

Promulgation of this law led John Milton to publish — without license — *Areopagitica,* the greatest and most noble of all defenses of the freedom of the press. " As good," said Milton in this book, " almost kill a man as kill a good book; who kills a man kills a reasonable creature, God's image; but he who destroys a good book kills reason itself; kills the image of God, as it were, in the eye." To the argument that truth needed the aid of the licenser and censor for its protection, Milton replied: " And though all the winds of doctrine were let loose to play upon the earth, so Truth be in the field, we do injuriously by licensing and prohibiting to misdoubt her strength; who ever knew Truth put to the worse in a free and open encounter."

The licensing and censorship of books and papers continued for a half-century after *Areopagitica* was published. When in 1694 Parliament at last allowed the Licensing Act to expire, it did so not for any of the arguments presented by Milton nor because it deemed censorship a thing essentially evil, but because administration of the law had led to many abuses, inconveniences, bureaucratic red tape, and the loss of a substantial part of the profitable foreign book trade.

Whatever the reason, the expiration of the Licensing Act brought an end to governmental pre-publication censorship in England. Publishers and authors could still be tried and punished for seditious libel, but they could no longer be required to submit their writings in advance of publication to a governmental licenser. By the time the American colonists were ready to declare their independence of the English king and Parliament, they well knew, through Blackstone, that one of the liberties of Englishmen was the freedom of the press from governmental censorship in advance of publication.

TAXING THE PRESS

The failure of licensing effectively to restrict the printing and circulation of books and papers led the English rulers to seek other means to control this medium for the widespread transmission of dangerous knowledge and ideas. They finally decided that if printing could not be prohibited it could perhaps be discouraged by making it costly. In 1711 Queen Anne prevailed upon Parliament to pass a measure imposing taxes on papers, periodicals, and books. Her purpose was to suppress objectionable comments and criticisms of the government. These taxes were imposed upon every newspaper, printed advertisement, book, or pamphlet. The sale of unstamped publications rendered the vendor, whether storekeeper or newsboy, liable to fine and imprisonment. The intended effect of these taxes was to curtail the circulation of newspapers by keeping the price high and to reduce the size of those that were published. Hardest hit were the lower-priced popular papers that circulated among the masses. Radical papers reached fewer readers, and the launching of new publications by malcontents faced serious financial obstacles. Any man who carried on printing and publishing for a livelihood was at the mercy of the Commissioners of Stamps, whenever they chose to exert their powers. Printers and publishers could hardly fail to assume that the degree of the Commissioners' diligence in the performance of their duties would vary proportionately with the degree of a paper's objectionable criticism of the ruling classes. During the period the tax was in effect more than seven hundred persons were prosecuted for publishing untaxed journals and more than five hundred served jail terms, some for long periods. These multitudinous prosecutions failed to suppress all obnoxious publications, although they may have been effective in keeping within manageable limits the harm threatened by what England's rulers considered to be the more dangerous publications.

While licensing and pre-publication censorship had disappeared in England by the time the American colonists were beginning to record their grievances against the Crown, the law imposing taxes on printing was still in effect; it was not to be repealed until 1855. But, if accepted by the English, it was not acceptable to the Americans. In 1765 Parliament extended the British stamp tax to America by requiring all publications and documents to bear stamps. The Stamp Act was presumably a revenue measure whose purpose was to require the colonists to contribute to the cost of colonial defense and administration.

The colonists, however, did not treat it as such. They recognized its restrictive effect upon the dissemination of the printed word and denounced it as a " tax on knowledge." The Act was vehemently attacked in the press and from platforms and pulpits by such patriots as Sam Adams, Patrick Henry, and Paul Revere. Organizations known as Sons of Liberty were formed to protect colonial freedom; merchants boycotted British goods, and the Massachusetts legislature called for the convening of a general congress to find means to resist the law. The Stamp Act Congress, which met in New York City with representatives from nine of the colonies, adopted a " Declaration of Rights," a " Petition to the King," and a " Memorial to Both Houses of Parliament." These documents declared that freeborn Englishmen could not be taxed without their consent and that since the colonists were not represented in Parliament any tax imposed upon them without the consent of their colonial legislatures was void. Fearing the effects of the boycott, Parliament repealed the Stamp Act barely a year after its enactment.

FREEDOM OF THE PRESS WON IN AMERICA

The colonists were well acquainted with this history of governmental efforts to suppress or restrain the printed word, and they would have none of it. Of the three principal methods employed — punishment, censorship, and taxation — they were spared the second, since the Licensing Act had expired before printing was established in America. But they did have a short and turbulent experience with the third during the year in which the Stamp Act was in effect. And they also had experience with the first, one particularly dramatic incident involving the German-born printer John Peter Zenger.

Zenger, editor of the *New York Weekly Journal*, had been apprentice to William Bradford, who had set up the first press in the colonies and had himself been unsuccessfully tried in Philadelphia for anonymously printing a seditious paper. Zenger severely criticized the administration of Governor William Crosby. He charged that the liberties and properties of the people " are precarious, slavery is like to be entailed upon them and their posterity if some things be not amended " and that judges were " arbitrarily displaced, new courts erected without the consent of the legislature, trials by jury taken away when a governor pleases." For this and similar articles, four issues of the *Journal* were publicly burned and Zenger was summarily arrested in 1734 and kept in prison for ten months, where he managed clandestinely to continue editing his paper regularly. Finally, he was brought to trial for seditious libel in bringing the government into disrepute and, because all New York lawyers who ventured to defend him were promptly disbarred, he was represented by a prominent Philadelphia lawyer named Andrew Hamilton. When the jury ultimately acquitted Zenger, the news was received with tremendous acclaim by the people, and accounts of the trial were published throughout the colonies.

The Zenger acquittal and its widespread popular approval indicated the high estate held in the minds of the colonists by the concept of the freedom of the press. This was further indicated by the *Letter to the People of Quebec,* issued by the Continental Congress as an appeal to Quebec to send delegates to a meeting of the Congress. In the *Letter* the Congress listed the five liberties of Americans that they prized most highly and felt were being denied them by the Crown. These were: representative government and self-rule; trial by jury; habeas corpus; free ownership of land; and, finally, freedom of the press. Of this last right the *Letter* said: "The importance of this consists, besides the advancement of truth, science, morality and arts in general, in its diffusion of liberal sentiments on the administration of government, its ready communication of thoughts between subjects, and its consequential promotion of union among them, whereby oppressive officials are shamed or intimidated into more honorable and just modes of conducting affairs."

When, after the Declaration of Independence, the States adopted constitutions for themselves, nine of the original thirteen States included guarantees of the freedom of the press in their constitutions. (Paradoxically, in 1785 Massachusetts, which had led the resistance to the British Stamp Tax, itself enacted a law imposing a stamp tax on all newspapers and magazines, but this met with such violent popular opposition that it was quickly repealed.) The omission of a bill of rights from the original Federal Constitution was, as we have seen, a source of severe criticism, and one of the omitted rights frequently mentioned was freedom of the press. Hence, when the Bill of Rights was added to the Constitution, included in the First Amendment was the provision that "Congress shall make no law . . . abridging the freedom . . . of the press . . ."

CENSORSHIP THROUGH THE MAILS AND CUSTOMS

The history of the freedom of the press after the establishment of our republic, like its earlier history in England and the colonies, largely concerns governmental efforts to suppress or restrict objectionable publications through the three tried methods: punishment, censorship, and taxation. Punishment for the publication of objectionable matter has been discussed in the chapter dealing with freedom of speech; the issues involved are not different from those in cases concerning punishment for oral expressions, and they were therefore treated together. Our discussion here is limited to censorship (including post-publication suppression as well as pre-publication licensing) and taxation.

The chief instrumentality of the Federal government for censorship of printed matter is its control of the mails. Theoretically a publisher deprived of the use of the mails can circulate his publication through a private agency, but the cost of this procedure is prohibitively high so that denial of the use of the mails to a particular publication is probably the most effective means of suppressing it.

What appears to be the first official suggestion that the mails be used as a means of suppressing objectionable publications was made by no less a libertarian and democrat than Andrew Jackson. In his annual message to Congress in 1835 he proposed the enactment of a law prohibiting, under severe penalties, the circulation through the mails in the Southern States of incendiary Abolitionist publications that might instigate the slaves to insurrection. The proposal came to naught when it was opposed in the Senate by John C. Calhoun, the slaveowner's chief spokesman, primarily because he deemed it an invasion of States' rights in determining what is and what is not likely to disturb the security of the States, but perhaps partly also out of concern for freedom of the press. The object of publication, said Calhoun, is circulation; and to prohibit circulation is in effect to prohibit publication. If Congress were to be empowered to bar Abolitionist publications from the mails, the freedom of the press on all subjects would be completely subject to its will and pleasure. (Calhoun had no objection if the post office were to refuse to deliver, in a State, mail declared by the *State* to be incendiary; but his colleagues could not see the fine distinction.)

During the Civil War there was some suppression of the press, particularly by the military. Lincoln, another great libertarian and democrat, while unhappy about it, nevertheless reluctantly acquiesced on the ground of military necessity. All in all some twenty newspapers were suppressed, and occasionally circulation was restricted. Suppression, however, was for short periods and was not sufficiently continuous or extensive to bring the problem to the courts.

At the conclusion of the Civil War, Congress enacted the first of a series of measures designed to utilize its control of the mails as an instrumentality of censorship. These laws exclude from the mails publications that are fraudulent or immoral. The constitutionality of these statutes was first sustained by the Supreme Court in *Ex parte Jackson*, where the Court upheld the exclusion, under the morals provision, of circulars advertising lotteries. The Court held that the right of Congress to designate what shall be carried involves necessarily the right to determine what shall be excluded. Later, the fraud provision was upheld in *Public Clearing House* v. *Coyne*, again on the ground that Congress, in establishing a postal service, may annex such conditions to it as it chooses.

The reasoning of these decisions would seem to confer unlimited power upon Congress to determine what may or may not be carried through the mails and would seem to negate Calhoun's contention that the Government is subject to the First Amendment guarantee of freedom of the press in its operation of the postal system. The result reached by the Court in upholding the exclusion is justifiable under the principles which justify some restraints on freedom of expression discussed in our chapter on freedom of speech; and, although the Court has not had occasion expressly to repudiate the reasoning, it has strongly intimated that it is likely to do so should the occasion arise. In *Hannegan* v. *Esquire*, shortly to be discussed, it asserted that grave constitutional questions are immediately raised once it is said that the use of the mails is a privilege which may be extended or withheld on any grounds whatever.

The issue of the use of control over the mails as an instrument of censorship again arose during the administration of another great libertarian and democrat, Woodrow Wilson, who like his predecessors pleaded military necessity as justification for restricting freedom of the press. The Espionage Act of 1917 declared seditious publications unmailable. The constitutionality of this provision never reached the Supreme Court, although it was upheld by the Circuit Court of Appeals in a decision sustaining the exclusion of *The Masses,* a radical monthly that attacked the war. In view, however, of the Supreme Court's post-war decision in *United States ex rel. Milwaukee Social Democratic Publishing Co.* v. *Burleson,* it is a fair assumption that had the Court passed upon the *Masses* case it would have affirmed the exclusion.

In the Burleson case, the Supreme Court upheld an order of the Postmaster General depriving all future issues of the *Milwaukee Leader* of the benefit of second-class mailing rates because of seditious matter contained in preceding issues. Denial of the low second-class mailing rates to a publication is perhaps not necessarily fatal, as is total exclusion from the mails; nevertheless, in most cases and certainly in the case of a publication issued by impecunious radicals and malcontents, the requirement that first-class postage rates be paid is an effective death blow to the publication. The Court's decision was based, not on the ground asserted in the earlier cases that the power of Congress over the mails is absolute, but on practical considerations. A newspaper that has published seditious matter in several issues may reasonably be expected to continue violating the law. The government cannot maintain a censor in every newspaper office in the country to approve every issue in advance. Hence an offending newspaper may have its privilege revoked until it submits satisfactory evidence of repentance. Government, said the Court, is a practical institution, adapted to the practical conduct of public affairs.

(The *Leader's* second-class mailing privilege was restored by Will Hays, Postmaster General under the non-democrat and non-libertarian Warren Harding, who, incidentally, pardoned many and commuted the sentences of many other persons convicted under the Espionage Acts, in whose behalf Wilson refused to exercise clemency. Hays himself later became chief censor for the motion-picture industry.)

The issue of the validity of denying second-class mailing rates to an objectionable publication again came to the Supreme Court in the case of *Hannegan* v. *Esquire* (1946). The statute providing for second-class mailing rates requires that a number of conditions be satisfied to entitle a publication to the privilege. One of these conditions, the fourth, is that it be "published for the dissemination of information of a public character, or devoted to literature, the sciences, arts or some special industry." *Esquire* is a "slick" magazine, undoubtedly containing articles and stories of some literary merit, but having a style and content which the less sophisticated might consider to border on the immoral. In any event, Postmaster General Hannegan felt that it did not "contribute to the public good and the public welfare" and accordingly ordered its second-class mailing privilege suspended.

The Supreme Court set aside the Postmaster General's action. It did so on the ground that the statute conferring the second-class mailing privilege authorized the Postmaster General only to determine if an applicant satisfied the conditions imposed by Congress, not to add conditions of his own and certainly not to decide on his own whether a particular publication positively contributes to the public good or public welfare. The Court, therefore, did not find it necessary to decide whether the statute would have been constitutional if it had authorized the Postmaster General to deny second-class mailing privileges to publications which he did not adjudge to contribute to the public good and the public welfare. Nevertheless, the language and tenor of the opinion intimate strongly that if that had been the issue the statute would have been declared unconstitutional.

What is good literature, said the Court, what has educational value, what is refined public information, what is good art, varies with individuals as it does from one generation to another. There doubtless would be a contrariety of views concerning Cervantes' *Don Quixote*, Shakespeare's *Venus and Adonis*, or Zola's *Nana*. The requirement that literature or art conform to some norm prescribed by an official smacks of an ideology foreign to our system. The basic values implicit in the requirements of the statute's fourth condition can be served only by uncensored distribution of literature. From the multitude of competing offerings the public will pick and choose. What seems to one to be trash may have for others fleeting or even enduring values. To withdraw the second-class rate from *Esquire* today because its content seemed to one official not good for the public would sanction withdrawal of the second-class rate tomorrow from another periodical whose social or economic views seemed harmful to another official. Acceptance of the Postmaster General's contention would mean that the second-class rate would be granted on condition that certain economic and political ideas not be disseminated. Such a statute, the Court concluded, would immediately raise grave constitutional questions.

A lesser instrumentality for Federal censorship of objectionable material, applicable to foreign publications, is control of customs. A Federal statute authorizes the Collector of Customs to seize any obscene or seditious book and directs the Federal district attorney to bring suit against the book for judgment ordering it to be destroyed. This results in cases having such intriguing titles as *United States* v. *One Obscene Book Called "Married Love."* None of these cases has reached the Supreme Court, but the decision of the District Court and its affirmance by the Circuit Court in the case arising from the attempted exclusion of Joyce's *Ulysses* indicate an attitude of strict judicial scrutiny of customs officials' claims that books of genuine literary value should be excluded for obscenity.

STATE CENSORSHIP AND TAXATION

As with the Federal government, the States use post-publication punishment as the chief means to control offensive publications. While the Federal government's concern has been principally with seditious publications, the States' concern has been mainly with immoral and obscene publications — not that the States have completely ignored seditious publications, as *Gitlow* v. *New York* attests. Before the Gitlow case the constitutionality of State statutes punishing the publication of objectionable material was not reviewable in the Federal courts. As we have seen, after that case the test of constitutionality for State statutes punishing publishers of seditious literature is the same as that for Federal statutes.

With respect to obscene and immoral publications, there can be no doubt that within its police power a State may constitutionally punish their publishers. The recent public concern over what is believed to be an alarming rise in juvenile delinquency with the simultaneous phenomenal growth in the popularity among youth and adolescents of uncomical comic books has set off a spate of statutes and ordinances making punishable the publication of at least the most lurid of the comics. These statutes are enacted generally as extensions of the anti-obscenity laws but are predicated on a somewhat different premise. The lewd and the obscene are constitutionally punishable because they are in effect verbal acts which by their very utterance, rather than their ultimate consequence, inflict injury and are therefore not within the protection of the First Amendment. Comic books dealing excessively and realistically with crime and violence are made punishable on a different assumption, i.e., that they are likely to cause suggestible youth and adolescents to emulate what they read (if " reading " is the correct term to apply to comic books). It would seem, therefore, that the First Amendment is relevant to a consideration of the constitutionality of these statutes and that the " clear and present danger " test, at least to the extent that it is still part of our constitutional law, should measure their validity. Specifically, it would seem that to sustain State infringement upon the liberty of adult Americans to publish comic books and young Americans to read them, the legislature would have to make a fairly convincing case for a causal relationship between comic books and juvenile delinquency.

In the one case that reached it, the Supreme Court carefully avoided passing on this difficult question. In the 1948 case of *Winters v. New York* the Court passed on the constitutionality of a statute making it a penal offense to publish or distribute " any printed matter principally made up of criminal news, police reports, or accounts of criminal deeds or pictures or stories of deeds of bloodshed, lust or crime." The New York courts had construed the statute " not to outlaw all commentaries on crime from detective tales to scientific treatises " but only to prohibit " such massing of accounts of deeds of bloodshed and lust as to incite to crimes against the person."

The Supreme Court invalidated the statute on the ground that even as construed by the New York courts it was too vague and indefinite to give publishers a reasonable idea of what is and what is not permissible under the statute. Terms such as " obscene " and " lewd " may be used in a criminal statute because their use has a long history in the law and their meanings have therefore acquired a reasonable degree of certainty. But the term " so massed as to incite to crime " is a new term having no history to shed light on its intended meaning. The absence of any definition of the term in the statute makes it impossible for a publisher of comics to know whether a particular book he plans to publish would be within or without the law. The constitutional prohibition against deprivation of life, liberty, or property without due process of law requires that laws making certain acts criminal should be sufficiently clear and unambiguous so that the people may know what they may do and not be innocently trapped into violating the law.

The States have also tried their hand at pre-publication censoring and licensing of the press. This has been a comparatively recent development, and in those cases in which the question of constitutionality has reached the Supreme Court, the Court has manifested a marked hostility to all previous restraints upon the press, whether by outright censorship or by licensing. In *Near* v. *Minnesota* (1931), the Court passed on the constitutionality of what the press called the Newspaper Gag Law. This was a statute authorizing the suppression by court injunction of obscene, scandalous, and defamatory newspapers and periodicals. The *Saturday Press,* published in Minneapolis, printed a series of articles charging that a Jewish gangster controlled all gambling, bootlegging, and racketeering in the county and that the chief public officials, the chief of police and the prosecuting attorney, were either corrupt or grossly neglectful in the performance of their duties. The prosecuting attorney replied by suing under the " gag law " to suppress the newspaper, and he succeeded in obtaining a court order directing destruction of all printed issues for the past two months and forbidding any further publication of the newspaper.

The Supreme Court set aside the injunction and declared the statute unconstitutional. Except in rare cases — as when the government during wartime seeks to prevent the publication of the sailing dates of transports or the location of troops — the First Amendment guarantee of the freedom of the press bars previous restraints upon publication. The State may constitutionally enact criminal libel laws providing for the punishment *after* publication of egregiously defamatory matter; but it may not by suppression, through injunction or otherwise, interfere in advance with publication. Whatever else freedom of the press may mean, its history shows conclusively that at the very least it bars previous restraints upon publication.

Licensing, like pre-publication censorship and suppression, has likewise been held unconstitutional by the Supreme Court. In 1938 the Court, in *Lovell* v. *Griffin,* held unconstitutional under the First Amendment an ordinance requiring a license from the city manager in order to distribute printed matter within the city. The case was one of the first brought by Jehovah's Witnesses to the Supreme Court, and while it could have been decided under the freedom-of-religion provision of the Amendment, the Court preferred to set it aside under the freedom-of-the-press guarantee.

The Court made short shrift of the city's argument that Alma Lovell, a Jehovah's Witness, was not a member of the press; that the freedom of the press does not encompass pamphlets and leaflets; that it protects only printing and publishing, not circulating and distributing; and, finally, that in any event a licensing requirement does not infringe upon the freedom of the press. Freedom of the press, the Court held, protects the amateur no less than the professional, and includes pamphlets and leaflets no less than books, periodicals, and newspapers. Pamphlets and leaflets have been historic weapons in the defense of liberty, as the pamphlets of Thomas Paine and others attest. The First Amendment protects circulating as well as printing. Liberty of circulating is as essential to freedom of the press as liberty of publishing; without circulation publishing would be of little value. Finally, the Court held, licensing no less than censorship and suppression is barred by the First Amendment. The struggle for the freedom of the press was primarily directed against the power of the licenser. The liberty of the press became initially a right to publish without a license what formerly could be published only with one.

In a number of other decisions (*Hague* v. *CIO*, *Schneider* v. *Irvington*, *Jamison* v. *Texas*, and others) the Supreme Court invalidated statutes and ordinances that either completely forbade the public distribution of pamphlets and leaflets or required a license from a public official in order to do so. These decisions show quite convincingly that except in rare and extraordinary situations all governmental previous restraints on publication, whether by prohibition, censoring, or licensing, are likely to be held by the Supreme Court to be unconstitutional infringements of the freedom of the press.

The Court's decision in *Grosjean* v. *American Press Co.* indicates that a like fate probably awaits governmental efforts to restrict the freedom of the press through "taxes on knowledge." In that case the Court invalidated a Louisiana statute (passed in the heyday of Huey Long's domination of the State and during his feud with the big city press) that imposed a tax of 2 per cent of gross receipts upon newspapers and periodicals having a circulation of more than 20,000 a week. The Court's opinion set out the history of taxes on printing outlined earlier in this chapter and came to the conclusion that, although such taxes were in force and legal in England at the time the First Amendment was adopted, nevertheless it was the purpose of the framers of the Amendment to outlaw such "taxes on knowledge" in their guarantee of the freedom of the press. Newspaper publishing, like any other commercial enterprise, is subject to the general non-discriminatory taxes imposed for the maintenance of government and public institutions. But the Louisiana imposition was not such a tax; its history and setting showed clearly that it was a deliberate and calculated device in the guise of a tax to limit the circulation of information to which the public is entitled by virtue of the constitutional guarantee of freedom of the press. A free press, the Court said, stands as one of the great interpreters between the government and the people; it may not be fettered by oppressive taxes.

RADIO AND TELEVISION

To deny the government the power to license printing creates no great practical problems. Any American dissatisfied with the editorial policies or news treatment of the newspapers in his community may, if he can scrape up the necessary dollars, buy himself a printing press and publish a newspaper nearer to his heart's desire. The same is not true of radio and television. There are only a limited number of radio and television frequencies physically available, and a discontented listener cannot start his own broadcasting station. Our government might have taken the position that whoever first occupies a particular frequency thereby obtains the right of permanent exclusive possession; to a limited degree (i.e., long-term rather than permanent) we adhere to that policy in respect to patents and copyrights. But patents and copyrights are rewards for creative ingenuity and intellect, not for expeditious acquisitiveness. We have long since outgrown the social philosophy that the race belongs only to the swift; and the licensing of enterprises that by their very nature enjoy a monopoly has long been part of the Anglo-American tradition. The Supreme Court, therefore, has had little hesitation in upholding Federal statutes that authorize the government to license radio or television broadcasting in the public interest; the Court has overruled contentions that issuance of radio and television licenses to ensure balanced programming (or on any other basis than first-come first-served) unconstitutionally abridges freedoms secured by the First Amendment. (*Federal Radio Commission* v. *Nelson Brothers; National Broadcasting Co.* v. *U.S.*)

On the other hand, it is of the essence of American liberty that, when a government official exercises power to grant or withhold a privilege, that power may not be exercised arbitrarily or capriciously. Arbitrary power tends to corrupt and is characteristic of despotism, not constitutional democracy. Corollary to this proposition is the principle that when a legislature delegates to an administrative body or official the power to grant or withhold a privilege, the delegation of power must spell out the standards to be employed in granting or withholding the privilege and may not leave it to the unbounded discretion of the administrative body or official.

Here again we have a problem of accommodating competing values. Democratic constitutionalism would dictate that these standards be spelled out by the democratically elected and politically responsible legislature in the utmost detail, leaving little or no discretion to the administrative official. But government is a practical institution adapted to the practical conduct of public affairs. As a practical matter, the legislature cannot generally spell out the standards and criteria in specific detail. The members of the legislature do not have the technical competence to enable them to do so; they cannot anticipate all the circumstances which might require the modification of the standards more expeditiously than can be accomplished by a slow-moving legislature; and, finally, statute books, excessively voluminous as they are, would be completely unmanageable if they were cluttered up with detailed standards for the issuance or withholding of the innumerable licenses required in the conduct of modern affairs.

Different licensing statutes effect the accommodation in different ways. Our concern here is with the Federal Communications Act, which provides for the licensing of radio and television broadcasting. The Act spells out a few standards in specific detail; it requires, for example, that licenses be distributed in such a way as to provide fair, efficient, and equitable service to each State and community. By and large, however, the Act confers a good deal of discretion upon the

Federal Communications Commission and sets forth its principal standard in terms of broad generality; it requires only that the Commission grant or withhold licenses on the basis of "public convenience, interest or necessity." This standard, though undoubtedly broad, has been held by the Supreme Court to be sufficiently definite, in view of the nature of the medium, to satisfy constitutional requirements.

While the First Amendment does not bar governmental licensing of radio and television broadcasting, the licensing power must be exercised within the limitations of the Amendment. The Federal Communications Act forbids the Commission to censor broadcasts; but even in the absence of such a prohibition it is likely that the Supreme Court would hold, should the occasion arise, that pre-broadcast censorship violates the First Amendment. Post-broadcasting punishment, conversely, is punishable within the constitutional principles permitting post-publication punishment of some written or oral utterances.

The fact that broadcasting is a monopoly enterprise nevertheless justifies not only licensing but some degree of control over content. Both public interest and enlightened democratic government demand that all sides of public issues be aired publicly. A newspaper may not constitutionally be compelled to print editorials on both sides of every question or perhaps even to accept political advertisements from candidates it opposes. This is so because, theoretically at least, dissatisfied readers can start their own newspapers and a laissez-faire policy is sufficient to assure diversity of views. Since, because of physical limitations, this is not so in the case of radio or television broadcasting, the Federal Communications Commission has taken the position that in deciding whether "public convenience, interest or necessity" justifies renewal of a station's license, it may consider as a pertinent factor whether the station has given equal treatment to opposing views on public issues, or has allocated adequate program time for the discussion of public issues, or has refrained from advertising excesses. Although the radio and television industry has disagreed with the Commission's interpretation of its powers, contending that the Commission may act only as a kind of traffic manager and may consider only technical and financial factors, such as whether the station owner has sufficient capital to run it, the Federal courts have uniformly upheld the Commission's position;

and, while the issue has never reached the Supreme Court, it is probable that when it does so the Court will take the same position.

MOTION PICTURES

Like printing presses, and unlike radio and television frequencies, motion-picture studios and theaters are available to all who can afford to build or buy them. Hence there are no physical factors that dictate governmental licensing and therefore no fundamental reason other than novelty to justify a holding that pre-exhibition licensing of motion pictures is consistent with the First Amendment even though pre-publication licensing of books and newspapers is not. However, when the issue first reached the Supreme Court in 1915, the factor of novelty was sufficient to dispose of it. In *Mutual Film Corporation* v. *Industrial Commission of Ohio* the Court said that the exhibition of moving pictures " is a business, pure and simple, originated and conducted for profit like other spectacles and is not to be regarded as part of the press or as organs of public opinion." Accordingly, the Court held, exhibitors may be made subject to licensing requirements, and the restrictions of the First Amendment are irrelevant.

Perhaps in 1915, in the early days of the magic lantern, this pure and simple analysis was an adequate disposition of the problem. True, the fact that motion-picture exhibition was a profit-making enterprise should not have been adequate ground to deny it the protection of the First Amendment; even in 1915 newspaper publishing was a business conducted for profit, and that fact did not deprive it of the Amendment's protection. But without doubt the motion picture was then a " spectacle " like professional boxing and circuses, and not a medium for the transmission of knowledge, ideas, or art within the contemplated purview of the First Amendment (although the circus in Nero's day, undoubtedly a spectacle, was nevertheless an effective medium for conveying the government's displeasure with the ideas adhered to by the Christians devoured therein to the edification as well as delight of the populace).

By 1952, however, it was clear that the 1915 solution was no longer adequate. Motion pictures such as *Ten Days That Shook the World*, *Grapes of Wrath*, *Blockade*, *All Quiet on the Western Front*, and scores of others had indicated fairly convincingly that motion pictures can be an effective medium for the communication of ideas on matters of public concern. The recent Congressional investigations of Communism in the motion-picture industry proceeded on that premise. In *Winters* v. *New York,* in extending the protection of the First Amendment to comic books, the Court rejected the claim that what is designed primarily to entertain is not within the scope of the Amendment. The line between the informing and the entertaining, the Court had held, is too elusive for the protection of the basic right of freedom of the press. Propaganda through fiction is a familiar matter. What is one man's entertainment teaches another doctrine.

When, therefore, the *Miracle* case (*Burstyn* v. *Wilson*) reached the Supreme Court, it was generally expected in the legal profession that the Mutual Film case would be overruled. *The Miracle* was a forty-minute Italian-language film relating the tale of a simple peasant girl who is seduced by a bearded stranger she imagines to be Saint Joseph and who later gives birth to a baby she believes to have been divinely conceived.

New York has a statute requiring that all commercially exhibited films receive a license from the Department of Education. The statute further provides that licenses shall be denied to films that are obscene, immoral, crime-inciting, or "sacrilegious." *The Miracle* had been duly granted a license, but after a furor against the film was raised by the Catholic Church under the leadership of Cardinal Spellman, the Department of Education reversed itself and revoked the license on the ground that the film was sacrilegious, presumably because it casts doubt on the authenticity of the Biblical account of the conception and birth of Jesus.

The Supreme Court, as expected, overruled the 1915 decision and held that motion pictures are protected by the First Amendment. Besides rejecting the argument that motion pictures are exclusively a medium of entertainment produced for profit-making purposes, it rejected the further argument that they possess a greater capacity for evil, particularly among the youth of a community, than other modes of expression. That fact, said the Court, may be relevant in determining the permissible scope of community control but it does not disqualify motion pictures from First Amendment protection nor authorize substantially unbridled censorship.

The Court did not hold that in all cases pre-exhibition restraints upon exhibition of motion pictures are unconstitutional. Neither are pre-publication restraints on printing in all cases unconstitutional; the publication of transport sailing dates, for example, may be restrained during war. But the protection against previous restraint, though not absolutely unlimited, is the rule, not the exception. A State seeking to uphold a previous restraint upon motion pictures, just as upon the press, has a heavy burden to demonstrate that the situation is exceptional.

It may be that a State may censor motion pictures under a clearly drawn statute designed and applied to prevent the showing of obscene films. This the Court did not find it necessary to decide. All the Court found it necessary to decide was that the interest of the State of New York in seeing to it that no religion be treated with contempt, mockery, and ridicule does not justify prior restraints upon the expression of views. It is not, said the Court, the business of government in our nation to suppress real or imagined attacks upon a particular religious doctrine, whether they appear in publications, speeches, or motion pictures.

As has been indicated in the first chapter, decisions of the Supreme Court interpreting the Constitution are dynamic and evolutionary and frequently acquire expanded meanings through later citations of them as authorities. The *Miracle* decision was based upon the holding that protection of religion from ridicule does not constitutionally justify prior restraints on motion pictures. In *Gelling* v. *Texas*, decided a week after the *Miracle* case, the Court, without opinion but merely citing the *Miracle* decision (and *Winters* v. *New York*), held unconstitutional the censorship by a Texas municipality of the motion picture *Pinky*. That picture relates the story of a Negro girl who passes as a white in the North and, after becoming engaged to a white man, pays a visit to her home in the South. The censors objected to the film because it depicts a white man retaining his love for a woman after learning that she is a Negro; it depicts a white man kissing and embracing a Negro woman; and it includes a scene in which two white ruffians assault the heroine after she tells them she is a Negro. The picture was shown in Texas without any incident other than the arrest of the theater owner. The ordinance on which the censors acted authorized them to deny a license for the showing of a motion picture which the board was " of the opinion " is " of such character as to be prejudicial to the best interests of the people of said City." Their ruling had been upheld by the Texas courts (before the *Miracle* decision was handed down) on the ground that motion pictures are not protected by the First Amendment.

In 1954, also without opinion other than a citation of the *Miracle* decision, the Supreme Court, in *Superior Films* v. *Department of Education,* set aside a decision of the Ohio motion-picture licensing officials refusing a license to the picture "*M*" on the ground that it tended to promote crime, and was not, as the statute required, "of a moral, educational, or amusing and harmless character." Similarly, on the same day in the companion case of *Commercial Pictures Corporation* v. *Regents of the University of New York,* the Court set aside a refusal by the New York licensing officials, acting under the same statute involved in the *Miracle* case, to issue a license to the picture *La Ronde* on the ground that it was "immoral."

While these decisions do not necessarily add up to banning all previous restraints upon motion-picture exhibition, it may be suggested that their cumulative effect is to accord to motion pictures substantially the same protection under the First Amendment as is enjoyed by the press.

FREEDOM OF TEACHING

Like all liberties of Americans, the liberty to teach is not absolute; its exercise must in each case be weighed against competing communal values. As we have seen, it does not encompass freedom to teach the forcible overthrow of the government as soon as circumstances permit. Nor is it likely to encompass the freedom of Fagin to teach little children the gentle art of pickpocketing and petty larceny. The communal interest in preventing the commission of crimes justifies restriction on the freedom to teach how to commit crimes, just as it justifies restriction upon attempts and conspiracies to commit crimes.

Moreover, one who undertakes to teach in the public schools yields his right to teach whatever he wishes. The terms of his employment require him to teach only what the community, acting through the school board and officials, believes should be taught to its children. This was what was decided in the famous (or notorious)

Scopes case, in which the highest court of Tennessee upheld the validity of a statute making it unlawful to teach in schools supported out of public funds " any theory that denies the story of the Divine Creation of men, as taught in the Bible, and to teach instead that man has descended from a lower order of animals." While this decision was never appealed to the United States Supreme Court, it is at least questionable that the Supreme Court would have upset it.

Not that the state is complete master of what shall be taught in its schools. There is, it is true, language in the Scopes decision (as in not a few other decisions in various courts) to the effect that, in managing its properties and in its relationships with its employees, government has the unrestricted freedom enjoyed by private individuals in the management of their properties and in their relations with their employees. But, aside from the fact that private individuals do not enjoy unrestricted freedom in dealing with their employees — witness wage and hour laws, for example — the fundamental difference between despotism and democracy lies in the fact that in democracy the state does not possess the individual's right to act capriciously or arbitrarily. The state must act within the limitations of a constitution that forbids it to act arbitrarily, whether it be a written constitution as in the United States or an unwritten yet equally real one as in England.

A few examples will illustrate this point. Since the American Constitution requires government to be neutral among believers and as between believers and non-believers, public schools, as we have seen, may not teach as true (or false) a particular religion or all religions — although, of course, private schools may and do. Since, too, as we shall see later, a plea of the Fifth Amendment does not constitute an admission of guilt, a State acts arbitrarily and therefore unconstitutionally if it discharges a teacher merely because he has asserted his privilege against self-incrimination before a Congressional committee (as the Supreme Court held in the 1956 case of *Slochower* v. *Board of Higher Education*). Finally, since the American Constitution requires the States to teach their citizens equally and without discrimination because of race or color, the States may not refuse to teach Negro children, nor may they teach them separately from white children, nor may they refuse to employ Negro teachers or pay them lower salaries than white teachers receive for comparable teaching services.

With a few exceptions, the Constitution's commands apply only to governments, Federal and State, and therefore do not prohibit private schools and individuals from refusing to teach Negro children or from teaching them separately or from refusing to employ Negro teachers or teachers who have pleaded the Fifth Amendment. As we shall see in a later chapter of this book, the Constitution does not bar a State from forbidding private schools and individuals to practice the racial discrimination that is forbidden to the States by the Constitution. A number of States do have laws forbidding private schools to practice racial discrimination in the selection or treatment of students, and while the constitutionality of these statutes has not yet been directly passed upon by the Supreme Court, their constitutionality is hardly open to serious question.

Subject to these qualifications, private individuals, unlike the States, are complete masters of their schools. Indeed, the right to teach what and how one wants to is among the constitutionally protected liberties of Americans. This was established in a number of cases arising out of the xenophobia and excess nationalism that characterized the period of World War I and the 1920's when many Americans believed that the welfare of our country demanded the elimination of cultural differences. Then the preservation of the "American type" was deemed of paramount importance. Homogeneity was the goal sought and its attainment was pursued through a variety of ways. One was the establishment of a restrictive immigration system based upon national quotas. Another, with which we are here concerned, was the enactment of a number of State laws controlling private education.

The first of these cases, *Meyer* v. *Nebraska,* reached the Supreme Court in 1923. It arose out of a prosecution under a State statute — one of several enacted in a number of Midwestern States — that prohibited "teachers in any private, denominational or parochial school to teach any subject in any foreign language other than the English language" and further prohibited the teaching of any foreign language until the pupil should have successfully passed the eighth grade.

The purpose of the statutes — according to the attorney general of Nebraska arguing before the Supreme Court — "was to create an enlightened American citizenship in sympathy with the principles and ideals of this country." It is, he argued, within "the police power of the States to compel every resident . . . so to educate his children that the sunshine of American ideals will permeate the life of the future citizens of this Republic."

In reversing the conviction of the defendant, a teacher of German in a Lutheran parochial school, the Supreme Court recognized as valid the desire of the legislature to foster a homogeneous people with American ideals, prepared readily to understand current discussion of civic matters. Nevertheless, the Court held, the means adopted to achieve that end exceeded the limitations imposed by the Fourteenth Amendment upon the powers of the States and interfered with the teacher's constitutional rights without adequate reason therefor, at least in time of peace and domestic tranquillity. No emergency existed that rendered knowledge by a child of some language other than English so clearly harmful as to justify its inhibition with the consequent abridgment of rights so long freely enjoyed.

Two years later the Court decided the famous Oregon parochial-school case — *Pierce* v. *Society of Sisters.* Actually this was two cases, one involving a parochial school conducted by an order of nuns, the other a private secular military academy. However, a single opinion was written for both cases, and they are generally referred to under the single title of *Pierce* v. *Society of Sisters.*

In 1922, largely under the influence of Ku Klux Klan elements, the people of Oregon enacted a law aimed at eliminating parochial and private schools. While it did not expressly outlaw these schools, it sought effectively to achieve the same end by requiring all children, with limited exceptions, to attend only public schools.

The attorney general of Oregon urged in support of the law that the notorious and alarming increase in juvenile crime (what generation of adults has not experienced a notorious and alarming increase in juvenile crime?) could be attributed to the lack of public-school education by many children; that religious prejudice might result from religious segregation; that subversive economic doctrines might be taught in non-public schools; and that a system of compulsory public education was necessary to encourage the patriotism and insure the loyalty of future citizens.

Relying upon *Meyer* v. *Nebraska,* the Supreme Court declared the Oregon statute unconstitutional on the ground that it unreasonably interfered with the liberty of parents and guardians to direct the religious upbringing and education of children under their control.

The fundamental theory of liberty upon which all governments in this Union rest, the Court said, excludes any general power of a State to standardize its children by forcing them to accept instruction from public teachers only. The child is not the mere creature of the state; those who nurture him and direct his destiny have the right, coupled with the high duty, to recognize and prepare him for additional obligations.

The suits to invalidate the Oregon statute were brought, not by parents who wished to have their children educated in parochial and private schools, but by the operators of these schools. Thus, the decision, coupled with *Meyer* v. *Nebraska,* makes it clear that the liberties of Americans, protected by the Bill of Rights, include the liberty to teach how and what one wishes without government restraint or interference, except where clearly and immediately necessary for the protection of a superior communal interest.

Farrington v. *Tokushige* made this even clearer. The statute there involved, enacted by the legislature of the Territory of Hawaii, was aimed at the numerous Japanese-language schools in the Territory. The statute did not purport to outlaw private schools; what it did was to subject them to detailed and minute government regulation that would have made their operation difficult if not impossible. That its motivation was the same as that of the Oregon and Nebraska statutes is indicated by the "declared object of the Act," which was "to fully and effectively regulate the conduct of foreign language schools and the teaching of foreign languages, in order that the Americanism of the pupils may be promoted." The fear underlying the statute, according to the attorney general of Hawaii, was that "foreign born guests" were conducting "a vast system of schools of American pupils, teaching them loyalty to a foreign country and disloyalty to their own country."

The Supreme Court invalidated the Hawaiian statute on the authority of the Meyer and Pierce cases. The Court stated that, while it appreciated the grave problems incident to the large alien population of the Hawaiian islands, the limitations of the Constitution might not be transcended in the search for a solution of these problems.

FREEDOM OF LEARNING

These three decisions established freedom of teaching as a constitutionally protected liberty of Americans. Their tenor and language accorded similar protection to freedom of learning. In the Meyer case the Court specifically stated that the liberty secured by the Bill of Rights encompassed the right "to acquire useful knowledge," including the right to learn foreign languages. In the Pierce case the Court's emphasis was on the right of parents to have their children educated in non-public schools.

To a certain extent freedom of learning is probably broader and enjoys greater constitutional protection than freedom of teaching. In the Dennis case the Court held that the *teaching* "of the principles of Marx, Lenin and Stalin with the intent that they be acted upon as speedily as circumstances would permit" could constitutionally be made a punishable crime. It is more than doubtful, however, that a similar ruling would be made in respect to a statute that made the *reading* of these books or the *learning* of these principles a punishable offense.

Nevertheless, freedom to read and learn, broad as it is, is not absolute. Members of a jury in a criminal case, for example, may be forbidden by the judge to read newspaper accounts of the case while the trial is in progress, and if they violate the judge's injunction they may constitutionally be punished for contempt of court. The right to read and learn must in this situation yield temporarily to the community's interest in providing accused persons with a fair trial by an unbiased jury. Subject to such rare exceptions, however, freedom to read and learn is, theoretically at least, as close to an absolute liberty of Americans as can be conceived — perhaps even more nearly absolute than freedom to believe, for many disqualifications are imposed by law upon those who cannot truthfully swear that they do not believe in the overthrow of the government by force or violence.

(The near absoluteness of freedom to read and to learn may be more theoretical than real. One of the standard questions on loyalty examinations relates to the reading habits of the witness. It is a rare government official who will readily employ a regular reader of the *Daily Worker*, notwithstanding his protestation that he reads it only out of intellectual curiosity. Regular students at Jefferson School and other educational institutions believed to be Communist-controlled are likewise considered poor security risks and can expect to find themselves dismissed from employment not only by Federal, State, and municipal governments but even by many private firms. As a practical matter, therefore, it can hardly be said that freedom to learn and to read is nearly absolute, at least in the present political climate.)

Freedom *not* to learn may likewise be a liberty of Americans. However, the communal interest in an educated citizenry is so great that this liberty is largely restricted to adults and to citizens. An applicant for naturalization may be denied citizenship unless he learns and expresses an awareness of the principles and institutions of American democracy. In *West Virginia Board of Education* v. *Barnette* the Supreme Court, in holding that a State could not compel public-school children to recite the Pledge of Allegiance, nevertheless made it clear that children could be compelled to study and learn " our history and . . . the structure and organization of our government, including the guaranties of civil liberty which tend to inspire patriotism and love of country."

In the Pierce case the Court pointed out that no question was raised regarding the power of the State "to require that all children of proper age attend some school." In the Everson case, too, the Court assumed the power of the States to require all children to receive a minimum secular education. Finally, in *Donner* v. *New York*, the Supreme Court held squarely that a State could constitutionally compel all children to obtain a minimum secular education even if their religious convictions forbade them to do so. On the basis of these cases it may reasonably be said that if freedom of ignorance is a liberty of Americans, it is one much subject to government restriction in the interest of the needs of the community and the welfare of children.

Chapter 6. *Liberty and Justice: Fair Play and Fair Trial*

FROM MAGNA CARTA TO BILL OF RIGHTS

The First Amendment, to which the first half of this book has been devoted, concerns laws that government in our democracy may not make: laws respecting an establishment of religion or prohibiting its free exercise, or abridging freedom of speech or of the press or of the right of the people peaceably to assemble and to petition for a redress of grievances. The other Amendments in the Bill of Rights deal mainly with laying down the rules of fair play in accordance with which laws that may constitutionally be made shall be enforced. Lawyers, as we have seen, call the rights secured by the First Amendment "substantive," those secured by the other Amendments "procedural."

Mention of procedures and methods of enforcing laws gives rise to images of lawyers quibbling over technicalities, throwing rules of pleading and evidence at each other — rules generally unintelligible to the non-lawyer — and apparently doing everything to avoid coming to grips with the simple question to be decided: Is the accused guilty or innocent of the crime with which he is charged? Particularly when the accused is charged with an especially heinous crime, such as committing a violent sex offense against a child or being a Communist, is there likely to be popular impatience with procedural technicalities.

The popular image is false, and the popular impatience lacks understanding. Neither appreciates the tremendous stake all Americans have in making sure that the accused rapist or Communist receives the full protection of all procedural requirements. It was such impatience with technicalities and procedures that for centuries justified the use of torture to exact a speedy confession from an accused person who everyone well knew was guilty — so why waste time on long-drawn-out trials? Justice Frankfurter has sagely noted that the "history of liberty has largely been the history of observance of precedural safeguards."

Nor is the story of how these procedural safeguards developed a dull, uninteresting chronicle. On the contrary, it is one of the most fascinating chapters in human history. The temptation is great to recount it in detail here, but to accord it even minimal justice would require a volume at least as large as this book, whose purpose, after all, is to portray the contemporary scene. We must therefore content ourselves here with little more than a bare mention of the highlights of the struggle.

That part of the story which concerns procedural safeguards is generally considered to have begun at Runnymede on the Thames in 1215, when the rebellious barons and clergy of England, under the leadership of Stephen Langton, Archbishop of Canterbury, exacted the Magna Carta — the Great Charter — from King John. But the story goes back long before that. The Mosaic code imposed a number of procedural safeguards, such as public trial and the right of confrontation. Some of these were even more stringent than those imposed under our present constitutional system; Moses required at least two eyewitnesses for conviction in any capital case; our Constitution imposes this requirement only in trials for treason.

The Romans too enjoyed certain procedural safeguards now included among the liberties of Americans. According to the Acts of the Apostles, Porcius Festus, Roman procurator of Judea, deemed it "unreasonable to send a prisoner and not withal to signify the crimes laid against him." "It is not," Festus reported, "the manner of the Romans to deliver any man to die, before that he which is accused have the accusers face to face, and have license to answer for himself concerning the crime laid against him."

Thus, when King John consented to the thirty-ninth article of the Magna Carta — that "No freeman shall be taken, or imprisoned, outlawed, or exiled, or in any way harmed, nor will we go upon or send upon him, save by the lawful judgment of his peers or by the law of the land" — he was establishing no new precedent. This article itself was apparently taken from an earlier Continental source and reflected usages well established in England when the Great Charter was given.

The importance of the Charter in the history of the struggle for civil liberties is not primarily intrinsic. The Charter had its greatness thrust upon it; it was not born great. Indeed it was to some extent a reactionary instrument. Its purpose was to insure feudal rights and protect baronial privileges against royal encroachment. Little in the seventy articles protected the vast majority of Englishmen, the villeins and the tenants. The intended beneficiaries of Article 39 and Article 40 ("To none will we sell, to none deny or delay right or justice") were not the common people but the noblemen.

Even to the limited extent that it sought to regulate governmental relations the Charter was largely ineffectual. No sooner had the barons returned to their castles than John repudiated it as having been obtained under duress. Pope Innocent III, with whom John had made his peace, sided with John as against the pope's own appointee Langton, and released John from its observance. The committee of barons set up to insure the king's adherence to the Charter never had an opportunity to function, since civil war broke out again shortly after the Charter was granted.

To infer, nevertheless, that the Charter was a completely reactionary document and without intrinsic significance in the struggle for democratic liberties would be unfair and inaccurate. It did, for the first time in England, give written, constitutional form to libertarian advances that had been achieved. It recognized the rightful existence of representatives of those protected, with authority to insure observance of the guarantees. It constituted an acknowledgment by a divinely appointed monarch that he could be required to judge not according to his own will but according to "the law of the land." Repudiated by John, the Charter was reissued after his death in the name of his young son — although with some of its libertarian provisions conspicuously omitted. In 1354 its protection, limited as it may have been, was extended by statute to every man "of what estate or condition that he be," a statute that first used the modern equivalent for "law of the land" in assuring that no man should be harmed in any way except by "due process of law."

But the real importance of the Charter is extrinsic to it. Its greatness was ascribed to it by succeeding generations, and therein lies its real significance. For the Charter, whether as the result of bad historical research, romanticism, wishful thinking, or any other reason, in time came to be looked upon as truly the Charter of liberties of free Englishmen. Through the centuries Englishmen in trouble with the authorities invoked the Charter as guarantor of rights — such as trial by jury and habeas corpus — whose relationship with it was, if not fanciful, then certainly remote and tenuous. English public opinion was quick to rally around any claim for liberty made in the name of the Charter. By the time Madison and his colleagues added the Bill of Rights to the American Constitution, the Charter had acquired a gloss of centuries that made of it a world of liberties which the barons at Runnymede never dreamed of, and which would have shocked and terrified them if they had.

The one figure most responsible for this development was Sir Edward Coke, one of England's greatest jurists, whose writing and thinking were known to every American lawyer of the eighteenth century and profoundly influenced American constitutional development. As Chief Justice of the Common Pleas, Coke became the champion of Parliament against James I and Charles I, attacking the royal prerogative and setting the precedent for judicial supremacy in the United States by declaring that royal decrees contrary to law were null and void. His arguments and reasoning were based upon history as he saw it and upon historical documents such as the Magna Carta as he interpreted them. Although neither his history nor his historical interpretations were entirely accurate, his reasoning was brilliant and his arguments impressive — in no small measure because they harmonized so well with the growing libertarian spirit of seventeenth-century England and with the democratic libertarianism of eighteenth-century America. Coke's *Institutes,* published in 1628, contained a commentary upon the Magna Carta in which he showed to the satisfaction of the American colonists the identity in meaning between the Charter's "law of the land" and the prevalent "due process of law" and that the purpose of these provisions was to protect the citizen from governmental oppression. Coke it was also who, in the same year, was probably chief draftsman of the Petition of Right, sent by Parliament to Charles I, which reaffirmed the principle of habeas corpus by asserting that no person might be imprisoned without cause shown, and declared that martial law might not be employed in time of peace.

The only other figure we can mention in this brief chronicle is the radical Puritan pamphleteer, John Lilburne — "Freeborn John"

— as obnoxious a character as one is likely to come across in history. (How much civilization owes to obnoxious characters!) It was Lilburne who contributed much to the abolition in 1641 of the Star Chamber, that secret tribunal of judges, clergy, lawyers, and laymen that for a century and a half acted as the Crown's instrument for tyranny and oppression. The Star Chamber's proceedings were totally devoid of the procedural safeguards that later became the liberties of Americans. One who incurred the displeasure of the Crown could be arrested in secret and tried in secret. He had no right to be informed of the charges leveled against him nor to face or examine his accusers. He could be tortured to exact a confession. If by any chance the jury should acquit him, the members of the jury could themselves be fined and imprisoned. If he was convicted, his nose could be slit, his ears cut off, his tongue drilled, and his cheeks branded. Whipping, pillory, and staggering fines were imposed. The Star Chamber could (and did) impose any penalty short of death.

Lilburne's troubles began in 1637, when he was barely twenty. Accused of importing unlicensed Puritan books from Holland, he was brought before the Star Chamber and ordered to take the usual inquisitorial oath. This he refused to do, claiming the right not to incriminate himself. For this he was sentenced to be publicly whipped and placed in the pillory. While this was going on he exhorted his hearers to resist the tyranny of the bishops and threw among them copies of the condemned books. The Star Chamber ordered him gagged and placed in solitary confinement, and immediately decreed that persons thereafter sentenced to whipping or pillory be searched before the sentence was carried out.

The Long Parliament, which abolished the Star Chamber, voted Lilburne £300 reparation (little of which was ever paid), declaring that his punishment had been " illegal and most unjust, against the liberty of the subject, and the law of the land and Magna Carta." But Lilburne — of whom it was said that " if the world was emptied of all but John Lilburne, Lilburne would quarrel with John and John with Lilburne " — soon found himself at odds with Oliver Cromwell and his Puritan Commonwealth. A left-wing Puritan himself, he nevertheless protested the illegal court that condemned Charles I to death. For this he was tried for treason and, though acquitted, later banished. Returning to England, he was again tried and, though again acquitted, placed in confinement as a dangerous character. Indeed, most of his adult life was spent shuttling between the prison walls and the courtroom chamber. But throughout his many trials, he continually and loudly asserted his procedural rights (such as the privilege against self-incrimination, the right to be informed of the crime charged against him, assistance of counsel, and public trial) and by doing so helped secure them for succeeding generations of Englishmen and Americans.

The long but ultimately successful struggle for procedural safeguards in criminal proceedings was an integral part of the long and ultimately successful struggle for constitutional democracy. These procedural safeguards rest upon two underlying assumptions of democracy, the integrity of the individual and government by law rather than men.

When Sir Walter Raleigh was tried for treason in 1603 he claimed that he was entitled to acquittal unless two eyewitnesses testified against him. To this one of the judges replied: ". . . many horse stealers may escape if they may not be condemned without witnesses." Both before that time and since then, every assertion by an accused of the benefits of a procedural safeguard not established by ancient precedent — from the assertion of the right not to be tortured into confessing, to an accused Communist's claim of the right to confront secret informers — has been met with the same objection: that, if it is granted, many guilty persons may escape. The fact that, notwithstanding this objection, procedural safeguards have developed and have become part of our legal system manifests the deliberate judgment of the people that the integrity of the individual in a democracy is so valuable that it is more important that he be accorded a fair trial than that every culprit be punished.

It is clear that observance of the procedural safeguards designed to insure a fair trial assumes the supremacy of laws over the arbitrary will of men. Under the Anglo-American legal system a criminal case is entitled "*The King* v. *Jones*," or "*State* v. *Jones*"; and it is prosecuted in exactly that way — a contest between the government and the individual. But, with all its power, the government, whether king or state, must abide by the rules of the game. When Edward Coke contested the claimed right of James I to remove from the law courts and to judge for himself whatever cases he wished, the king replied that, if Coke was correct, then the king was "under the law, which was treason to affirm." But Coke stood his ground and replied that the king " ought not be under men but under God and the law." The inclusion in the Bill of Rights of the procedural safeguards deemed necessary to insure fair play for accused Americans constituted a recognition that in our democracy the state, like the king, is not above the law.

DUE PROCESS — FEDERAL AND STATE

By the time the colonies declared their independence of the king, the struggle for fair play in criminal trials had long been won in England. Indeed, one grievance against the king listed in the Declaration of Independence was that he had deprived the colonists of a number of important elements of fair play in criminal cases, such as trial by jury and trial at the place of commission of the charged offense. The concept of fair trial had been slow in developing and had come about by the gradual and erratic accretions of seemingly unrelated procedural safeguards. When, therefore, the Constitution and the Bill of Rights were framed here, the framers included specifically the more important components of fair trial that had by that time become established as liberties of Englishmen and Americans. These were:

1. Privilege of habeas corpus (Constitution, Art. I, sec. 9)
2. No bills of attainder (Art. I, sec. 9, 10)
3. No ex post facto laws (Art. I, sec. 9, 10)
4. Trial by jury (Art. III, sec. 2; Amendment 6)
5. No unreasonable searches and seizures (Amend. 4)
6. Right to indictment by grand jury and to be informed of crime charged (Amend. 5, 6)
7. No double jeopardy (Amend. 5)
8. No compulsory self-incrimination (Amend. 5)
9. Speedy and public trial at place of crime (Amend. 6)
10. Confrontation of witnesses (Amend. 6)
11. Compulsory process for defense witnesses (Amend. 6)

12. Right to counsel (Amend. 6)
13. Reasonable bail (Amend. 8)
14. No cruel and unusual punishments (Amend. 8)

These, of course, are not all the components of fair play in criminal proceedings. For example, while Amendment 6 guarantees trial by an " impartial jury," there is no specific guarantee that the *judge* be impartial. Nor is there any express abolition of the judge's power, which had survived to Freeborn John's day, of fining a jury for bringing in a verdict with which he disagreed. Nor is there anything expressly prohibiting a State from rushing an accused to trial immediately after indictment without affording him a reasonable time in which to prepare his defense. These unmentioned procedural safeguards are surely important elements of a fair trial.

To provide for unmentioned established safeguards and perhaps for those not yet established, Madison and his colleagues who drafted the Bill of Rights included an omnibus guarantee. No person, the Fifth Amendment states, shall " be deprived of life, liberty or property without due process of law." The phrase " due process of law " is much broader than its Magna Carta ancestor " law of the land," which guaranteed only that no person should be proceeded against except for violation of an existing law. " Due process of law " includes this but goes much further; it guarantees that, when a person is proceeded against for violation of a law, the government will act fairly and will accord him all the procedural safeguards comprising fair play and within the concept of ordered liberty. The short phrase " due process of law " thus leaves unlimited room for the evolution and expansion of the Anglo-American concept of fair play.

Before the Civil War the requirements of fair play were applicable only to the Federal government. The only exception was the ban on bills of attainder and ex post facto laws, which Article I, Section 10, of the Constitution made applicable to the States as well as to Congress. The Fourteenth Amendment, enacted after the Civil War to secure the rights of Americans against infringement by the States, incorporated the " due process " clause but did not expressly declare that the specific procedural safeguards set forth in the Bill of Rights should be applicable to the States. As we have seen, Justices Black and Douglas believed that this was the purpose of the Amendment, but the majority of the Supreme Court has never accepted this view.

The position of the Court is that the " due process " clause of the Fourteenth Amendment requires the States to accord defendants only such procedural safeguards as are at the particular time considered essential components of ordered liberty or fair play.

In most cases this interpretation will not result in any practical difference between State and Federal procedures. Thus, a " third degree " confession is barred to the States as outside the limits of fair play, and barred to the Federal government by the express ban on compulsory self-incrimination. On the other hand, there are many instances where permissible State procedures may differ from those in the Federal courts, such as elimination of jury trials in State non-criminal suits, noted in our first chapter. Further illustrations will appear throughout the remainder of this chapter.

Since the Federal government is also subject to the " due process " clause, which in the Fifth Amendment means all that it means in the Fourteenth, the net result is that the States have substantially more leeway than the Federal government in the conduct of criminal proceedings, and correspondingly an accused American's procedural liberties are less comprehensive in the State courts than in the Federal courts. To a substantial degree the practical difference is lessened by the fact that most State constitutions themselves contain many of the specific guarantees of the Bill of Rights, and the State courts generally interpret these in the same way that the Supreme Court interprets those in the Bill of Rights. Despite this, however, a large difference exists.

Before considering the specific procedural safeguards constituting fair trial, one fact should be noted. With minor exceptions, these developed in the criminal law and relate to criminal trials. A serious and as yet largely unanswered question is to what extent they are applicable to non-criminal matters between the government and the individual. One often hears, in defense of the denial of many of these safeguards (e.g., confrontation, right of cross-examination) in Congressional investigations, that investigations by legislative committees are not criminal proceedings and that procedural safeguards are therefore irrelevant. The same is said in respect to the dismissal of government employees on security grounds, and the deportation of aliens.

We shall see as we proceed to what extent this contention has been accepted by the Supreme Court. Two comments, however, are appropriate here. In the first place, it rests upon an extremely legalistic if not fictional distinction. A person discharged as a security risk by the government or uprooted from his family and home of many years and deported to a foreign land suffers consequences far more serious than ensue from many criminal proceedings. In the second place, and more important, the contention recognizes only the procedural trees and is completely oblivious to the democratic forest. It is only because of historical accident that the procedural safeguards developed in criminal proceedings; there is nothing inherent in criminal proceedings that makes procedural safeguards relevant only there. Procedural safeguards evolved in criminal proceedings as part — and only part — of the development of constitutional democracy out of despotism and tyranny. Democracy differs from despotism in that in the former the government deals fairly with the people in all its relations with them — not in a selected few. A government that adheres to fair play only part of the time is only a part-time democracy.

THE LAW OF THE LAND

Fair play, as envisaged by the American Constitution, contemplates punishment only for violation of a law duly enacted by the legislature. Common-law crimes — acts deemed offensive by virtue of judicial decisions alone — existed in England for centuries, but the Supreme Court has consistently held in many cases that there are no Federal crimes other than those that Congress has by duly enacted statutes declared to be crimes. Although the Court has never had occasion expressly to make the same ruling with respect to State common-law crimes — i.e., offenses deemed criminal by the State courts in the absence of a specific statute making them criminal — there would seem to be little doubt that the Court would interpret "due process" to require that punishment in the State courts shall be imposed only for violation of the "law of the land," that is, a duly enacted State statute. This follows from the express ban on ex post facto laws and from the oft-held principle that criminal laws, State no less than Federal, must be sufficiently clear to be understandable by the ordinary, reasonable citizen. A law that has never been enacted but exists solely by virtue of judicial decisions is not likely to be held to be clear and understandable.

The requirement that a criminal statute be reasonably clear is simply a requirement that the government play fair with the people and not entrap innocent persons into unintentional commission of crime. A statute, the Supreme Court said in the Winters case, that is so vague and indefinite as to fail to give fair notice of what acts will be punished does not constitute " due process of law." A penal statute must set up ascertainable standards of guilt so that men of common intelligence are not required to guess at its meaning.

EX POST FACTO LAWS

Few would dispute the proposition that it is unfair and offensive to our concepts of justice to punish a person for an act innocent when done but only later declared criminal by the legislature. That is why the Constitution forbids both Congress and the States to enact ex post facto laws, i.e., laws which either make criminal an act innocent when done or impose a greater punishment than was provided by law when the act was committed.

It was probably the intention of the framers of the Constitution that the ban on ex post facto laws should apply to civil no less than criminal statutes, that is, a person could not constitutionally be made liable for damages in a civil court for an act which did not give rise to liability when it was done. However, in *Calder* v. *Bull,* an early case decided in 1798, the Supreme Court held that the ban was limited to criminal statutes. On the basis of this decision and upon subsequent decisions holding that deportation, no matter how much hardship it causes, does not constitute punishment for a crime, the Vinson Court in *Harisiades* v. *Shaughnessy* upheld as constitutional (with Justices Black and Douglas dissenting) a provision in the Alien Registration Act of 1940 providing for the deportation of any alien who ever had been a member of the Communist Party. The Court refused to interfere with the deportation of an Italian, father of an American-born child, who had come to the United States in 1920, joined the Communist Party in 1923 when he was nineteen years old, and resigned from it in 1929; nor with the deportation of a mother of three American-born children who between 1919 and 1936 had on three separate occasions signed up for membership in the Party and paid dues (but taken no other part in its activities) for a total of four or five years. It was immaterial, the Court held, that both these aliens had resigned from the Party long before the Alien Registration Act was adopted and at a time when the Communist Party was still a legal party entitled to be on the ballot and elect its members to public office.

Yet the Court has not always accepted the full implications of the holding in *Calder* v. *Bull*. A year after the close of the Civil War the Court, in *Cummings* v. *Missouri,* invalidated as unconstitutionally ex post facto a State statute that barred from the right to vote, hold office, teach, or practice law any person who did not first take an oath that he had never borne arms against the United States government. In the same year, in *Ex parte Garland,* it invalidated on the same ground a Federal statute barring from practice in the Federal courts any attorney who refused to take a similar oath. The difference between these cases and the deportation case, said Justice Jackson speaking for the majority of the Court in the latter case, is that the earlier cases proceeded from the view that the novel disabilities there imposed were really criminal penalties disguised in civil forms whereas deportation has long been held not to be a criminal penalty in any form.

In view of the fact that, as we shall see in a later chapter, an alien subject to deportation is entitled to at least some of the procedural safeguards that the " due process " clause imposes upon criminal proceedings, this distinction does not appear entirely satisfactory. A more realistic explanation, a cynic might suggest, is that in the heat of the Korean War the United States was not prepared to accord to ex-Communists the liberties it was willing to accord to ex-Confederate soldiers after the Civil War.

In support of this explanation the cynic might point to the 1951 case of *Garner* v. *Los Angeles Board*. The Supreme Court (Justices Black, Douglas, and Burton dissenting) upheld an ordinance enacted in 1948 which required the discharge and permanent disqualification of any municipal employee who had been a member of the Communist Party after 1943. The Court distinguished the Cummings and Garland cases on the ground that the purpose of the statutes invalidated in those cases was punishment, whereas the purpose of the Los Angeles ordinance was merely to set up standards for public employment. The Court cited the case of *Hawker* v. *New York,* wherein it had upheld a statute disqualifying from the practice of medicine any person who had previously been convicted of a felony. The Court had held that the Constitution did not prevent States from improving the practice of medicine by imposing higher standards, and that the standard for physicians set up by the statute was not unreasonable. Here, too, said the Court in the Garner case, the standard set up for public employment is not unreasonable. The fact that the Los Angeles ordinance makes no provision for sincere and honest repentance may be unfortunate and unwise, but it does not render the ordinance unconstitutional.

BILLS OF ATTAINDER

Both the Federal government and the States are forbidden by the Constitution to enact bills of attainder. A bill of attainder is an act of the legislature inflicting punishment upon a person or persons who have not been convicted in a judicial trial. It needs little argument to show that punishment by legislative act without judicial trial does not accord with democratic concepts of fair play, besides being inconsistent with the American system of the separation of powers.

Historically bills of attainder concerned themselves only with punishment, but, as in the case of ex post facto laws, the Supreme Court held that a disqualification for an office or profession imposed upon individuals by act of the legislature may constitute punishment and thus be a bill of attainder. This is illustrated by the case of *United States* v. *Lovett.*

Robert Lovett, Goodwin Watson, and William E. Dodd, Jr., had been government employees who had been called before the House Un-American Activities Committee, then headed by Martin Dies. Dies called them " irresponsible, unrepresentative, crackpot, radical bureaucrats," affiliated with " communist front organizations " and unfit to hold government posts. Following this, a rider was added by the House of Representatives to an appropriation act, providing that no part of the funds should be used to pay the salaries of the three men — who were specifically named in the rider. Because the appropriation was needed to carry on the operations of the government during the critical war period, the Senate accepted the rider and President Roosevelt signed the act, although both believed the rider unconstitutional. And so did the Supreme Court, on the ground that the rider effectively barred the three from government employment and this constituted punishment in substance if not in form.

Although historically, too, bills of attainder usually identified the victims by name (as in the Lovett case), this, the Supreme Court has also held, is not necessary to condemn it as an unconstitutional bill of attainder; it is equally a bill of attainder if the victims are members of an identifiable class. In the Cummings and Garland cases, it will be remembered, the victims were all persons who had participated on, or actively sympathized with, the Confederate side during the Civil War, and this was held to be a sufficiently identifiable class to invalidate the statutes not only as ex post facto laws but also as bills of attainder. The stated reason a contrary result was reached in *Garner* v. *Los Angeles* was that the purpose of the ordinance in that case was merely to set up standards for municipal employment and not to punish ex-Communists; if the latter had been its purpose, it would have been a bill of attainder, since ex-Communists are an identifiable class.

Like an ex post facto law, the Supreme Court has held, a bill of attainder is retroactive in operation. If opportunity for repentance is provided, the statute is not an unconstitutional bill of attainder. On that basis the Court, in *American Communications Association* v. *Douds,* upheld the non-Communist oath in the Taft-Hartley Act, for under the Act a Communist could always resign and disassociate himself from the Party and thus remove his disqualification for union office.

HABEAS CORPUS AND ARBITRARY ARREST

" The habeas corpus," Samuel Johnson said to Boswell, " is the single advantage our government has over that of other countries." This may sound like a typical Johnsonian hyperbole; yet it is undoubtedly true that, as much as if not more than any other procedural safeguard, habeas corpus typifies government under law rather than the arbitrary rule of men, even men anointed by God to rule over other men.

The writ of habeas corpus is simply a command by a court of law — originally to a government official, later also to private persons — to bring before the court a person held in custody by the official and to show the court under what law the prisoner is being held. If the official is unable to satisfy the court that the prisoner is held justly under the law of the land, the court may command the official to release the prisoner.

An illustration of the use of habeas corpus occurred in 1772 when a slave, being transported for sale in Jamaica, applied for a writ of habeas corpus in England, where the ship had stopped over. The ship captain, upon explaining the cause of the slave's detention, was directed by the great English jurist Lord Mansfield to release him, because slavery was " odious " to the law and morals of Englishmen, and the slave therefore was being detained contrary to the law of the land.

The writ of habeas corpus was well established by the time of the Magna Carta, Article 36 of which provides that it should be issued gratuitously and " not be refused." However, during the reign of Charles I, the judges held in Darnel's case that the command of the king was a sufficient answer to a writ of habeas corpus, i.e., that the detention was lawful if the king commanded it. Acceptance of this decision would have meant that the king was above the law, and Parliament was not prepared to accept it. In its Petition of Right, adopted the same year, it protested against the principle that a person could lawfully be detained on the mere command of the king, and, in the statute of 1641 abolishing the Star Chamber, Parliament provided that the court issuing a writ of habeas corpus should pass upon the legality of an imprisonment even if it was ordered by the king.

The protection of the writ was finally secured by the enactment in 1679 of the great Habeas Corpus Act, which provided for issuance of the writ on behalf of any person detained on a criminal charge. The importance attached to the writ by the English people is indicated by the fact that the Act provided heavy fines against judges who wrongfully delayed or refused to issue the writ. The American colonists shared this view, as is indicated by the fact that, in the *Letter to the People of Quebec* issued by the Continental Congress in 1774, habeas corpus was listed as one of the five great rights enjoyed by Americans. A final indication of its importance to Americans lies in the fact that it was one of the few liberties (along with jury trial and bans on ex post facto laws and bills of attainder) which were included in the original Constitution rather than being added in the Bill of Rights.

Section 9 of the first Article of the Constitution provides that " the privilege of the writ of habeas corpus shall not be suspended, unless when in cases of rebellion or invasion the public safety may require it." Acting under the authority of this provision, Congress in 1867 enacted a law entitling any person who claims to be confined in violation of his rights under the Constitution to apply for a writ of habeas corpus in the Federal courts. Moreover, since the person may be held incommunicado or may otherwise be unable to invoke the court's aid, the writ may be applied for on his behalf, not merely by a relative but by a " next friend," a technical term meaning anybody at all, even one completely unknown to the prisoner. When Julius and Ethel Rosenberg were in the death cell in Sing Sing in 1953 awaiting execution for espionage, a total stranger, who knew about the case only from newspaper accounts and the court opinions, applied for habeas corpus on their behalf without consulting them or their attorneys and was able to obtain a stay of execution until the novel legal issues raised in his application were disposed of as untenable by the Supreme Court.

The Constitution permits suspension of the writ in case of rebellion or invasion, but it does not expressly say who may suspend it in such case. The fact that the provision for suspension is contained in the article of the Constitution dealing with the powers of Congress would seem to indicate that the framers of the Constitution intended that only Congress should have power to suspend it, and this was the view taken during the Civil War by Chief Justice Taney. This view, too, would seem to be consistent with the history and tradition of habeas corpus and its underlying premise of the supremacy of law over the executive. Lincoln, however, believed that the power to suspend the writ belonged to the President, since it was an emergency power which could not be exercised effectively if it had to await the slow course of Congressional action. When Taney overruled Lincoln's contention and issued a writ of habeas corpus on behalf of a civilian arrested by the Army in Baltimore after Lincoln had suspended habeas corpus, Lincoln directed the Army to ignore Taney's writ. The controversy ended, without settlement of the fundamental issue, when Congress enacted a law ratifying Lincoln's action in suspending the writ.

INDICTMENT BY GRAND JURY

The Anglo-American legal system has developed a division of responsibilities in criminal proceedings, as in lawmaking and law enforcement: the grand jury investigates, the government attorney prosecutes, the (petty) jury determines whether the accused has actually committed the crime, and the judge passes on questions of law and decides the punishment within the limits prescribed by law.

Since investigation by grand jury is a rather cumbersome device, it has been refined through the centuries. In the first place, its function has been restricted to serious offenses (felonies), i.e., those punishable by death or imprisonment in a penitentiary, generally for a year or longer. Lesser offenses (misdemeanors) may be prosecuted without grand-jury action merely on an information, a complaint sworn to either by a private citizen, by a police officer, or by the prosecutor himself. Secondly, the indictment — wherein a police official or government attorney does the investigating and the latter presents the evidence to the grand jury — has largely displaced the presentment, wherein the grand jury acts upon its own investigation and knowledge. Traditionally, the grand jury consists of twenty-three persons and hands down a true bill — a certification that it has found sufficient evidence to warrant a trial of the accused by a jury — on the affirmative vote of twelve members.

The Fifth Amendment provides: " No person shall be held for a capital or otherwise infamous crime, unless on presentment or indictment of a grand jury, except in cases arising in the land or naval forces or in the militia, when in actual service in time of war or public danger." As we have seen, the Fifth Amendment does not apply to the States, which are required by the " due process " clause of the Fourteenth Amendment to provide only such procedural safeguards in criminal proceedings as are necessary to insure justice and fair play.

Indictment or presentment by a grand jury serves two necessary functions in assuring fair play in criminal proceedings. First, it secures a person against the necessity of undergoing a possibly long, expensive, and harrowing trial merely on the basis of suspicion or rumor; the true bill is a representation by at least twelve citizens that they have found substantial evidence that the accused has in fact committed the crime. Secondly, it operates to satisfy the requirement of fair play — expressly specified in the Sixth Amendment — that the accused be informed " of the nature and cause of the accusation " so that he can adequately prepare his defense. It follows, therefore, that if another procedure instituted by a State satisfies both requirements, an accused is not denied " due process " even if he is proceeded against without indictment by grand jury.

So the Supreme Court held in 1884 in *Hurtado* v. *California*. California had adopted a constitution which permitted prosecution of felonies by the simpler procedure of information by a magistrate who, after examining the witnesses and permitting the accused's counsel to cross-examine them, certifies that he is convinced of the accused's probable guilt. Since this procedure assured that the accused would not be required to undergo a trial on mere rumor or hearsay, and since it adequately informed him of the nature of the accusation, it thus provided the elements of fair play and satisfied the " due process " clause. The Court's decision in the Hurtado case has been followed and reaffirmed in many later cases arising in the State courts, although indictment by grand jury is still necessary in proceeding against a person for committing a *Federal* felonious offense.

While the States are not required to proceed by grand-jury indictment, they are required to accord an accused fair play, and if they do proceed by grand-jury action, that procedure too must comply with the requirements of fair play. In *Norris* v. *Alabama*, the second Scottsboro case, the Supreme Court decided that an indictment against a group of Negro boys for allegedly raping two white girls did not satisfy the requirements of due process where Negroes were systematically excluded from serving on grand juries. The exclusion of Negroes from trial juries will be more fully discussed later in this chapter in connection with trial by jury; here we need point out only that the requirements of fair play cannot be assured to accused Negroes by the actions of a grand jury from which Negroes are systematically and deliberately excluded.

BAIL

The right of an accused to be released on bail before conviction has long been considered an element of fair play in the Anglo-American system of justice. In 1681 the House of Commons voted for the impeachment of the Chief Justice of the King's Bench because, among other reasons, he denied bail in prosecutions coming before his court. By the time our Bill of Rights was added to the Constitution, the right to bail was universally considered to be one of the liberties of Americans.

Right to freedom on bail before conviction is an aspect of fair play for two reasons. First, it permits the unhampered preparation of a defense; preparation of the defense is obviously made more difficult if the accused is confined to prison before trial. Secondly, it serves to prevent the infliction of punishment prior to conviction. A person later acquitted will have been punished for a crime he did not commit if he was confined in jail before the acquittal. Unless the right to bail before trial is preserved, the presumption that every person is innocent until he is proved guilty, secured after centuries of struggle, would lose its meaning. For these reasons, it is reasonable to assume — although the Supreme Court has never had occasion to pass on the question — that the "due process" clause of the Fourteenth Amendment encompasses the right to bail before conviction, even though the provision of the Eighth Amendment that "Excessive bail shall not be required" applies only in the Federal criminal courts.

The Eighth Amendment prohibits "excessive bail" but does not define what constitutes "excessive." The purpose of fixing bail is to assure the accused's presence at trial, and this can be assured by fixing bail sky-high — that is, so high that the accused cannot furnish it. Admission to bail in an amount that the accused can supply, thus obtaining temporary liberty, always involves a risk that the accused will take flight; but that is a calculated risk which the Constitution requires the government to take as the price of our system of justice.

In *Stack* v. *Boyle* the Supreme Court was faced with an appeal by a number of Communists indicted by a Federal grand jury in California for violation of the Smith Act. The Federal judge had fixed bail at $50,000 for each defendant. The penalty on conviction was fixed by the Smith Act at no more than five years imprisonment and a fine not exceeding $10,000 — or one-fifth the amount fixed as bail. The Federal district attorney conceded that $50,000 was far higher bail than usually fixed in cases of crimes punishable by five years and $10,000; but he justified the demand on the ground that each defendant was a pawn in a conspiracy and would, in obedience to his superiors, flee from the country if allowed his freedom on bail. (Note again the assumption that Communists as members of a criminal conspiracy are not entitled to the liberties enjoyed by other Americans.)

The Court refused to accept this contention without evidence to support it. If bail in an amount greater than that usually fixed for serious charges of crime is required in the case of any of the defendants, the Court said, that fact must be established by proof, and will not be assumed. In the absence of such proof the defendants have been denied their constitutional rights and the amount of bail should be reduced.

SEARCHES AND SEIZURES

One of the principal grievances of the American colonists against the British king was the issuance by his judges of general writs of assistance. These were search warrants, unlimited either in time or place, allowing the king's agents to search any place during the day or night for contraband goods. In 1761 James Otis made an historic, though unsuccessful, court argument against the issuance of the writ on the ground that "the freedom of one's house" is an essential of liberty, that a man in his home must be as secure "as a prince in his castle," and that a law violating that privacy is an instrument of "slavery" and "villainy."

As a result of these experiences the framers of the Bill of Rights declared in the Fourth Amendment: "The right of the people to be secure in their persons, houses, papers and effects against unreasonable searches and seizures shall not be violated, and no warrants shall issue but upon probable cause, supported by oath or affirmation and particularly describing the place to be searched and the persons or things to be seized."

The Amendment bans warrants on mere suspicion. And it requires that, before a warrant may be issued by a court for the search of premises or the seizure of property, the official seeking the warrant must present sworn evidence showing that the search or seizure is reasonably necessary for the apprehension and conviction of one who has committed a crime. The warrant issued by the court must state specifically the premises to be searched or the property to be seized; blanket or roving warrants are outlawed by the Amendment.

The only exception to the ban on searches without a prior search warrant is in the case of a search that is incidental to a lawful arrest. It had long been held that the person of one lawfully arrested could be searched for incriminating evidence without the necessity of obtaining a separate search warrant. In *Agnello* v. *United States* the Supreme Court extended this rule to permit the search without warrant of the immediate premises in which the accused is arrested, as well as of the accused's person. In *Harris* v. *United States* the Court, in a 5-to-4 decision, upheld the validity of a search without warrant of a four-room apartment occupied by the person arrested, and also upheld the seizure by the Federal officers of papers evidencing a crime unrelated to the one for which the arrest was made. Three years later, in *United States* v. *Rabinowitz,* the Court sustained as valid the act of Federal officers, armed with a valid warrant for arrest but none for search or seizure, in searching the desk, safe, and file cabinets of the accused and seizing a large number of forged and altered stamps.

Although the Fourth Amendment applies only to the Federal government, freedom from unreasonable searches and seizures is unquestionably required by our concepts of fair play. In *Wolf* v. *Colorado* the Supreme Court held, in 1949, that the security of one's privacy against arbitrary intrusion by the police — which is at the core of the Fourth Amendment — is basic to a free society. It is therefore implicit in " the concept of ordered liberty " and as such is enforcible against the States through the " due process " clause of the Fourteenth Amendment.

While there is theoretically no difference under the Constitution between an unlawful search or seizure by Federal officers and one by State officers, as a practical matter there is all the difference in the world. Ever since the decision of *Weeks* v. *United States* a half-century ago, the Court has held that evidence seized in violation of the Fourth Amendment may not be used against the accused in a *Federal* criminal court. The reason for this rule is to remove the temptation to resort to unconstitutional short cuts by Federal law-enforcement officials seeking convictions. Where, however, the unlawful search or seizure is made by State officials, the Court held in *Wolf* v. *Colorado* (1949) that the unconstitutionally seized evidence could be used against the accused in a *State* criminal court. According to the majority opinion (with three justices dissenting) the violation of fair play consists in the act of searching and seizing and not in the use of the seized evidence in the trial. The remedy, said the Court, is to discipline the offending police officer or to sue him for damages — a remedy which the minority thought more theoretical than real.

The Court has also taken a narrow view as to what constitutes search and seizure. It interprets a search to mean a physical entry of premises and a seizure to mean the taking of something tangible. This is what search and seizure meant in 1791 when the Fourth Amendment was adopted, and the Court has felt that to extend its meaning would unduly hamper government officers and would result in the escape of many guilty persons. For that reason the Court, by a vote of 5 to 4, held in *Olmstead* v. *United States* that wiretapping by Federal officers and their testimony in court as to what they overheard the accused say did not violate the Fourth Amendment, for there had been no searching of the accused's person or premises, nor had anything tangible been taken from him.

Justice Holmes in his dissent called wiretapping a " dirty business " and expressed the view that it is less an evil that some criminals should escape than that the government should play an ignoble part. Justice Brandeis, another dissenter, stated that the makers of our Constitution sought to protect Americans in their beliefs, their thoughts, their emotions, and their sensations. They confirmed, as against the government, the right to be let alone — the most comprehensive of rights and the right most valued by civilized man.

These forceful dissents ultimately resulted in the enactment by Congress of a law prohibiting disclosure of any information obtained through wiretapping unless both parties to the telephone conversation consented. In 1937 the Court held in *Nardone* v. *United States* that the statute barred use of wiretap evidence in the Federal courts; two years later, in the second Nardone case, the Court went even further and held that evidence obtained through leads developed by the wiretapping could likewise not be used against the accused. If, for example, the accused discloses in the illegally intercepted telephone conversation the hiding place of certain incriminating evidence, that evidence may not be used against him even if the Federal officers then obtain a warrant for its seizure.

The Nardone rule applies only in the Federal courts; the Supreme Court so ruled in *Schwartz* v. *Texas*. Wiretapping is extensively practiced by State police officers, and wiretap evidence is widely used in State courts. This is so even though the State officers commit a Federal crime in the very act of divulging the intercepted communication in the courtroom. One need hardly comment on the morality of violations of law by government officers — particularly government officers who take an oath to uphold the law — in order to punish other law violators.

Even in the Federal courts, the ingenuity of electronic engineers and the eagerness of prosecuting officers to obtain convictions has outrun the indignation of Congress and the restrictions of the Nardone case. In *Goldman* v. *United States* the Court held that neither the statute nor the Fourth Amendment applied to the use by Federal officers of a Detectophone which enabled them to overhear a conversation taking place in an adjoining hotel room.

In *On Lee* v. *United States* the following facts were disclosed. A man named On Lee ran a laundry in Hoboken. A customers' room opened on the street; back of it was a room for ironing tables, and in the rear were his living quarters. Chin Poy, an old acquaintance and former employee, sauntered in and, while customers came and went, engaged On Lee in conversation, during which the latter made incriminating statements concerning the selling of narcotics. On Lee did not know that Chin Poy was an " undercover agent " or " stool pigeon " for the Federal Bureau of Narcotics; nor that Chin Poy was wired for sound, with a small microphone in his inside coat pocket and a small antenna running along his arm; nor that a Narcotics Bureau agent was standing outside with a receiving set properly tuned to pick up any sounds the Chin Poy microphone transmitted. The Supreme Court held, following the Goldman case, that the bureau's agent could testify in court as to what he thus overheard. The act of Congress applied only to communications transmitted over telephone wires; it no more barred testimony of a conversation overheard through an electronic device than one overheard through the garden variety of eavesdropping or ear-straining. Four of the nine justices strongly dissented.

TRIAL BY JURY

The origin of the Anglo-American jury system is clouded in uncertainty. Although some historians trace it to Anglo-Saxon or even earlier times, most believe it was brought to England by the Normans. The first jurors did not decide disputes, but were neighbors who were acquainted with the facts and spoke from their own knowledge. In criminal proceedings the jurors at first presented the accusations; it was only later that their function became to determine whether the accusations were true.

By the time of the American Revolution trial by jury had become a cherished protection against tyranny. It was one of the five " grand rights " listed in the *Letter to the People of Quebec;* and among the abuses charged against the king in the Declaration of Independence was that he deprived " us in many cases of the benefits of Trial by Jury." So important did Americans deem trial by jury in criminal cases that this is the only liberty of Americans secured both in the Constitution itself and in the Bill of Rights.

Despite this history and surprising as it may seem, the right to trial by jury in criminal cases is not today considered a fundamental liberty of Americans. In 1900 the Supreme Court in *Maxwell* v. *Dow* ruled that the Sixth Amendment guarantee of trial by jury is not applicable to the States. Since then a number of Supreme Court cases have ruled in effect that the " due process " clause of the Fourteenth Amendment does not require the States to provide a jury trial in all criminal cases. Hence, while a person charged with any Federal crime is entitled to a trial by a jury of twelve persons, all of whom must agree if he is to be found guilty, some States provide for non-jury trial even of felonies, and in most States persons charged with lesser crimes such as misdemeanors are likewise tried by judges without juries.

Though the States are not constitutionally required to provide jury trial in criminal cases, if they do the jury trials they provide must accord with our concepts of fair play; less than that would violate " due process." While a jury of eight rather than twelve, or conviction by five-sixths vote, would not offend our sense of justice and is therefore not unconstitutional, in a long series of cases beginning in 1880 with *Strauder* v. *West Virginia* the Supreme Court has held that systematic exclusion of Negroes from juries that try Negroes violates the Fourteenth Amendment and requires reversal of convictions handed down by such juries. Since direct proof that Negroes have been systematically excluded from juries is difficult to obtain, the Supreme Court held in *Patton* v. *Mississippi* (1947) that absence of Negroes from the jury rolls over a long period of time creates an inference of discriminatory exclusion in a county where a substantial percentage of the adult population is colored and thus would normally be expected to be represented in the juries.

These decisions were based upon the " equal protection " clause of the Fourteenth Amendment (discussed more fully later in this volume) rather than the " due process " clause; but the principle is the same. The Sixth Amendment requires trial by an " impartial " jury, and the fair-play requirement of the " due process " clause means that if a State provides a jury it must provide an impartial jury. While a Negro defendant has no constitutional right to have Negroes on the jury that tries him, he does have a constitutional right that Negroes not be excluded from serving on the jury merely because they are Negroes.

" Impartial jury " means a jury representing a cross-section of the community. Exclusion from the jury of persons because of their race, and probably too because of their economic status, does not satisfy this requirement; disqualification from jury service of all laborers or all low-income citizens would probably be held to violate due process. However, in *Fay* v. *New York* and in *Moore* v. *New York* the Court, by a vote of 5 to 4 in each case, upheld the " blue ribbon " jury for special cases allowed under New York law. The majority found unconvincing the argument that such juries, reflecting relatively high economic and social positions, are undemocratic and are more likely to return verdicts of guilty than normal juries; the majority held that a jury of better-educated citizens did not offend our concepts of fair play. The minority opinion argued that an accused is constitutionally entitled to be judged by a fair sampling of his neighbors, not merely those who are of superior intelligence or learning; any method that permits only the " best " of the community to judge the guilt or innocence of an accused opens the way to grave abuses and does violence to the fundamental concept of fair play.

RIGHT TO COUNSEL

Some of the most spirited colloquies between "Freeborn John" Lilburne and the judges of King Charles's court who tried him concerned Lilburne's repeated requests — repeatedly denied — for counsel to assist him in his defense. The judges assured him that he needed no counsel since they would protect his legal rights; Lilburne replied, pertinently though undoubtedly irreverently, that he feared just such protection.

Yet the judges were right and Lilburne was wrong in his day. Under the English common law, well into the nineteenth century a person charged with a felony had no right to counsel but had to rely upon the judge who tried him to act as his counsel. It was only when charged with a minor crime that an accused since the twelfth century had the right to counsel to assist him in his defense.

Englishmen and American colonists alike constantly attacked as barbarous the practice of denying counsel to one needing it most. Even Blackstone, the ardent defender of the common law, queried: "For upon what face of reason can that assistance be denied to save the life of a man, which yet is allowed him in prosecutions for every petty trespass?" The colonies refused to follow the English practice, and by the time the Constitution was adopted practically every State provided for assistance of counsel in criminal cases. When, therefore, the Sixth Amendment was added to the Constitution in 1791, there was no dispute as to the necessity of the guarantee that in "all criminal prosecutions, the accused shall enjoy the right . . . to have the assistance of counsel for his defense."

The Sixth Amendment applies directly only to the Federal government, and in the Federal courts the constitutional right to counsel is strictly adhered to. An accused charged with a Federal crime must be advised by the court of his right to counsel, and if he is financially unable to secure counsel for himself the court must provide him with counsel. The accused may waive the right to counsel and defend himself, but the court may allow him to do so only if it has advised him fully of the consequences of a conviction and is convinced that he has sufficient intelligence and education to understand his right and to waive it.

In prosecutions in the State courts the question is far more difficult and complicated. It is probable that more appeals are made to the United States Supreme Court to upset State court convictions on the claim that the defendant was deprived of his right to counsel than for any other ground. In 1932 the issue first reached the Supreme Court in *Powell* v. *Alabama,* the first Scottsboro case. There seven young, uneducated, derelict Negro boys were accused of raping two white girls aboard a freight train in Alabama. All were indicted, arraigned, tried, found guilty, and sentenced to death. They were not advised of their right to counsel, nor were they offered court-appointed counsel or the opportunity to communicate with their relatives to obtain counsel. Before the morning of the trial the trial judge had generously "appointed all the members of the bar" for the limited "purpose of arraigning the defendants," but this was hardly more than an expansive gesture. At the morning of the trial two attorneys stepped forward and volunteered to assist the defendants. The trial then proceeded without any preparation or opportunity to prepare for it by the two attorneys. It was only after their conviction that the defendants first obtained the benefit of adequate legal assistance.

The Supreme Court reversed the conviction in a decision which, while it did not hold that the Sixth Amendment was incorporated in the Fourteenth (as we have seen, the majority of the Court has consistently refused so to hold), nevertheless in effect held that the "due process" clause of the Fourteenth Amendment imposed upon the States the same requirements in respect to the right to counsel in criminal cases as the Sixth imposed upon the Federal courts.

Ten years later, in *Betts* v. *Brady*, the principle of the Powell case was severely limited. In the Betts case an indigent farm hand in Maryland was indicted for robbery. Being unable to hire a lawyer, he requested the court to appoint one for him. The court refused on the ground that it was not the practice in that county to supply lawyers except in murder and rape cases. Forced to defend himself, the defendant was tried, convicted, and sentenced to eight years imprisonment. The Supreme Court refused to upset the conviction and held that the doctrine of the Powell case was limited to *capital* offenses. While, the Court said, the Fourteenth Amendment prohibits punishment of one whose trial was offensive to common and fundamental ideas of fairness and right, and while want of counsel in a particular case may result in a conviction lacking in such fundamental fairness, the Fourteenth Amendment does not embody an inexorable command that no trial for any crime or in any court can be fairly conducted and justice accorded a defendant who is not represented by legal counsel.

The principle of *Betts* v. *Brady* has been severely criticized; Justices Black and Douglas (and during their lifetimes Justices Murphy and Rutledge) have never accepted it. Nevertheless, it does reflect the majority view of the Supreme Court today. The rule today may be stated somewhat as follows: Unlike the Sixth Amendment, the Fourteenth does not require assistance of counsel in all criminal cases, but only in cases of crimes punishable by death. In all other cases, the defendant is constitutionally entitled not to counsel but to a fair trial. If under the circumstances of the case the absence of counsel deprives him of a fair trial, the conviction will be set aside; but if he has a fair trial even without being accorded counsel or advised of his right to counsel, his conviction will be left undisturbed.

For example, in *Palmer* v. *Ashe* the Court upset the conviction of a person of subnormal intelligence, formerly an inmate of a mental institution, who, without being afforded counsel or advised of his right to counsel, was sentenced for armed robbery although he had assumed he was charged only with the much lesser offense of breaking and entering. In *Gibbs* v. *Burke* the Court set aside the larceny conviction of an adult who, not being advised of his right to counsel, conducted his own defense, with the result that a good deal of prejudicial hearsay evidence was admitted (which a lawyer would have objected to and caused to be excluded) and he took no objection to the judge's biased comments to the jury.

On the other hand, in *Gryger* v. *Burke* the Court refused to disturb the life sentence as a fourth offender imposed upon one who had eight times previously been convicted of violent crimes and had been represented by counsel in two of the previous cases. The Court refused to believe that such a hardened criminal, who had had so many previous encounters with the law, did not know of his right to engage counsel or was prejudiced by the trial judge's failure to advise him of that right. Similarly, in *Bute* v. *Illinois* the Court upheld the plea of guilty under a morals charge of a 57-year-old non-lawyer who, though not advised of his right to counsel, was fully advised by the judge as to the consequences and penalties of the plea.

It might be noted in conclusion that the distinction between capital and non-capital offenses does not appear to rest upon any logical base. If the Fourteenth Amendment entitles accused Americans only to the right to a fair trial, it is hard to see why the Supreme Court will set aside a death sentence where the accused receives a fair trial even without benefit of counsel. The explanation may be more psychological than logical; it offends our conscience to send a man to his death without having afforded him counsel to defend himself. (The same conscience motivates the rule in most States that a person may not plead guilty to an offense punishable by death.) The most that can be said for the distinction is that it is infinitely preferable to the old common-law rule that allowed counsel only in minor non-capital offenses.

CONFRONTATION AND CROSS-EXAMINATION

At a time when the Senate Investigating Committee under the chairmanship of Joseph McCarthy had engaged in a particularly egregious violation of civil liberty, President Eisenhower told a press conference: " In this country, if some one dislikes you or accuses you, he must come up in front. He cannot hide behind the shadows, he cannot assassinate you or your character from behind without suffering the penalties an outraged citizenry will inflict . . ." The American code, the President continued, encompasses " the right to meet your accuser face to face."

With respect to the specific subject under discussion, Congressional investigations (as well as with respect to government employee security cases and deportation proceedings), the President was perhaps expressing an ideal rather than a reality. With respect, however, to criminal proceedings he was stating in non-technical language the Sixth Amendment right of an accused " to be confronted with the witnesses against him." The " faceless accuser " is banned in Federal criminal trials by the Sixth Amendment, and probably in State criminal trials by the " due process " clause of the Fourteenth. A plea that considerations of national security prevent disclosing undercover agents, confidential informers, or secret evidence is not acceptable in a criminal court. The government must choose between prosecuting the accused or keeping its secrets; it cannot constitutionally do both.

The Sixth Amendment speaks of confrontation but does not mention cross-examination. Nevertheless, there can be no doubt that the right of an accused to cross-examine witnesses testifying against him is an essential element of fair trial and due process, protected in the Federal courts by the Fifth and Sixth Amendments, and in the State courts by the Fourteenth. Our trial system is based upon the belief that the best way to arrive at the truth is by examination and cross-examination of witnesses in open court. The Supreme Court has held, in the case of *In re Oliver*, that a person's right to examine the witnesses against him is basic in our system of jurisprudence, and that a conviction of a crime without according the accused this right will not be allowed to stand.

COERCED CONFESSIONS AND THE FIFTH AMENDMENT

A volume much longer than this one and devoted exclusively to the subject would not begin to do justice to an account of the history and meaning of the short clause in the Fifth Amendment that "no person . . . shall be compelled in any criminal case to be a witness against himself." In the popular mind the term "Fifth Amendment" has in our time come to mean the privilege against self-incrimination — even though that is but one of five liberties secured by the Amendment. The history of the guarantee against compulsory self-incrimination is a long one, going back to the Inquisition and the Star Chamber, and is marked by blood, faggots, and the screw. The clause was included in the Bill of Rights as a liberty of Americans because the framers recognized that, in the words of Dean Erwin Griswold, "the privilege against self-incrimination is one of the great landmarks in man's struggle to make himself civilized."

The constitutional prohibition of compulsory self-incrimination has two aspects; the first involves coerced confessions, the second the right of an accused not to testify to matters that might incriminate him. There is an important constitutional distinction between these two aspects, even though they differ only in degree. Torturing a suspect on the rack until he cries out, "I am guilty," and throwing him in prison for contempt of court or of Congress if he refuses to utter words having an equivalent significance — these differ basically only in degree. Constitutional differences are nevertheless frequently differences in degree, and such is the case here.

The constitutional difference lies in this: A forced confession offends our sense of justice and fair play and is accordingly barred not only in the Federal courts by the Fifth Amendment but also in the State courts by the " due process " clause. On the other hand, it is not inherently offensive to Western concepts of justice to require an accused to take the stand and testify to what he knows about the crime; this method of procedure is used in all the courts of Europe and the West outside the Anglo-American system, and it would be arrogance to suggest that we alone possess a true sense of justice. True enough, the privilege against self-incriminatory testimony contained in the Fifth Amendment is duplicated in the constitutions of most States in the Union; but this does not mean that States that do not wish to accord the privilege, or which modify and qualify it, violate fundamental concepts of justice.

Hence, in a series of cases beginning in 1908 with *Twining* v. *New Jersey*, the majority of the Supreme Court has consistently held that the " due process " clause of the Fourteenth Amendment does not preclude a State from compelling a defendant to take the stand and testify in a criminal case. In that case the Court upheld the practice in the New Jersey criminal courts (impermissible in Federal criminal courts) by which judges instruct juries that they may infer guilt from the defendant's refusal to take the stand, even though the obvious effect of such power of instruction is to compel the defendant to take the stand. This holding was reaffirmed in *Palko* v. *Connecticut* and again in *Adamson* v. *California*.

The Supreme Court, however, has given a different treatment to forced confessions and has consistently upset State court convictions based upon such confessions. " Compulsion by torture to extort a confession is a different matter. . . . The rack and torture chamber may not be substituted for the witness stand." So said the Court in *Brown* v. *Mississippi*, where in 1936 it set aside a conviction based upon a confession extorted by strangulation and whipping by a sheriff assisted by a mob.

Rochin v. *California* has already been discussed in the first chapter of this book. There the Supreme Court held that forcing a suspect to disgorge narcotic capsules that he had swallowed, and using them in evidence upon his trial, shocked the conscience, offended procedures implicit in the concept of ordered liberty, and thus violated the " due process " clause.

Psychological coercion or " third degree " methods have likewise been condemned by the Court. In *Chambers* v. *Florida* (1940) it set aside a conviction based upon the confession of a prisoner who had been arrested on suspicion and without warrant, had been confined incommunicado, and had been subjected to protracted questioning by police officials under circumstances calculated to break the strongest nerves. Similarly, four years later, in *Ashcraft* v. *Tennessee*, the Court ruled violative of the " due process " clause the use of a confession obtained near the end of a 36-hour period of practically continuous questioning under powerful electric lights by relays of police officers, investigators, and lawyers. In *Malinski* v. *New York* (1945) a confession was held unconstitutionally coerced where it was obtained from a suspect who had been held incommunicado in a hotel room from 8 A.M. to 6 P.M., completely unclothed so as to " let him think that he was going to get a shellacking."

The Court has gone even further and has thrown out a confession based primarily upon fraud. In *Leyra* v. *Denno* a confession (of murder) was obtained through apparently sympathetic and solicitous interrogation by a psychiatrist with considerable knowledge of hypnosis, introduced by the police officials to the suspect as a physician who was going to give him medical relief. The Court held violative of due process not only the admissions of guilt made to the psychiatrist but also the signed confession given immediately thereafter to the police officers who had been waiting in an adjoining room for the opportune moment to enter.

In the Malinski case and a number of others that followed it the Court held that if a coerced confession played any part in a conviction, the conviction would be thrown out and a new trial would be held in which the confession would be excluded. However, in *Stein* v. *New York* a majority of the Court (Black, Douglas, and Frankfurter dissenting) appeared to overrule this principle. In the Stein case the Court seemed to hold that a conviction (in this case of a robbery murder) would not be disturbed if there was sufficient untainted evidence presented to establish the defendant's guilt even if the coerced confession had not been used against the accused. In such case, the Court argued, the defendant has not been hurt by the denial of his constitutional right and therefore has no cause to complain.

The Malinski and Stein holdings are based upon two disparate rationales for the exclusion of coerced confessions. Under the Malinski principle, coerced confessions are offensive to our standards of justice and morality; they should not be obtained because it is uncivilized to do so; the only way to ensure their not being obtained is to remove from prosecuting officials the temptation to get them, and this can best be accomplished by throwing out any conviction after a trial in which they are used. The Stein case proceeds on the premise that it is not the business of the United States Supreme Court to tell State police officials how to perform their duties or to deter them from doing wrong; it is the Court's business only to protect the constitutional rights of Americans. Coerced confessions are excluded because they are unreliable, and a defendant convicted on the basis of a coerced confession has been deprived of his constitutional right to a fair trial in having been convicted on the basis of unreliable evidence. If, however, there has also been an abundance of other reliable and unimpeachable evidence clearly showing the defendant's guilt, then he has not been prejudiced, has received his just deserts, and has no valid cause to complain.

THE PRIVILEGE AGAINST SELF-INCRIMINATION

As we have seen, the privilege against self-incrimination is conferred only by the Fifth Amendment in respect to the Federal government; it is not deemed an integral part of fair play or ordered liberty so as to encompass it in the "due process" concept of the Fourteenth. While most State constitutions do recognize the privilege, they are not required by the United States Constitution to do so. Hence, the only cases under this provision considered by the Supreme Court concern application of the privilege in respect to the Federal government.

The Sixth Amendment, in setting forth the elements of a fair trial, begins with the phrase "In all criminal prosecutions," and the Court has interpreted the Amendment to require the specified procedural safeguards only in criminal prosecutions. The Fifth Amendment, too, in respect to the immunity against self-incrimination specifically states that "in any *criminal* case" no person shall be compelled to be a witness against himself. However, it was long assumed by Congressional investigating committees that the privilege is not limited to criminal proceedings but extends to any situation in which a branch or agency of the Federal government seeks to compel a witness to testify regarding incriminating matters. In *Emspack* v. *United States* and *Quinn* v. *United States,* the Supreme Court took it for granted, without finding it necessary to discuss the point, that a witness before a Congressional committee is constitutionally entitled to refuse to answer questions that might incriminate him.

It is frequently assumed that the privilege extends to testimony that might degrade the witness or subject him to popular opprobrium. This is not so; if the witness is immune from prosecution for the crime concerning which he is questioned — as, for example, where the statute of limitations has run out — he may not refuse to answer even though the answer will disgrace him in the eyes of the community. Similarly, the Supreme Court held in *Brown* v. *Walker* and in *Ullman* v. *United States,* if a so-called immunity statute is enacted providing that the witness shall not be prosecuted on account of anything to which he testifies, he may not assert the constitutional privilege but may be punished for contempt if he refuses to answer.

On the other hand, the privilege is not limited to answers which in themselves incriminate the witness; it extends to answers that may supply a link in the chain of evidence needed in the prosecution of the witness for the commission of a crime. For example, in *Blau* v. *United States* the Supreme Court upheld the right of a witness not to answer the question whether she was a member of the Communist Party. At that time (1950) it was not considered a crime to be a member of the Communist Party. (Whether it is today is uncertain.) But, as the Dennis case showed, it was a crime under the Smith Act to be an organizer for the Communist Party or to teach its doctrines. If the witness testified that she was a member, that could well provide evidence that might be used against her for violation of the Smith Act.

This case shows what the Court emphasized in the Quinn and Slochower cases — that the term "Fifth Amendment Communist," popularized by Senator McCarthy, is misleading if not false, that the purpose of the privilege against self-incrimination is to protect the innocent and not to shield the guilty, and that assertion of the privilege should not be construed as an admission of guilt.

Another illustration is the Owen Lattimore case. Lattimore denied under oath before a Senate committee that he had ever followed the Communist Party line. He was indicted for perjury, but after two court setbacks the Justice Department finally dropped the prosecution. Since under our system a person is presumed innocent until proved guilty, it must be presumed that Lattimore had not followed the Party line and had not committed perjury. But to obtain this vindication Lattimore had to spend thousands of dollars in attorneys' fees and had to live for several years under the fear of conviction and the penitentiary. (A person may fear conviction even if he knows he is innocent.) Lattimore could have avoided all this by the simple expedient of asserting the privilege against self-incrimination. Yet, had he done so, he would no more have been guilty than he is now. It can safely be assumed that many other persons, less courageous or perhaps less foolhardly, have not followed Lattimore's example, and though innocent have pleaded the privilege.

When a person pleads the privilege against self-incrimination he usually says: " I refuse to answer on the ground that my answer may incriminate me." But no specific formula is required. It is sufficient if the witness makes reasonably clear his intention to invoke the privilege. In the Quinn case the first witness had refused to answer a question as to his membership in the Communist Party on the basis of " the First and Fifth Amendment " and on " the First Amendment to the Constitution supplemented by the Fifth." Quinn, the next witness, said in reply to a similar question: " I should like to say that I support the position taken by Brother Fitzpatrick yesterday." This, the Court held (realistically) sufficiently apprized the committee of Quinn's intent to invoke the privilege. It would obviously be unfair to hold a lay witness, who frequently is not permitted to have counsel with him, to the technical skill expected of a lawyer in asserting a constitutional privilege.

Like most constitutional rights, the privilege against self-incrimination may be waived; that is, the witness need not avail himself of it if he does not wish to. He may waive it in various ways. One way is by signing what is generally called a " waiver of immunity." Many States provide by law that a State employee who refuses to sign such a waiver of immunity when questioned by a grand jury, legislative committee, or other governmental body is subject to automatic dismissal from his post. (In the Slochower case, such a statute was held unconstitutional when applied against a State employee who had asserted the privilege in a Federal investigation.) A defendant in a criminal case waives the privilege by taking the stand to testify in his own defense. Once he does that, he has given up his immunity and like all other witnesses must answer all relevant questions put to him.

In *Rogers* v. *United States* the Supreme Court held that a witness before a grand jury who, in answer to a question, admitted that she had been treasurer of the local Communist Party had thereby waived the privilege. For that reason, the Court held, she could not claim the privilege when asked to whom she had turned over the party membership and dues records.

It is for this reason — that the answering of one question might be construed to constitute a waiver — that many lawyers advise their clients not to answer even those questions which they could safely answer in the negative. Thus a careful lawyer will frequently advise his client to assert the privilege when asked if he ever spied on the United States for the Soviet government even though he would answer in the negative; for the interrogator in cross-examining him on this point might well ask if he was a member of the Communist Party, and the witness might then find that he had waived the privilege and could no longer refuse to answer. This is another illustration of a case where assertion of the privilege does not require an inference that the witness is guilty of the crime concerning which he is questioned (in this case, espionage).

FAIR TRIAL

A number of other elements of fair trial are guaranteed by the Fifth, Sixth, and Fourteenth Amendments as they have been interpreted by the Supreme Court. These include: (1) a civil trial, (2) speedy but not too speedy, (3) local and (4) public, (5) by an impartial and unintimidated tribunal, (6) at which the accused has the benefit of compulsory process for obtaining witnesses for his defense.

(1) *Civil trial*

As early as the seventeenth century the English took political action against aggressive military rule. When James I and Charles I authorized martial law for the purpose of speedily punishing all types of crimes committed by civilians, Parliament in the Petition of Right protested this arbitrary procedure and prayed that it be stopped and never repeated. One of the causes that impelled the colonies to the separation from the king of England, specified in the Declaration of Independence, was that "He has affected to render the military independent of and superior to the civil power."

The superiority of civil over military government is an indispensable element of democracy. One aspect of that superiority is the immunity of civilians from trial by military tribunals even in theaters of war if the civil courts are open and functioning. The reason for this is that military trials do not have many of the procedural safeguards that are required by democratic concepts of fair trial. Thus the Supreme Court held in 1866 in the case of *Ex parte Milligan,* when the Court set aside a sentence of hanging handed down by a military commission in Indiana against a civilian charged with actively aiding the Confederate cause. The conflict between civil liberty and martial law, the Court said, is irreconcilable. They cannot endure together; one or the other must perish.

This case was followed in *Duncan* v. *Kahanomoku* where, more than two years after the Pearl Harbor attack, a military court in Honolulu tried and sentenced a civilian navy-yard employee who had engaged in a brawl with two armed Marine sentries. The Supreme Court, in upsetting the conviction and sentence, held that Congress had not authorized the trial of civilians by military tribunals where the civil courts were open and unobstructed. While the Court's opinion did not find it necessary to discuss the question of constitutionality, the tenor of the opinion indicated that, even if Congress had authorized military trials for civilians where the civil courts are functioning, the Milligan holding would have been followed and the authorization held unconstitutional.

This was borne out in 1955 in *U.S. ex rel. Toth* v. *Quarles.* Here the Court not only held military trials of civilians to be unconstitutional but went even further and voided a Federal statute authorizing military trial after discharge from the armed forces for crimes committed before discharge. Under our Constitution, the Court held, a civilian may not be tried by court martial even for crimes committed while in military service.

(2) *Speedy but not too speedy trial*

The purpose of the Sixth Amendment guarantee of a speedy trial is obvious and needs little comment. If the accused is unable to provide bail it will avail him little to be ultimately acquitted after waiting in jail for a period as long as or longer than the sentence which would have been imposed had he been found guilty. And even if he is admitted to bail, his liberty is restricted to a substantial extent, and he is entitled to speedy removal of the cloud of suspicion under which he lives. Moreover, while waiting for a long-delayed trial, his evidence may be lost and his witnesses may disappear. For these reasons, one of the procedural safeguards exacted by the barons from King John at Runnymede was the undertaking that "To none will we . . . delay right and justice," an undertaking sought to be secured by the further provision that two judges would travel to every county four times a year to hold court. For these reasons too it is the uniform practice today in all criminal courts, Federal and State, to dismiss a prosecution and release the accused if the government delays unduly in bringing the case to trial.

But, as we have seen in the first Scottsboro case, a too speedy trial is likewise an unfair trial. The defendant is entitled to a reasonable time to prepare his defense, and if, as in the Scottsboro case, he is forced to trial in a capital case on the same morning that he obtains counsel he has not been accorded due process and his conviction will be set aside.

(3) *Local trial*

Another of the grievances that the Declaration of Independence listed against the king consisted of his "transporting us beyond the seas to be tried for pretended offenses." Out of this grievance came the command in Article III of the Constitution that "the trial of all crimes . . . shall be held in the State where the said crimes shall have been committed," and its extension in the Sixth Amendment to require further that the jury which tries the accused shall come from the State and district wherein the crime shall have been committed.

Both English and colonial history had shown the framers of the Constitution the unfairness of requiring a person to defend himself before a tribunal distant from the place where he was alleged to have committed the crime and where his friends and witnesses lived, and before a jury of strangers and foreigners.

Occasionally fairness does require trial at a distant place. In some instances the passions and prejudices of the community in which a particularly horrendous crime has been committed make it difficult if not impossible to obtain an impartial and unintimidated jury. In such case it would constitute a denial of fair play and due process on the part of the court to refuse the accused's request for a change of venue and to require him to defend himself in a hostile community.

(4) *Public trial*

The history of the Inquisition and of the Star Chamber had convinced the fathers of the Bill of Rights that a fair trial would best be secured if it were a public trial. While grand juries traditionally conduct their investigations behind closed doors, the Sixth Amendment and the constitutions of almost all the States require that the trial itself be open to the public and the press. A secret trial is anathema to concepts of liberty and democracy, and does not accord the accused due process of law. So the Supreme Court held in the case of *In re Oliver;* the Court stated that it had been unable to find a single previous instance of a criminal trial conducted *in camera* in any Federal, State, or municipal court in the history of the United States, nor, for that matter, in England since the abolition of the Star Chamber in 1641.

The Oliver case is an interesting example of what may happen when, in the name of more efficient prosecution of criminals, experiments are taken with our liberties. Michigan has a procedure, apparently unique in the United States, whereby any judge may act as a one-man grand jury. In that capacity he may investigate crimes, compel witnesses to attend secret sessions called by him at any time and place, and question them in secret. If a witness refuses to answer, or if he gives evasive testimony, or if the one-man grand jury believes he is lying, the judge may then transform himself into a one-man petty jury, find the witness guilty, and as a sentencing judge summarily throw him into jail for sixty days. When the witness comes out, the procedure may be repeated and the witness sent back to jail for another sixty days.

All this may take place in absolute secret, without the presence of any outsiders, at any time and at any place — a hotel room, an office building, the back room of a bar; in fact, this one-man grand jury is popularly referred to as the "portable grand jury." The witness-defendant has no right to counsel, no time for the preparation of his defense, to examination of witnesses, or to any of the usual procedural safeguards incident to criminal trials. The attorney general of Michigan justified the absence of these safeguards by claiming that the witness was not being punished for the commission of an ordinary crime but for contempt of court, and that both the common law and the Supreme Court had long recognized the power of a judge summarily to punish a person for an act of contempt committed in the judge's presence.

The Supreme Court in the Oliver case refused to accept this argument. Even for an act of contempt of court, it held, a person may not under the "due process" clause be tried and condemned in secret. Secret trials have no place in a democracy.

(5) *Impartial and unintimidated tribunal*

Due process of law implies trial by an impartial judge and jury. One of the most serious charges leveled against the conduct of the trial of Sacco and Vanzetti in the 1920's was that the trial judge had indicated off the bench his conviction that the defendants should die and his determination to see to it that they would. For technical reasons, the United States Supreme Court was never able to pass on the trial or upon the charge of the judge's bias.

All will agree that a trial by a biased tribunal is not a fair trial. Nor is a trial by a judge having a financial stake in finding the accused guilty. For that reason the Supreme Court, in *Tumey* v. *Ohio,* held that a system under which a police judge was paid only for convictions and received no compensation for acquittals was inconsistent with due process of law and unconstitutional.

A fair trial implies a tribunal not only free from bias and pecuniary interest but also free from fear. In *Moore* v. *Dempsey,* decided in 1923, the following facts appeared. A group of Negro sharecroppers met in a church in Phillips County in eastern Arkansas, near the Mississippi border, to discuss the employment of counsel to protect their rights against their white landlords. The white citizens of the community got word of the meeting and descended upon the church. Gunfire broke out, and a white man was killed. A posse of white men was formed to hunt down the Negroes and avenge the white man's death. Many Negroes were caught, tortured, and slain. Finally, saner heads prevailed; when five captured Negroes were about to be lynched, a "Committee of Seven," representing the more responsible white citizenry, prevailed upon the mob to disperse by solemnly promising them that the Negroes would be hanged after trial. To make sure that this "solemn promise" would be carried out, the committee called Negro witnesses and had them whipped and tortured until they promised to testify as the committee wanted them to. The courtroom was filled with angry white citizens; outside hundreds more milled about, shouting threats at anyone who interfered with the desired result. The trial of all five Negroes before an all-white jury took about forty-five minutes. Five minutes later the jury, to the surprise of no one, returned with a verdict of guilty of murder in the first degree against all the defendants.

Eight years earlier, in the Leo Frank case in Georgia (*Frank* v. *Mangum*) the Supreme Court refused to interfere with a similar mob-dominated trial involving a Jew charged with the rape murder of a Christian girl. (Although the Court upheld the conviction, the citizens finally grew impatient with the law's delays and brought the protracted legal proceedings to an end by lynching Frank.) In the Frank case Justice Holmes dissented, but in *Moore* v. *Dempsey* he was able to get a majority of the Court to agree with him that a mob-dominated trial is not a fair trial and does not comply with due process of law. Accordingly the conviction of the five Negroes was set aside by the Supreme Court.

While one cannot expect a prosecuting attorney to be impartial and unbiased, he still is a representative of the State and must act fairly toward its citizens, even those accused of crimes. A frame-up is not fair treatment and does not accord with American principles of justice and fair play. So the Supreme Court said in *Mooney* v. *Holohan* where, although for technical reasons it found itself unable to interfere with the murder conviction of Tom Mooney, it nevertheless asserted that, if the State prosecuting attorney knowingly used false evidence and perjured testimony against Mooney, the conviction would be set aside for violation of the " due process " requirement. (In 1939 Mooney was pardoned by Governor Olsen after having served in jail for twenty-two years.)

(6) *Compulsory process for defense witnesses*

There can be no question that a trial at which the accused is not permitted to present witnesses to testify in his defense is not a fair trial and violates due process of law. The Constitution, however, goes further than that. It recognizes that many persons, either from timidity, or from unwillingness to spare the time or suffer the inconvenience, or for other reasons, will not willingly testify. Accordingly, the Sixth Amendment requires the government in Federal criminal cases to compel the attendance of defense witnesses just as it compels the attendance of prosecution witnesses. While, as we know, this Amendment is not applicable to the States, it is probable that a State criminal trial in which only the prosecution could issue subpoenas for the compulsory attendance of witnesses would be held by the Supreme Court not to be a fair trial or to comply with the requirements of due process of law.

DOUBLE JEOPARDY

No person, the Fifth Amendment commands, " shall . . . be subject for the same offense to be twice put in jeopardy of life or limb." This means that a person put on trial for a crime in a Federal court may not thereafter be tried for the same crime, whether he is acquitted or convicted and punished. If he is convicted and appeals and the higher court reverses the conviction, it may order a new trial, either because that new trial is considered part of the original jeopardy or because by appealing the defendant has waived his constitutional privilege against double jeopardy. But if he is acquitted or if he is convicted of a lesser crime or lesser degree than the prosecution sought, the prosecution may not appeal.

This is the rule in the Federal courts. Some States, however, do allow the prosecutor to appeal where he is dissatisfied with the verdict. In *Palko* v. *Connecticut* (1937), the defendant was convicted of second-degree murder. Dissatisfied, the prosecutor appealed and obtained a reversal. On the second trial the jury returned a verdict of first-degree murder. The Supreme Court rejected the defendant's appeal based upon the claim that he was unconstitutionally subjected to double jeopardy. The Fifth Amendment ban on double jeopardy, the Court held, is not applicable to the States. Only if double jeopardy shocks the conscience of the court, or violates the fundamental principles of liberty or justice which lie at the base of all our civil and political institutions, or offends the American concepts of ordered liberty does it violate the Fourteenth Amendment guarantee of due process of law. Such might be the case if a defendant is tried, convicted, serves his sentence, and then is tried again for the same offense. Or perhaps if he is harassed by a multitude of trials, after acquittals, all for the same offense. But the specific situation in the Palko case, the Court held, did not appear shocking and therefore was not unconstitutional.

Under the common law, which developed the principle of no double jeopardy, once a jury was impaneled the case had to be continued until a verdict was reached. If in the course of the trial the prosecutor found that the case was going badly for him and that the evidence he had available against the defendant was less convincing than he had anticipated, he had no choice but to go on and make the best of what he had. During the latter Stuart period this rule was changed, and the prosecutor could request the judge to declare a mistrial so as to enable the former to present a better case against the defendant at a future day. But long before the American Revolution this practice had become abhorrent and the earlier rule was revived.

Today, only North Carolina adheres to the Stuart rule. *Brock* v. *North Carolina* was a criminal prosecution against a mill striker for violence in the course of the strike. In the middle of the trial the prosecutor suddenly discovered that two witnesses upon whom he was counting to corroborate the sheriff's testimony were not going to be able to testify. Accordingly, he asked the court to declare a mistrial so that he could try again later. The court did so, and upon the second trial the defendant was convicted. The Supreme Court, following the Palko decision, refused to set aside the conviction, saying that the case did not disclose a situation shocking to American concepts of justice and fairness.

CRUEL AND UNUSUAL PUNISHMENTS

The Eighth Amendment prohibits excessive fines and cruel or unusual punishments. While this Amendment does not apply to the States, the Supreme Court in 1890 indicated in *Ex parte Kemmler* that the " due process " clause of the Fourteenth Amendment bars punishments involving torture or a lingering death, such as burning at the stake, crucifixion, breaking on the wheel, and the like. It held, however, that the novel method of executing a death sentence by electrocution was not within that category of uncivilized punishments. Some eleven years earlier, in *Wilkerson* v. *Utah,* it had made the same ruling in respect to death by shooting.

In *Louisiana ex rel. Francis* v. *Resweber* the following occurred. Willie Francis, a young Negro, had been convicted of murder and sentenced to the electric chair. On the day set for the execution he was strapped in the chair and the switch was thrown. Nothing, however, happened. Apparently some mechanical defect had occurred that prevented the current from passing through Willie's body. For three hours Willie was kept in the chair while the electricians vainly sought to get the current to flow. After that he was removed from the chair and returned to the death cell.

Several days later the chair was finally fixed and a new date for execution was about to be set. Willie appealed to the Supreme Court, claiming that a second execution under the circumstances would constitute cruel and unusual punishment. By a vote of 5 to 4, the Court rejected his claim. The majority held that while the traditional humanity of modern Anglo-American law forbids the infliction of unnecessary pain in the execution of the death sentence, the fact that an unforeseeable accident prevented prompt consummation of the sentence does not make the subsequent execution cruel. To the minority of the Court, however, death by installments, whether intended or accidental, constituted cruel punishment and offended what they considered to be American standards of civilized conduct on the part of State officials.

Justice Frankfurter, in his opinion concurring with the majority's decision, hopefully suggested that this was an appropriate case for executive clemency, but the governor did not take the hint. On the second appointed day Willie Francis finally paid his debt to the sovereign State of Louisiana.

Chapter 7. *Liberty of Franchise*

THE POOR MAN'S VOTE

Most Americans would probably be shocked at the suggestion that the right to vote for public office should be restricted to the wealthy or to those above a specified income level. During the depression of the 1930's one occasionally heard of proposals that persons on relief should not be allowed to vote. These proposals never got very far because it is offensive to our present-day concepts of democracy to make participation in the election of the people's representatives in government depend upon possession of a purse. Since our President, governors, mayors, and legislators will govern all, rich and poor alike, modern principles of democratic fairness require that all be entitled to participate in their selection.

It is striking evidence of the evolutionary and progressive nature of American democratic concepts that this was not always so. When the men met at Philadelphia in 1787 there was sharp division among them as to the poor man's right to vote. Hamilton, to whom the people was a beast, was frightened by the radical notion, advanced by a few Jeffersonians, that the franchise should be as broad as possible. Since no agreement could be reached, the question was dropped and the Constitution remained silent on qualifications for voters. It was left for each State to decide for itself which of its citizens would be entitled to vote.

This compromise appeared eminently satisfactory to the Hamiltonians, for all the States, following the English and colonial tradition, imposed property qualifications upon the right of franchise. But the Hamiltonians proved shortsighted; they had not foreseen the imminent surge of democracy. Barely had the ink dried on the Constitution when agitation for extension of the franchise by removal of property qualifications began to be heard throughout the land.

Hamiltonian Canutes sought to hold back the tides. In Massachusetts, Daniel Webster declaimed: "In the nature of things, those who have not property and see their neighbors possess much more than they think them to need, cannot be favorable to laws made for the protection of property. When this class becomes numerous, it grows clamorous. . . . It would seem then to be the part of political wisdom to found government on property."

In New York, Chancellor James Kent considered universal suffrage "an extreme democratic principle . . . regarded with terror by the wise men of every age." It had, to him, the tendency "to jeopardize the rights of property, and the principles of liberty."

The protests of Webster, Kent, and other Hamiltonians proved futile. One by one the States eliminated property qualifications from their election laws. In some States there still are laws on the books providing that payment of a tax or possession of property may qualify a person who because of non-residence or illiteracy would otherwise be disqualified. But State laws directly restricting the right to vote to those possessed of a minimum amount of property have practically disappeared. The constitutionality of those that may still be in effect is questionable. The Fourteenth Amendment prohibits the States from denying to any person the equal protection of the laws. While this provision permits reasonable qualifications, it is questionable whether the Supreme Court today would consider a classification based upon the possession of property as reasonable in the exercise of the elective franchise.

Indirect economic restrictions on the right to vote have, however, not entirely disappeared. Five Southern States still impose poll taxes, payment of which is a prerequisite of voting. In *Breedlove* v. *Suttles* the Supreme Court in 1937 upheld the validity of these statutes. It did so on the ground that the tax does not deny or abridge the right to vote. Women and men over sixty were exempt from the tax, although they were entitled to vote. Aliens, on the other hand, though ineligible to vote were liable for the tax. Therefore, the Court held, the poll-tax law was an ordinary revenue measure and making payment of the tax a prerequisite of voting was merely a means adopted for its collection. The Court considered immaterial the fact that no attempt was made by the State to collect the tax except from persons seeking to vote.

The extent to which poll taxes actually restrict the right to vote is variable and uncertain. While theoretically it is payable whether the person votes or not, as a practical matter it is not enforced against any but voters. The amount of the tax is small, only one or two dollars a year. In a few States it is cumulative and back taxes must be paid before voting is permitted, but even this requirement cannot make the tax substantial in prosperous times. In times of economic depression or recession, on the other hand, it probably does exercise a substantial deterrent effect on voting by members of the lowest income groups.

The poll tax is a dying institution. Six of the eleven States that have had poll-tax laws have repealed them. They are retained in the others primarily as a means to restrict Negro voting. How effective they are for this purpose is questionable. With the increasing industrialization of the South they are certain to become increasingly ineffective. It may safely be predicted that they will not last much longer in the five States that still retain them.

FREE ACCESS TO AN HONEST BALLOT

While the framers of the Constitution provided (in Article I, Section 4) that the " times, places and manner of holding elections for Senators and Representatives shall be prescribed in each State by the legislature," they did retain some Federal control by providing further that " the Congress may at any time by law make or alter such regulations." It is this retained power which allows Congress to fix a uniform day for Federal elections in all States and otherwise to control elections for Federal office.

More important, however, is the inherent power of the Federal government to protect the integrity of elections to that government. The government of the United States is a government of " We, the People," not of the States. The right to vote for the President of that government (theoretically through Presidential electors) and for its Senators and Representatives is a right conferred not by the States but by the Constitution of the national government. Hence that national government has inherent power to see that this right is secured.

For that reason, Congress may take appropriate measures to protect the polling place, and need not rely solely upon the laws and police of the States. In 1884 the Supreme Court so held in *Ex parte Yarbrough,* where it upheld the conviction of a number of Southern whites who severely beat and wounded a Negro in order to frighten him out of voting in a Federal election. The defendants were convicted under a Federal statute making it criminal to conspire to intimidate a person to keep him from voting in a Presidential or Congressional election, and the Court held that Congress had inherent power to enact the statute. It is the duty of government, said the Court, to see that citizens exercise freely their right to vote, a duty which is not solely for the citizens' benefit but arises out of the interest a democratic government has in assuring that its representatives are elected by the free votes of the people.

The integrity of the polling place implies not only that the ballot shall be free but also that it shall be honest. Congress, therefore, has the power to insure an honest count in Federal elections, as it has to insure unintimidated access to the polling place. Hence, the Supreme Court held in *United States* v. *Classic* (1941), Congress may constitutionally make it a Federal crime for State election officials to certify a false count in an election for President, Senators, or Representatives.

In the same case the Court went even further. It held that Congress could also make it criminal falsely to certify the results of a party *primary* election for candidates for Federal office. The fact that the ultimate selection of the Federal officials is carried on in two stages rather than one is immaterial. Nor is it material that the framers of the Constitution did not contemplate the selection of Congressional candidates by direct primary (any more than they contemplated the application of the clause conferring on Congress power to regulate interstate commerce to the telephone, the telegraph, or the radio). In determining whether a provision in the Constitution applies to new subject matter it is not important that the subject matter is one with which the framers were not familiar. They established a constitution for the indefinite future to carry out certain fundamental purposes, among which was the free and honest election of the people's legislative representatives in the government.

The full significance of this holding will become apparent shortly in our discussion of the Negro's vote. For in the one-party South, the only area in the country where the Negro's right to vote is subject to substantial restrictions, the all-important thing is the primary election. One who is selected in the Democratic Party primaries is as good as elected. Hence, unless a free and honest *primary* ballot is assured, the most scrupulous supervision of the *election* ballot is meaningless.

Because of the federal nature of our government, the constitutional power of Congress to secure the integrity of the ballot is limited to the Federal ballot. If Federal and State officials are elected on a single ballot at the same time and place (as is the case in even-numbered years everywhere except in Maine), both the Federal and State governments have the power and duty of insuring the freeness and honesty of the election. In respect, however, to elections exclusively for State and municipal officers, the responsibility rests entirely upon the States. Accordingly, the Supreme Court held in *Snowden* v. *Hughes* that no Federal law was violated by State officials who falsely certified the results of a primary election held for exclusively *State* officers.

THE NEGRO'S VOTE

By the middle of the nineteenth century the poor man had won his right to vote; but it has taken the Negro much longer to win his. Indeed, he has not even today entirely won it; restrictions on Negro voting in the South are still substantial and still have an important effect upon Southern politics. Here too, however, the onward surge of democracy cannot be stopped. The number of Negroes effectively participating in Southern elections and primaries is increasing from year to year; it is only a question of time before the lily-white elections of the South will be no more than a sorry chapter in the evolutionary history of American democracy.

The struggle to secure the Negro's right to vote has been long, violent, and bitter, in and out of the courts. In the last several decades it has largely resolved itself into a sort of protracted chess game between the Supreme Court on one side and, on the other, Southern lawyers, legislators, and politicians, who have taxed their ingenuity to find legal loopholes in or devious ways around each previous Court decision seeking to insure the Negro's constitutional right to vote. (A similar chess game around racial segregation in the public schools has already begun.)

To insure the Negro the right to vote (among other rights), the Reconstruction Congress adopted the Fourteenth Amendment, which conferred State and Federal citizenship upon Negroes and forbade the States to abridge their privileges or immunities to deprive them of life, liberty, or property without due process of law, or to deny them the equal protection of the laws. (The Amendment sought to secure the right to vote by providing for proportionate reduction in the representation in Congress of any State that denied the Negroes the right to vote, but this provision was a dead letter from the very beginning.)

In addition, Congress also adopted the Fifteenth Amendment, which specifically forbade the United States or any State to deny or abridge the right of any person to vote because of his race, color, or previous condition of servitude. The Fourteenth and Fifteenth Amendments also confer upon Congress power to enforce their provisions by appropriate legislation. Accordingly, Congress passed the Enforcement Act of 1870 to carry out the purpose of the Amendments and to insure Negroes free access to an honest ballot.

We have seen that the Federal government's inherent power (as well as the power derived from the retained control over the ballot provided in Article I, Section 4) to protect the integrity of the ballot is limited to the Federal ballot. No such limitation is expressed or implicit in the " equal protection of the laws " clause of the Fourteenth Amendment, which sought to confer equality in all civil rights. Nor is any expressed or implicit in the Fifteenth Amendment, which speaks of " the right . . . to vote," without qualification. There are, however, two important limitations in the Fifteenth Amendment, the second of which is also applicable to the " equal protection " clause of the Fourteenth. First, only such denial or abridgment of the right to vote as is based upon " race, color or previous condition of servitude " is within the scope of the prohibition. Second, the prohibition is limited to action by a State and does not (as does the Federal government's power to protect the Federal ballot) extend to action by private individuals not acting under color of State law.

Thus, six years after the Enforcement Act of 1870 the Supreme Court threw out one of its important provisions. In *United States* v. *Reese* the Court set aside the indictment of two Kentucky election inspectors who refused to receive and count the vote of a Negro cast in a *municipal* election. The provision of the statute under which they were indicted, the Court held, could not be sustained under the Federal government's inherent powers or the power conferred by Article

I, Section 4, since the statutory provision was not limited to Federal elections. Nor could it be sustained under the enforcement clause of the Fifteenth Amendment, since it apparently sought to penalize all infringements upon the right to vote and was not expressly limited to infringements on account of race, color, or previous condition of servitude. Since this failure to limit the scope of the provision made it unconstitutional, it did not matter that the person deprived of his vote was in fact a Negro, for no one may be punished for doing an act declared criminal by an unconstitutional law.

In 1903 the Court struck down another provision of the Enforcement Act. In this case, *James* v. *Bowman,* two persons were indicted for preventing a Negro from voting in a Congressional election. The provision, the Court held, could not be sustained under Article I, Section 4, because, like the provision in the Reese case, it went too far; just as the other provision did not expressly say that it was limited to abridgments on account of race, color, or previous servitude, so too the present provision did not say that it was limited to abridgments in connection with Federal elections. That a Congressional election was in fact involved in the present case was held as immaterial as the fact that the victim in the Reese case was actually a Negro. Nor could the provision be upheld under the Fifteenth Amendment, for, although that Amendment is not limited to Federal elections, it is limited to infringement by State officials and does not authorize enactment by Congress of a statute penalizing infringements by private persons unconnected with the State and not purporting to act under color of a State law.

The effect of these two decisions was largely — though not entirely, as the Yarbrough case shows — to grant to unlawful, violent infringements upon the Negro's right to vote immunity from Federal punishment. However, resort to violence could not be counted on by the South as an effective means of keeping the ballot from the Negro. After all, most Americans are law-abiding and except in periods of extreme passion are not likely to resort to violence. Hence, after the decline of the first Ku Klux Klan, violence and intimidation could at best be of sporadic effectiveness in assuring that government of the whites, by the whites, and for the whites should not perish from the South. Besides, American traditions and mores, to which Southerners are as committed as Northerners, require that some legal façade cover all infringements upon others' rights and liberties.

So the search began in the South for a legal way to disenfranchise the Negro. The poll tax, as we have seen, was one of the methods tried. It was effective so long as the Negro in the South remained impecunious — although it also affected many poor whites. But with the arrival of the war industries employing large numbers of Negroes and paying them high wages, the poll tax probably ceased to be a substantial deterrent to Negro voting.

Another method essayed was manipulation of literacy requirements. Conditioning eligibility to vote upon attainment of literacy is unquestionably reasonable and unquestionably constitutional. The Court so held in 1898 in *Williams* v. *Mississippi.* The submerged status of the Southern Negro made it reasonable to assume that such a condition would effectively disenfranchise the overwhelming majority of Negroes. The difficulty with this expedient was that it would also disenfranchise a large number of submerged whites. To avoid this, the ingenious Southern lawyer conceived the "grandfather clause," at one time adopted by seven Southern States.

The Oklahoma "grandfather clause" was typical. It exempted from the literacy requirement any person who either had been eligible to vote on or before January 1, 1866, or was a direct lineal descendant of such a person, or was a resident of a foreign nation at that time or the descendant of such a resident. Since Negroes were not eligible to vote in Oklahoma before 1866 and were not residents of any foreign nation at that time, the effect was to disenfranchise illiterate Negroes without prejudicing illiterate whites.

The vulnerability of this ingenious expedient lay in the fact that the Supreme Court would have none of it. By unanimous decision in the 1915 case of *Guinn* v. *United States* the Court held the clause invalid as a patent device to circumvent the mandate of the Fifteenth Amendment. The next move being up to Oklahoma, that State countered with a new law providing that all those who had voted in the 1914 election (when the "grandfather clause" was still in effect and the Negro largely disenfranchised) automatically remained qualified voters. All others (mostly Negroes) were given twelve days to register; if any failed to do so (whether they knew of the law or not) they permanently forfeited their right to vote.

The Supreme Court was not impressed. In *Lane* v. *Wilson,* decided in 1939, it struck this down too, remarking drily that the Fifteenth Amendment " nullifies sophisticated as well as simple-minded modes of discrimination."

Checked here, the defenders of the lily-white purity of the ballot tried a different approach. The most effective means of achieving this, of course, was the simple and direct one of expressly making possession of a white skin a prerequisite to entry to the polling booth. Unfortunately the Fifteenth Amendment and the " equal protection " clause of the Fourteenth barred this method. But both Amendments specifically refer to action by a " State " and were interpreted by the Supreme Court not to bar action by private individuals nor to authorize Congress to bar action by private individuals.

A political party, the white South reasoned, is a private association of individuals. As such it can admit or exclude whomever it wishes, for whatever reason it sees fit. Those excluded have a perfect right to form their own political party and run their own candidates for office. Moreover, a party primary is an internal affair of the party, engaged in so that the party may decide which candidates it will support for public office; it bars no one from running for office without the party's support. What is there in the Constitution to prevent the Democratic Party in the South from providing that only whites shall be eligible for membership in the party and thus eligible to vote in the Democratic primaries? The fact that in the one-party South success in the primary is equivalent to election and that the November election is merely a formality — this is purely a matter of coincidence and irrelevant to the constitutional issue.

So the Southern States began to pass statutes forbidding Negroes to vote in Democratic Party primaries. But it soon appeared that they had overplayed their hand. A statute passed by the State is patently action by the State and thus within the orbit of the ban in the Fourteenth and Fifteenth Amendments. The Supreme Court had no difficulty therefore in ruling in *Nixon* v. *Herndon* (decided in 1927) that such statutes were unconstitutional.

The South tried another move. It repealed these statutes and enacted others which simply authorized the executive committees of the respective parties to fix the qualifications of members; and the executive committees of the Democratic Party fixed whiteness of skin as one such qualification. But the Supreme Court refused to accept this either. Five years after *Nixon* v. *Herndon* it decided in *Nixon* v.

Condon that the action by the party executive committee was in fact and law the action of the State, for the committee acted as representative of the State and pursuant to authority conferred by the State.

The South then countered by bypassing the executive committee and having the racial qualification imposed by the party convention. The convention, like the governing body of any private association, acted without any specific statutory authority. The South appeared to have finally hit upon the solution to its problem. For in *Grovey* v. *Townsend*, decided in 1935, the Court held that a party convention was not an organ of the State and that whatever it decided as to the qualifications for party membership was of no concern to the State or to the Constitution or to the Supreme Court.

But the South's victory was short-lived. *Grovey* v. *Townsend* lasted nine years; in *Smith* v. *Allwright* the Roosevelt Court expressly overruled it. The United States, said the Court, is a constitutional democracy. Its organic law grants to all citizens the right to participate in the choice of elected officials without restriction by any State because of race. This grant to the people of the opportunity for choice is not to be nullified by a State through casting its electoral process in a form which permits a private organization to practice racial discrimination in the election. Constitutional rights would be of little value if they could be thus indirectly denied.

With *Smith* v. *Allwright* most of the South was ready to resign from the game. Texas (or most of it) — which had been the scene of the two Nixon cases, *Grovey* v. *Townsend*, and *Smith* v. *Allwright* — gave up the battle and made no further statewide effort to maintain the white primary. Tennessee and North Carolina quickly followed suit. So too, after some delay, did Alabama, Florida, Georgia, Louisiana, and Virginia.

Some parts of the South, however, still doggedly fought on. Since 1889 there was in one county in Texas a political club known as the Jaybird Association. Its membership was all white. Political aspirants submitted their applications to the association, which then decided who would run in the Democratic primaries. Almost invariably the Jaybird candidates were successful in the primaries, and of course in the general election that followed.

By the time this set-up reached the Supreme Court in 1953, the Court had become quite expert in Southern evasions of the Fourteenth and Fifteenth Amendments. In *Terry* v. *Adams* the Court invalidated this three-step method of denying the ballot to the Negro, as in the white-primary cases it had invalidated the two-step method, and as it had earlier in the " grandfather clause " cases invalidated the one-step method.

South Carolina experimented with a different approach. *Smith* v. *Allwright* had been decided on the ground that the Democratic primaries were part of the statutory electoral scheme and therefore within the Fourteenth and Fifteenth Amendments. So South Carolina repealed every one of its laws regulating primaries and then took the position that what remained were purely private Democratic " clubs." The Federal Court of Appeals, in *Rice* v. *Elmore,* a decision which the Supreme Court refused to review, held that no election machinery, statutory or not, could be sustained if its purpose or effect was to deny Negroes because of their race an effective voice in the government of their country, State, or community.

Following this defeat, the Democratic Party in South Carolina, although still excluding Negroes from membership, adopted a resolution permitting them to vote in the primaries, but provided that no person, white or Negro, could vote in a primary unless he took an oath that he believed in racial segregation and opposed " the proposed Federal so-called F. E. P. C. law." The Federal courts, in a decision not reviewed by the Supreme Court, promptly threw this provision out too.

Alabama (before it finally gave up the struggle) tried still another approach. In 1946 it adopted an amendment — popularly called the Boswell amendment — to the State constitution, limiting the ballot to those who could " understand and explain " any article of the Federal Constitution. Strictly applied, this requirement could probably disenfranchise a large majority of Americans, not excluding perhaps some Supreme Court justices as well as not a few professors of constitutional law. Fortunately, however, it was not strictly applied; with rare exceptions only Negroes were asked by election officials to " explain." These explanations were almost invariably found unsatisfactory. The result was that in Mobile county, of some 230,000 residents, fully 36 per cent of whom were colored, only 104 Negroes qualified to vote as compared with 28,000 whites.

In *Schnell* v. *Davis,* the Supreme Court in 1949 affirmed a lower-court decision holding the Boswell amendment unconstitutional on the ground that its purpose, as shown by its history, was to confer arbitrary power upon election officials to deprive Negroes of the right to vote.

So the situation stands today. Most of the South is learning to live with a ballot open to Negroes. In fact, in not a few communities white politicians vie for the Negro vote; in a few, but steadily increasing, instances Negroes have been elected to political office. Some communities are still fighting a desperate rear-guard action; in Mississippi, Negro voting is still practically insignificant, partly because of legal restrictions and partly because of intimidation. Nevertheless it cannot be long before the Negro will finally win his way to the polling place.

EQUALITY OF VOTES

The basic unit in our constitutional democracy is the individual. The " equal protection " clause of the Fourteenth Amendment merely voices the underlying assumption of democracy that in the eyes of government and law every individual is the equal of every other individual. It would seem to follow from this that every man's vote should count for no more and no less than every other man's vote.

This, however, is not the case. It has not been the case from the beginning. The men who gathered in Philadelphia sought to establish a republic, but they were not interested in founding a democracy — at least not an extreme democracy. That idea was completely abhorrent to most of them. There was a bitter struggle between the large States and the small States over representation in Congress, a struggle that threatened for a time to break up the convention. But the struggle was a struggle for power, not for democratic concepts. The struggle was compromised by establishing a bicameral legislature. In one chamber representation would be based upon population; in the other, representation would be equal among the States.

Since a Senator from a sparsely populated State has exactly the same rights, privileges, and powers as one from a heavily populated State, there is an obvious inequality in the value of votes. The vote of a citizen in a small State is considerably more valuable than the vote of a citizen in a large State.

Even in the House of Representatives representation is not always in accordance with population, and votes for Representatives are not always equal in value. The framers of the Constitution did not specify how Representatives should be chosen other than that they should be apportioned among the States according to their respective numbers. However, early in the nation's history Congress realized that different geographic areas have different interests and that the Congress should reflect this multiplicity of interests. To accomplish this end Congress provided in 1842 that Representatives should no longer be elected in a body by the people of a State at large, as had been the practice in some States, but that each State should be divided into districts, and each district should elect its own Representative.

If all districts contained equal numbers of residents, the aim of Congress would be achieved without sacrificing the democratic principle of equality. But because of the growth of cities through migrations from farm areas and immigration from abroad, combined with the use of antiquated population estimates and districting laws, deliberate gerrymandering, and a variety of other reasons, urban Congressional districts almost invariably are far more heavily populated than rural districts. The same is true with State legislative districts. The result is that the vote of a city dweller is less valuable and less effective than the vote of a farm dweller.

In 1911 Congress sought to ameliorate glaring inequalities, at least in the election of Congressmen, by requiring that Congressional districts be composed of contiguous and compact territories containing, as nearly as practicable, equal numbers of inhabitants. The Reapportionment Act of 1929 omitted this requirement, and the Supreme Court held in *Wood* v. *Broom* that the omission constituted an implied repeal of the provision.

Acting upon this assumption, a lower Federal court in Illinois refused to set aside a State apportionment law which created Congressional districts of glaring inequality. One of these districts, entitled to a Congressman, had some 112,000 inhabitants, whereas another, also entitled to one Congressman, had 914,000 inhabitants. The suit to invalidate the law was brought by a number of residents of heavily populated districts claiming that this gerrymandering denied them the equal protection of the laws in violation of the Fourteenth Amendment, for it made their votes only one-ninth as effective as the votes of residents of the sparsely populated districts.

In *Colegrove* v. *Green* (1946) the Supreme Court, by a narrow majority of the justices hearing the appeal, affirmed the lower court's dismissal of the complaint. The majority could not agree on the reason for affirming the dismissal. Three of the justices felt that the complaint should be dismissed because the question presented was a "political" one — that is, a question involving political rather than legal issues, one that the framers of the Constitution intended to be decided by political rather than judicial processes. (Other examples of non-judicial political questions are which of two candidates actually received the most votes in an election, and whether a particular State has a republican form of government.) These three justices, speaking through Justice Frankfurter, contended that the only remedy authorized by the Constitution to meet gerrymandering is to elect a new legislature which would undo the evil. (The obvious difficulty with this reasoning is that gerrymandering makes difficult if not impossible the election of legislators who would eliminate gerrymandering.) Justices Black, Douglas, and Murphy dissented.

Several years after *Colegrove* v. *Green* was decided, a legal attack was made upon the Georgia county unit system. Under the system, patterned after the Presidential Electoral College, candidates in primaries are elected by counties. The counties cast two to six votes, depending upon their population, and in each county the votes are cast for the candidate receiving the most votes in that county, the loser getting nothing. Under this system one county having a population just short of 400,000 casts six votes, while another with a population just under 3000 casts two votes. The result is that a vote in the latter county is worth 120 times as much as a vote in the former county.

When the case (*South* v. *Peters*) reached the Supreme Court, the Court affirmed the dismissal of the complaint on the ground that it would not act in cases posing political issues arising from a State's geographic distribution of electoral strength among its political subdivisions. Justices Black and Douglas dissented, pointing out that, since the State's Negro population is concentrated in the cities, the county unit system heavily disenfranchises the urban Negro population.

THE CIVIL SERVANT IN POLITICS

Andrew Jackson is supposed to have said upon his election that "to the victor belong the spoils." Whether or not he actually made that statement, there is no doubt that it represented the general political philosophy almost from the establishment of the nation. However, beginning with the assassination of President Garfield by a disappointed office seeker, strong public sentiment was expressed for the establishment of a merit system in the Federal service. The first Federal civil-service law was adopted in 1883, and since then the system has been steadily expanded and strengthened.

The purpose of the civil-service laws is to keep politics out of the Federal service except at the policy-making level, where, in a democracy, it properly belongs. To effect the converse of this objective — i.e., to keep the civil service out of politics — Congress in 1939 adopted the Hatch Act. This made it unlawful for any person in the Federal civil service to use his official authority or influence for the purpose of interfering with an election or influencing its result.

To this there could be no valid objection; it simply prohibited Federal officials from violating their trust by using their office for political purposes. But the Act went further. It prohibited all officers or employees in the Executive Branch of the Federal government from taking any active part in political management or political campaigns. They were, however, to retain their right to vote and could legally express their opinions on political subjects and candidates. Any Federal employee violating this prohibition was subject to immediate and permanent discharge from his position.

In *United Public Workers* v. *Mitchell* (discussed in an earlier chapter in connection with freedom of association), a roller in the Philadelphia mint, who had served as a ward executive committeeman, campaign literature distributor, and polls watcher on election day, brought suit to declare the Act unconstitutional. A majority of the Supreme Court upheld the Act. While the Act undoubtedly infringed upon the Federal employee's freedom to engage in political activities and thus at least indirectly upon his right of franchise, infringement was reasonably necessary for the protection of the integrity of the Federal civil service. Congress could well have believed, the Court held, that political activity on the part of a Federal employee might influence his superiors to promote or retard him depending on whether or not they concurred in his political judgment, thus impairing the merit system. Moreover, government employees are handy elements for political leaders to use in building a political machine. Finally, there would be a cumulative adverse effect on employee morale if all of them could be induced to participate in political activity. To prevent these evils Congress could constitutionally prohibit active participation in politics by Federal civil servants.

THE COMMUNIST'S VOTE

The Constitution lets each State fix the qualifications of voters. Several of the Amendments, however, restrict this power. The Fifteenth Amendment bars the States from making membership in the Caucasian race a qualification for voting. The Nineteenth Amendment does the same in respect to membership in the male sex. And the provision in the Fourteenth Amendment that no State shall deny any person within its jurisdiction the equal protection of the laws means that in fixing qualifications for voting, as in all its actions, a State may not arbitrarily discriminate between different classes or groups.

In determining whether a particular distinction (other than of race or sex) between classes or groups violates the "equal protection" clause, the test — simple to announce though greatly difficult to apply — is reasonableness. A distinction that is reasonable is constitutional; one that is not reasonable is unconstitutional. It is reasonable that the right to choose the officers of a government be limited to those who by birth or voluntary act owe allegiance to that government; hence, it is reasonable to distinguish between citizens and aliens in fixing qualifications for voters. Familiarity with the problems and personalities of a community may likewise be reasonably expected of voters, and residence within the community for a fixed minimum period is therefore a reasonable requirement of voters. So too is good character (convicted felons may constitutionally be barred from voting); and a minimum education (illiterates may be barred); and maturity (adolescents may be barred).

These are undeniably reasonable qualifications, and their constitutionality is not likely to be seriously challenged. But what of political qualifications; can they be reasonable and hence constitutional? Ordinarily, obviously not. Otherwise a party controlling the legislature could perpetuate itself in office by restricting the ballot to members of the party. Whatever may be said for or against such a system, it can hardly be called democracy. But is it unreasonable to bar from the ballot those who would destroy the ballot? An alien seeking to become a citizen must affirm his allegiance to our democratic system and swear that he does not believe in its overthrow by force or violence and is not a member of any organization committed to its forcible overthrow. Why should not a prospective voter be required to take a similar oath? Specifically, why may not a State or the Federal government close the polling booth to members of the Communist Party?

The Supreme Court has not had occasion to pass upon the question, and therefore a definite answer is not possible. Speculation, however, is permissible. The Court conceivably might refuse to pass upon the question at all on the ground that it is "political." The Court would almost certainly do so if the attack upon a State statute disenfranchising Communists were based on the claim that the Constitution guarantees to every State a republican form of government, and that a government that deprives members of a political party of the right to vote is not republican. Since, however, the statute would in all probability be attacked under the "equal protection" clause, it is less likely that the Court would adjudge the question to be exclusively "political" and hence outside its competence.

A plausible argument can be made in favor of the constitutionality of such a statute. Loyalty to the government does not appear to be an unreasonable demand upon voters. A State may constitutionally bar persons of bad morals or character from the ballot box, and it would not seem unreasonable to adjudge Communists to be persons of bad morals or character. In *Davis* v. *Beason*, it will be remembered, the Court upheld an Idaho statute which, as interpreted by the courts, disenfranchised all members of the Mormon Church. Many reasonable persons would refuse to concede that the Mormon advocacy of polygamy represented a greater threat to the security of the people than the Communist Party does today; if exclusion of Mormons from the polling booth is constitutional, certainly exclusion of Communists should be.

Yet the argument is not as one-sided as might appear at first glance. Restrictions upon constitutional rights are permissible only if they are clearly and presently necessary for the protection of a superior communal interest. It is doubtful that there are 50,000 Communist Party members in the whole United States. What real danger lies in allowing them to vote? Moreover, Communists profess not to believe that their Party is committed to the forcible overthrow of the American government; they contend that its objectives can be achieved by the legal and peaceful means of winning elections. But if they can constitutionally be deprived of this means, what recourse is left to them except to seek to achieve their objective by illegal and violent means?

In the Dennis case Chief Justice Vinson pointed out that, whatever theoretical merit there might be to the argument that there is a "right" to rebellion against dictatorial government, it is without force where the existing structure of the government provides for peaceful and orderly change. But if the existing structure does not permit peaceful and orderly change, then the theoretical merit of the argument may well become actual.

Here once more the answer to the constitutional question lies in what one considers to be the nature of the Communist Party. If, as Justices Black and Douglas contend, the Communist Party is a political party within an American tradition that has always recognized radical and even revolutionary parties, its members may not be denied access to the ballot box. If, on the other hand, as Justice Jackson asserted, it is not a political party at all but a criminal conspiracy masquerading as a political party, membership therein may be declared a disqualification to vote in the same way as membership in the criminal conspiracy to advocate or practice polygamy.

COMMUNISTS ON THE BALLOT

The right of the Communist Party to a place on the ballot is likely before long to reach the Supreme Court for adjudication. A number of States have already enacted statutes specifically excluding the Communist Party and its candidates from the ballot. In addition, Section 3 of the Communist Control Act of 1954, enacted in the closing hours of the Eighty-third Congress, declares that "whatever rights, privileges, and immunities which have heretofore been granted to said [Communist] party or any subsidiary organization by reason of the laws of the United States or any political subdivision thereof, are hereby terminated." It is quite clear that by this provision Congress intended to bar the Communist Party and its candidates from a place on the ballot.

Because of the federal nature of our government, both this Act of the Federal government and the State statutes raise the immediate question of how far one can validly regulate the ballot of the other. Can Congress direct a State as to who may or may not appear on the latter's ballot, and vice versa? Aside from this problem, there is a more important one: Even if each acts within the sphere of its jurisdiction, to what extent, if any, does the Constitution restrict both Congress and the State legislatures from excluding a political party or its candidates from the ballot?

In respect to members of Congress, who are elected Federal officials, it would seem clear that the States have no power to disqualify any party or candidate of a party. The States may impose qualifications for *voters* for Federal office, but not for *candidates* for the office. Nor is it by any means certain that even Congress may do so. The Constitution sets forth certain qualifications for Senators and Representatives (age, length of citizenship, residence); most constitutional authorities assume that these are exclusive, and that Congress has no power to add additional qualifications, such as non-membership in the Communist Party.

It may well be that when the issue does come before the Court, decision here too will be avoided on the ground that the question is "political" — one to be decided not by the judgment of the Court but by the judgment of the people, exercised democratically through the polls. This, as we have seen, is how the Court disposed of legal attacks upon gerrymandering, although here also the very existence of the statute makes it more difficult for the people to elect a Congress that would repeal it.

Realistically there appears to be little need for a statute disqualifying Communists from a place on the Federal ballot. Aside from the improbability that a candidate running on the Communist Party ticket would be elected to Congress (Vito Marcantonio, it will be remembered, was elected on the Republican and American Labor Party tickets), the Constitution provides that each House shall be the judge of the elections, returns, and qualifications of its own members. Nothing therefore prevents a majority in each House from refusing to seat an elected candidate who is a member of the Communist Party. The Socialist Victor Berger was twice rejected by the House of Representatives in 1919, although he received a majority of the votes each time he ran. Some twenty years earlier the House refused to seat a successful Mormon candidate from Utah because he practiced polygamy. In neither instance was the controversy taken to the Supreme Court, but it is highly probable that in both cases the Court would have refused to interfere on the ground that the question was "political."

The fact that the Supreme Court would not interfere does not mean that the exclusion is constitutional, any more than it means that gerrymandering is necessarily constitutional. It means only that each House is the sole judge of the constitutionality of its act of excluding the successful candidate, and that the Constitution has provided no way to appeal judicially from the decision. (It is even more obvious that the Court's non-intervention does not certify to the wisdom of the act or its consistency with democratic principles.)

Once again, one's view of the constitutional issue depends upon the view one takes of the Communist Party. If one considers it to be a bona-fide — though radical and unorthodox — political party, the exclusion, whether by statute of Congress or act of the particular House, is unconstitutional, even though there may be no practicable way of obtaining a decision by the Supreme Court declaring it to be unconstitutional. If, on the other hand, one considers the Communist Party to be a criminal conspiracy to overthrow the government by force or violence, the exclusion would appear to be quite constitutional.

Congress, in enacting the Communist Control Act, sought to supply the answer to the question. In Section 2 of the Act, Congress declared that the Communist Party, "although purportedly a political party, is in fact an instrumentality of a conspiracy to overthrow the Government of the United States." Inasmuch as a jury in the Dennis case found this to be so, and its finding was affirmed by the Supreme Court, it can hardly be said that the same finding by Congress is unreasonable. Indeed, one of the principal arguments urged for enactment of the Act was that it simply put into statutory form what had been found to be true in the Dennis case, and that it would avoid repetitious, protracted, and costly trials to determine the question in future cases.

Undoubtedly this finding in the Act supplies a convenient short cut; but the history of the Anglo-American struggle for fair play and fair trial has been the history of a struggle against convenient short cuts. A finding by a jury of one's peers on the basis of evidence and testimony presented under procedural safeguards is in harmony with our tradition of fair play; a similar finding by a legislative body is generally considered to be a bill of attainder and antagonistic to that tradition.

The " political question " rule is not likely to bar review by the Supreme Court of *State* statutes barring the Communist Party or its candidates from election to State office. The Court has already taken jurisdiction of one case involving the constitutionality of a loyalty-oath requirement for candidates to elected State offices, and there is thus no reason to believe that it would not take jurisdiction of a case involving a State statute specifically barring the Communist Party or its candidates from the State ballot.

The case that the Court did review in 1951 — *Gerende* v. *Board of Supervisors* — did not involve a statute specifically barring the Communist Party. The Maryland statute at issue required all candidates for State office to take an oath that they were not engaged in any attempt to overthrow the government by force or violence and were not knowingly members of any organization engaged in such an attempt. The Maryland courts had upheld the statute and had ruled that it did not unconstitutionally abridge freedom of speech, press, assembly, or association and that it was not a bill of attainder. Without any discussion of these issues, the Supreme Court unanimously affirmed the decision.

There is little reason to question the correctness of this decision, but its scope is extremely narrow. It permits a State to bar from public office those actually engaged in attempting to overthrow the government and those who knowingly are members of an organization actually engaged in the attempt. It does not bar anyone for *advocating* the forcible overthrow of the government or for knowingly belonging to an organization that so advocates or teaches. It does not bar anyone for membership in the Communist Party. If a Communist candidate took the oath and were challenged, it would be necessary to prove that the Communist Party is actually engaged in an attempt to overthrow the government by force or violence. Even the extensive evidence presented in the Dennis case would not suffice for this purpose, since that evidence showed only that the Communist Party advocated and taught the desirability of overthrowing the government — not that it was then actually engaged in an attempt to overthrow the government.

The Gerende case, therefore, offers little clue as to how the Supreme Court — or a majority of the Court — would treat a State statute expressly and specifically barring from the ballot the Communist Party or any candidate running for election under the emblem of the Communist Party. Here, again, the resolution of the issue would depend on whether a majority of the Supreme Court was prepared to hold — as Justice Jackson was prepared to hold — that the criminal and conspiratorial nature of the Communist Party is so widely recognized and has been proved by such abundant evidence that it is no longer necessary to prove it every time it becomes relevant, but that the legislature may declare it as a rule of law to be accepted and applied in every case without special further proof.

One final comment may be made here. It would be fatuous to suggest that there is no risk to democracy in allowing the Communist Party to appear on the ballot. The Nazi party in Germany achieved totalitarian power after it won parliamentary power at the polls. So too did the Communist Party in Czechoslovakia. Communists have been elected to public office in the United States, and there is no reason to be sure that, unless disqualified, they might not be elected in large numbers during a period of economic crisis. It is unlikely that in the foreseeable future a sufficient number of them will be elected to constitute the majority party in Congress or a State or municipal legislature; but neither the Nazis in Germany nor the Communists in Czechoslovakia were the majority party when they seized dictatorial power. Merely by getting into the government, Communists may be in a position to carry out a *Putsch* and establish a Soviet dictatorship here, as they did in democratic Czechoslovakia.

A risk, of course, there is; but risk is an inherent and indispensable element of democracy. Only a totalitarian government seeks to eliminate all risks and thus establish itself permanently or at least for a thousand years. History has shown that the search for a riskless security is futile, and that democracy is more likely to survive and grow if it willingly accepts some risks in order to preserve unimpaired the sole reason for its existence — the protection of its people's liberties. This, at least, was the premise upon which our fathers based the Bill of Rights. It may well be doubted that the health of America is so precarious as now to justify abandonment of that premise.

Chapter 8. *Liberty of Entry, Sojourn, and Exit*

THE RIGHT TO ENTER

In 1887 Chae Chan Ping, a Chinese laborer who had lived in the United States since 1875, decided to take a trip to his native land to visit his family and old friends and relate to them the wonders of this new land. As a careful, law-abiding resident (though not a citizen) of the United States, he consulted an attorney, who assured him he could take the trip in safety; for a solemn treaty between the sovereign governments of the United States and China provided that a national of either country residing in the other would be permitted to visit his native land and return to his new residence. Doubly to fortify himself, Chae obtained from the Federal authorities a certificate, issued pursuant to a statute of Congress, entitling him to re-enter the United States.

So armed, Chae left for China. After a pleasant visit, he returned to the United States. It is not difficult to imagine his feelings when, as his ship came into port, he was informed that he could not enter. It appeared that seven days before his arrival Congress had passed a law abrogating all outstanding certificates of re-entry.

Chae's lawyer sought a writ of habeas corpus. The suit reached the Supreme Court in a case which later became known as the Chinese Exclusion Case. Chae's complaints were many: The act of Congress violated a solemn treaty made by the United States; applied to him, it was a bill of attainder and an unfair ex post facto law, since it was adopted after he had acted in good-faith reliance upon the old law; it deprived him of his liberty without due process of law; he was a person of good character who had never gotten into trouble with the law, wherefore there was no valid reason to exclude him; the cancellation of his certificate was a breach of contract; and finally there was in any event nothing in the Constitution that authorized Congress to exclude anyone or to enact any immigration law. (The first Federal immigration law had been enacted in 1875, only fourteen years earlier, and it had provided merely for the exclusion of prostitutes and convicted criminals.)

In a unanimous opinion (and in *Nishimura Ekiu* v. *United States*, which followed three years later) the Court summarily disposed of all Chae's complaints. The absence of any provision in the Constitution expressly authorizing Congress to regulate or restrict immigration was immaterial; the power was vested in Congress as an inherent element of sovereignty. The power of Congress in the admission and exclusion of aliens is plenary. It is not subject to barter or trade and cannot be alienated by any treaty. Any license granted to Chae to come into the United States was revokable at the will and pleasure of Congress and conferred no enforcible rights upon Chae. The exercise by Congress of its plenary power over the exclusion of aliens is a political act in the field of international relations and as such is not subject to judicial review.

The rule of the Chinese Exclusion Case has never been seriously questioned by any member of the Court — not even by Justices Black and Douglas. It was reaffirmed in 1950 in the case of *Knauff* v. *Shaughnessy*, where the immigration authorities barred from entry into this country the war bride of an American citizen. The authorities gave no reason for their decision other than that they considered her admission to be prejudicial to the interests of the United States. They refused to say in what way it would be prejudicial, and they refused to accord her a hearing so that she might attempt to show that it would not be prejudicial.

The Supreme Court upheld the decision of the immigration authorities. An alien who seeks admission to this country, said the Court, may not do so under any claim of right. Admission of aliens to the United States is a privilege granted by the sovereign United States government. Such privilege is granted to an alien only upon such terms as the United States prescribes. It must be exercised in accordance with the procedure that the United States provides. An alien seeking admission into the United States is entitled only to such procedural safeguards and such elements of fair play and fair trial as Congress sees fit to give him; if Congress has seen fit to give him none, then he has none. Fair or unfair, reasonable or arbitrary, whatever the procedure authorized by Congress is, it is due process as far as an alien denied entry is concerned.

The 1875 law barred prostitutes and convicts. In 1882 lunatics and persons likely to become public charges were barred. In 1884 and 1886 Chinese were excluded. In 1903, after the assassination of President McKinley, anarchists were barred. In 1924 Japanese were barred, and the national-origins quota system was established; under this immigrants from north and west Europe were preferred over those from south and east Europe. The wisdom of some of these exclusions may be open to question. What is not open to question is the constitutional power of Congress to impose them.

Put simply, liberty of entry into the United States of America is exclusively a liberty of Americans. And in this context Americans are only those who are citizens of the United States of America. Continuous and lawful residence here, for no matter how long, does not make one an American so as to entitle him to re-enter the country after a temporary absence. Once he leaves our shores even for a short visit abroad, he is like unto one who had never been here. That, at least, was the holding in the Chinese Exclusion Case. And that was generally assumed to be the law until 1953 when, within about a month, the Supreme Court handed down two decisions which appeared to arrive at different conclusions and the first of which might seem to modify somewhat the severity of the Chinese Exclusion Case.

In the first of these two cases, *Kwong Hai Chew* v. *Colding*, the Court passed upon the rights of an alien Chinese seaman. Last admitted to the United States in 1945, he married a native American and after living here for five years was admitted for permanent residence. After service in the Merchant Marine during World War II, he applied for naturalization and continued his employment as a seaman. In 1951, before he had acquired American citizenship, he returned from one of his trips but was ordered "temporarily excluded" by the immigration authorities; they refused to give him any information concerning the reasons for his exclusion or the identity of his accusers.

With only one justice dissenting, the Supreme Court held that an alien who is a lawful permanent resident of the United States can claim the right to due process of law under the Fifth Amendment and may not be denied liberty or property without the elementary rights of notice of charges, a hearing, and an opportunity to defend himself. In view of this constitutional requirement, the Court continued, the authority granted to the Attorney General by the statutes and regulations to exclude temporarily any alien whose entry he deems prejudicial to public interest does not include authority to prevent the re-entry of a lawfully resident alien who temporarily leaves our shores.

In the second case, a dramatic one attracting nationwide attention, a result was reached that four of the nine justices strongly believed was inconsistent with the principles announced in the previous case. In *Shaughnessy* v. *U.S. ex rel. Mezei,* the Court considered the appeal of Ignatz Mezei, a Rumanian-Hungarian alien who had migrated to the United States in 1923 and lived in Buffalo, New York, for a quarter of a century. In 1948 he sailed for Europe to visit his dying mother in Rumania. Denied entry there, he remained in Hungary for some nineteen months because of difficulty in obtaining an exit permit. Finally, armed with a regular immigration visa issued by the American consul in Budapest, he sailed for New York. Upon his arrival he was temporarily excluded. Thereafter the Attorney General, without a hearing or any indication of detailed reasons, ordered the temporary exclusion to be made permanent on the ground that for security reasons Mezei's admission would be against the public interest. The immigration authorities then attempted to deport Mezei. But no country would take him. England, France, and other countries, including many in Latin America, refused to receive him. As Justice Jackson remarked tartly in his dissent: " Since we proclaimed him a Hercules who might pull down the pillars of our temple, we should not be surprised if people less prosperous, less strongly established and less stable feared to take him off our timorous hands." The result was that Mezei was detained and confined at Ellis Island.

Mezei applied for a writ of habeas corpus to obtain his release. The Federal district court requested the Department of Justice to disclose the reasons for Mezei's exclusion. When the Department refused to do so, even in the privacy of the judge's chambers, the court ordered Mezei's release on bail. The Supreme Court, however, reversed the order, and provided for Mezei's arrest and return to Ellis Island, where he had already been confined for three years.

The difference between this and the Chew case, the majority of the Supreme Court held, was that Chew left the United States in pursuit of his vocation as a seaman and with full security clearance and documentation, whereas Mezei, apparently without authorization or re-entry papers, simply left the United States and remained behind the Iron Curtain for nineteen months. By leaving this country even temporarily, the majority continued, Mezei lost whatever rights he may have had as a result of his long residence here. In all respects he was to be treated as if he were coming to the United States for the first time. According to well-settled law, a prospective immigrant may be excluded without hearing or other incidents of due process, even if " exclusion " means detention for life on Ellis Island. (The Department of Justice later relented and allowed Mezei to return to his family in Buffalo.)

It is difficult to reconcile the decisions in these two cases. The four justices who dissented in the Mezei case could not do so. Yet the majority in the Mezei case did not overrule the Chew case, which therefore must be assumed still to be the law. Nevertheless, the importance of the Chew holding should not be overestimated. It is true that the Court in the Chinese Exclusion Case held that the documents received by Chae from the government conferred absolutely no rights upon him, while similar documents in the 1953 case were held to confer some rights upon Chew. But the rights conferred, though undoubtedly important, are modest; they are procedural, not substantive, rights. They entitle Chew to notice of the charges against him and to some kind of a hearing on those charges. That is all they cover; they do not include the right to challenge the reasonableness of the exclusion. If, for example, Congress had passed a law saying that no alien with a relative behind the Iron Curtain would be permitted to enter the United States, all that Chew would be entitled to would be notice that he was charged with having a relative in Communist China and a hearing on that charge. This is more than Mezei was held entitled to, but it is still not very much. The Supreme Court could not pass on whether having a relative behind the Iron Curtain is a rational basis for excluding an alien. To this extent the rule in the Chinese Exclusion Case remains unaffected. It is still true that the right of entry is a liberty only of American citizens.

THE RIGHT TO STAY

Our nation had barely established itself when its leaders essayed a brief and abortive experiment in seeking to expel from the country those foreigners whose views they did not approve. One of the measures adopted by the Federalists to stem the rising tide of Jeffersonian Republicanism was the Alien Act of 1798. This authorized President Adams to order the deportation from our shores of any alien whom he considered to be dangerous to the peace or safety of the public or who he believed was plotting against the country. Although there were many prosecutions under the companion Sedition Act, the Alien Act expired two years after its enactment without a single alien having been expelled under its terms.

As we have seen, the Alien and Sedition Acts led to the demise of the Federalist Party. For a century the political leaders heeded the lesson, but with the extensive growth of nationalism and the growing fear of the "Yellow Peril," the experiment was revived in the milieu which also produced the Chinese Exclusion Act. This time the experiment succeeded, and the constitutional base of American deportation policy was laid.

In 1892 Congress enacted a law requiring all Chinese laborers lawfully in the country to obtain certificates of residence. Failure to possess such a certificate subjected the alien to arrest and deportation. One year after the law was enacted, the Supreme Court in *Fong Yue Ting* v. *United States* upheld its constitutionality. The power to expel aliens, like the power to exclude them in the first place, the Court held, is a political power which belongs to Congress as an incident of national sovereignty, to be exercised in accordance with Congress's views of national interest and not to be subject to judicial interference.

Although three of the members of the Court dissented, the principles of the Fong Yue case remain in full effect today. It was on the basis of these principles that the Alien Registration Act of 1940 and the Internal Security Act of 1950 directed the deportation of any alien who at any time during his stay in the United States was, for no matter how short a period, a member of the Communist Party or any other organization that advocated the violent overthrow of the government. These provisions were upheld in two cases decided on the same day in 1952: *Harisiades* v. *Shaughnessy*, and *Carlson* v. *Landon*.

In both cases the Court refused to overrule the Fong Yue case. Aliens in this country, the Court said, have no right to stay; that is a liberty belonging exclusively to American citizens. Aliens are here as a privilege and are subject to the plenary and unreviewable power of Congress under its sovereign right to determine which non-citizens shall be permitted to remain here. The decision of Congress in such a case is a political decision over which the courts have no control or power to review. The fact that the statute interferes with the alien's freedom of speech, press, and association cannot be considered by the courts. No matter how offensive to our traditions the judgment of Congress might be, the courts are powerless to act. The courts may not even consider the alien's claim, made by Harisiades, that if deported to his land of origin he would face persecution and even execution for his political views. The remedy, said the Court, is exclusively political — i.e., the election of a Congress that will repeal the law.

Deportation, the Supreme Court has consistently held, is not a criminal proceeding, even though the consequences to the alien may be far more drastic than fine or imprisonment. Therefore, the various procedural safeguards that Anglo-American law had so laboriously developed are for the most part irrelevant. The law under which the alien is deported may be completely arbitrary and irrational. It may be the equivalent of a bill of attainder, specifically naming a particular person or group, such as the Communist Party. It may be an ex post facto law directing deportation for the commission of an act, such as joining the Communist Party, that was entirely legal when done. The Court so held in *Galvan* v. *Press*, where it held also that the alien was deportable even if he was an innocent dupe without knowledge of the illegal purposes and aims of the Communist Party. The persons deported in the Harisiades, Carlson, and Galvan cases had quit the Communist Party at a time when membership was still legal and long before it was declared to be an offense subjecting the alien to deportation.

Since deportation is not a criminal proceeding, an alien who is arrested preparatory to deportation may be kept confined indefinitely without the right to release on bail. He is probably not constitutionally entitled to be defended by counsel or to compulsory process to obtain witnesses in his behalf. He may be questioned and compelled to furnish the evidence that will be used to sustain the deportation order, for such evidence does not incriminate him but merely subjects him to the civil liability of deportation. He is not entitled to trial by jury or even trial by a judge without a jury. A hearing before a petty official of the Immigration Service, who acts both as prosecuting official and as judge, is due process enough for an alien whom the government seeks to deport. Even if deportation means abandonment of family, home, and friends for exile to a country the alien never knew or where he may be persecuted and even executed, it is not punishment; therefore the courts may not set it aside as cruel or unusual or grossly disproportionate to the gravity of the offense that gave rise to it.

He may be deported into the hands of a government that seeks his death, and he may even be compelled to cooperate in his own deportation. In 1952 the Supreme Court, in *United States* v. *Spector*, upheld the validity of a Federal statute making it a felony for a deportable alien to fail to make application for travel documents necessary for his departure. The fact that evidence may have once been held to be insufficient to prove the alien's commission of the deportable offense does not bar a second or third attempt or any number of attempts by the immigration authorities to deport the alien on the same evidence. The Fifth Amendment ban on double jeopardy applies only to criminal proceedings. Deportation is not a criminal proceeding.

For some twenty years now — through Franklin Roosevelt's New Deal, Harry Truman's Fair Deal, and Dwight Eisenhower's Republican administration — the government of the United States has been engaged in a campaign to deport the radical West Coast labor leader, Harry Bridges. In 1945, about halfway through the history of the war of the United States against Harry Bridges, Justice Murphy, concurring in the decision of a majority of the Supreme Court in *Bridges* v. *Wixon* that Bridges' alleged affiliation with the Communist Party had not been proved, stated:

> The record in this case will stand forever as a monument to man's intolerance of man. Seldom if ever in the history of this nation has there been such a concentrated and relentless crusade to deport an individual because he dared to exercise the freedom that belongs to him as a human being and that is guaranteed to him by the Constitution.

Undeterred by this strong condemnation, the government resumed the campaign. As of this writing, the latest episode in the saga of Harry Bridges came to a close in 1955 when a Federal judge refused to accept the testimony of several bitter ex-Communists and dismissed a proceeding to denaturalize Bridges preparatory to deporting him. (After the third attempt to deport him had failed,

Bridges became a naturalized citizen, and a citizen is not subject to deportation. But the government claimed that Bridges had committed perjury in denying in his application for citizenship that he had ever been a member of the Communist Party, and that his naturalization should therefore be revoked for fraud.)

Despite all this, the Bill of Rights does afford some modest protection to the alien lawfully present here. The Fifth Amendment prohibits the Federal government from depriving any "person" of life, liberty, or property without due process of law. An alien has long been held by the Supreme Court to be a "person" within the meaning of this provision, and deportation is a deprivation of "liberty." The due process to which the alien is entitled is modest indeed. It requires only that he be given reasonable notice of the charge against him, that he have the opportunity of a fair hearing before some Federal official, and that there be some evidence to support the charge against him.

Modest as it is, the protection afforded aliens lawfully resident here is by no means negligible. Because of the requirement that a deportation order must be supported by evidence, Bridges was able to defeat the government's efforts to deport him. The fair hearing required in deportation proceedings entitles the alien to reasonable notice not only of the charges against him, but also of the evidence upon which the charges are based, and permits him to present evidence of his own to counter the charges.

These modest procedural safeguards, it should be remembered, are enjoyed only by aliens who are resident in this country and only while they are here. An alien who departs even temporarily from the country (except in pursuit of his vocation as a seaman, with full security documentation and clearance) is not constitutionally entitled to any procedural safeguards or to due process of law if he is barred upon seeking to return; for then he is subject to the completely unreviewable power of exclusion rather than the slightly reviewable power of expulsion.

THE RIGHT TO BE AN AMERICAN

The right to be an American is a liberty enjoyed only by Americans, i.e., those persons having the good fortune to be born in the

United States. Not all of even those persons have always enjoyed that right. In the famous or infamous Dred Scott decision (*Scott* v. *Sandford*), the Supreme Court precipitated a bloody Civil War by holding that the right to be an American citizen is a liberty possessed only by white Americans. The Dred Scott decision was overruled at Appomattox, and the reversal was made permanent by the opening sentence of the Fourteenth Amendment: "All persons born or naturalized in the United States, and subject to the jurisdiction thereof, are citizens of the United States and of the State wherein they reside."

This language appears to be clear and definite. The qualification "subject to the jurisdiction thereof" excludes children of foreign ambassadors; but otherwise the Amendment states clearly that everyone born in the United States is a citizen of the United States. Nevertheless, the Supreme Court held in the 1884 decision of *Elk* v. *Wilkins* that, of all people, American Indians born in the United States were not American citizens. Whether or not this decision would be followed by the Supreme Court today is questionable. In 1898 the Court ruled in *United States* v. *Wong Kim Ark* that the scope of the first sentence of the Fourteenth Amendment is not limited to Negroes, and that a child born here to Chinese parents is a citizen of the United States even though at that time an alien of Chinese descent could not become a naturalized citizen, thus implicitly though not expressly overruling the Elk case. The question has become academic by reason of the passage by Congress in 1924 of a statute providing that all Indians born in the United States thereby acquire citizenship.

Persons not born in the United States have no constitutional right to become American citizens, just as they have no constitutional right to come to America to live. Section 8 of Article I of the Constitution empowers Congress to "establish an uniform rule of naturalization"; but probably the power to regulate naturalization, like the power to regulate immigration, is inherent in Congress as an incident of sovereignty and would be recognized even if this provision were absent from the Constitution.

Although in the Dred Scott case the Supreme Court held that the power of Congress to regulate naturalization did not encompass the naturalization of natives but was limited to the foreign born, it is unlikely that this holding would be followed today. It is fairly clear from the Court's later decisions that the power of Congress over naturalization is absolute, in respect both to who may be naturalized and to who may not be naturalized. In the exercise of this power Congress acts "politically" and its judgment is therefore not subject to review by the courts.

For many years Congress exercised this power to withhold the privilege of becoming an American from all aliens whose skin was not white. After the Civil War, the bars were let down slightly to permit the naturalization of Negroes of African descent. Asians, Chinese, Japanese, Hindus, and others were for many years barred from becoming naturalized citizens, and the Supreme Court consistently upheld the power of Congress to exclude them. It was not until the enactment of the McCarran-Walter Immigration and Naturalization Act in 1952 that Congress finally eliminated all racial and color bars to becoming an American citizen.

The elimination of color and race as bars to naturalization was gradual, proceeding step by step from the passage of the Civil Rights Laws and the adoption of the Fourteenth Amendment after the Civil War until the passage of the McCarran-Walter Act. But as race and color factors were dropped, political considerations came to play an increasingly important role in our naturalization policy. As the bars were being lowered for Negroes, American Indians, and Asians, they were being raised against pacifists, radicals, and subversives.

Because the power of Congress over the privilege of naturalization is an incident of sovereignty and its exercise raises political questions not subject to court review, there is no restriction upon the decision of Congress as to who may and who may not be naturalized, other than its own judgment and the displeasure of the electorate manifested at the polls. Congress, said the Supreme Court in *Terrace* v. *Thompson,* may grant or withhold the privilege of naturalization upon any grounds or without any reason, as it sees fit.

Accordingly, in *United States* v. *Schwimmer* (1929) the Supreme Court held that 50-year-old Rosika Schwimmer, international pacifist and woman suffragist, was properly denied naturalization as a result of her negative answer to a question on the printed form of petition for citizenship whether if necessary she would be willing to take up arms in defense of this country. Two years later, in *United States* v. *Macintosh,* this decision was reaffirmed and a pacifist professor of divinity at Yale was denied the privilege of becoming a citizen. However, in *Girouard* v. *United States,* decided in 1946, these decisions were overruled; a majority of the Court held that religiously motivated refusal to bear arms did not manifest a lack of attachment to the principles of the Constitution. The Girouard decision was followed and extended in *Cohnstaedt* v. *Immigration and Naturalization Service,* where the Court held that refusal on religious grounds to manufacture munitions or deliver them to combat troops did not disqualify an applicant for naturalization.

The Girouard and Cohnstaedt cases, it is important to note, were not based upon the ground that Congress could not constitutionally make religiously motivated pacifism a bar to citizenship. On the contrary, only one year before the Girouard case the Court had decided in the case of *In re Summers* that a State could constitutionally make religious pacifism a bar to the privilege of practicing law. The Girouard decision was based upon the holding that Congress had not intended to disqualify from citizenship those aliens whose religious convictions barred them from combatant service. Had Congress clearly manifested its intent to do so, there would have been no doubt concerning its constitutional power. The McCarran-Walter Immigration Act removed all doubts on this score by requiring applicants for citizenship to take an oath of willingness to bear arms, while expressly exempting conscientious objectors from this requirement.

Beginning in 1906, when Congress barred believers in anarchy and polygamy from citizenship, Congress imposed ever-increasing political qualifications upon the privilege of becoming a citizen. The McCarran-Walter Act of 1952, now in effect, bars from citizenship any person who at any time within ten years before filing his application for citizenship was a member of or affiliated with the Communist Party. There is no question as to the constitutionality of this provision; the constitutional bars on ex post facto laws and bills of attainder have no relevance to naturalization proceedings.

EQUALITY BETWEEN CITIZEN AND ALIEN

"Ye shall have one manner of law," Moses commanded the children of Israel, "as well for the stranger, as for one of your own country." Indeed, the Lawgiver went even further: "Love ye therefore the stranger," he commanded. American social and political morality is undoubtedly based to a large extent upon the Bible; but it is at least doubtful that we apply one law for the stranger as for the citizen, and more than doubtful that we love the stranger within our gates.

The Fourteenth Amendment provides that no State shall deny to any person within its jurisdiction the equal protection of the laws. No similar mandate of equality is expressly imposed by the Constitution upon the Federal government. But — as will become more apparent in the next chapter — the grafting and pruning function of the Supreme Court, discussed in the first chapter, becomes evident here. It is probable that the Court would find little difficulty in invalidating an act of Congress which arbitrarily and unreasonably discriminated among persons in the same class, just as it would invalidate under the "equal protection" clause a similar law enacted by a State.

The "equal protection" clause refers to "persons," not "citizens." Equality, therefore, is a liberty of all persons legally in the United States, not just American citizens. But just as "due process of law" means considerably less when applied to an alien than when invoked by a citizen, so too what a citizen is entitled to as "equal protection" may be a good deal more than what an alien may legally claim under the same guarantee.

Certain distinctions between citizens and aliens are manifestly reasonable, and their imposition does not constitute a denial of equal protection. For example, it is hardly open to dispute that the right to vote or hold public office may validly be limited to citizens. The test is whether citizenship bears a reasonable relationship to the legitimate object of the particular legislation; if it does, a classification based upon citizenship is not a denial of equal protection. The object of election laws is to obtain public officials who will best and most loyally govern the nation and administer its laws, and it is reasonable to assume that those owing allegiance to the nation will be more likely to govern it loyally and administer its laws wisely than those owing allegiance to a foreign nation. For the same reason it is undoubtedly constitutional for a State to limit civil-service employment or the practice of law or teaching in the public schools to Americans who are citizens.

On the other hand, in the leading case of *Yick Wo* v. *Hopkins*, decided in 1886, the Supreme Court held unconstitutional the action of the city of San Francisco in discriminating against Chinese aliens in the issuance of licenses to operate hand laundries. No reasonable distinction in the operation of hand laundries may be made between citizens and aliens. If the legislature believes that aliens or Chinese aliens depress labor standards by working for lower wages or longer hours than American citizens, then the State may enact a minimum-wage or maximum-hour law, applicable to all, citizens and aliens alike; but it may not simply bar aliens from a particular occupation in which citizenship is not a natural qualification.

Following the Yick Wo case, the Court in *Truax* v. *Raich* held unconstitutional under the " equal protection " clause a State statute prohibiting private employers from hiring more than one-fifth of their labor force from among non-citizens. The Fourteenth Amendment, said the Court, does not permit a State to deny to lawful inhabitants the right to earn a livelihood merely because they are not citizens. (During the same year, however, the Court held in *Heim* v. *McCall* that a State could validly restrict *public* employment to citizens.) And in *Takahashi* v. *Fish and Game Commission,* before the 1952 McCarran-Walter Act removed all racial bars to citizenship, the Court invalidated a California law that barred from the right to engage in commercial fishing those aliens (chiefly Japanese) then ineligible for citizenship.

In *Terrace* v. *Thompson* the Court, in 1923, had upheld a State law forbidding aliens to own land; but the authority of this decision was greatly weakened twenty-five years later in the case of *Oyama* v. *California.* There the Court invalidated a statute which provided that, if an alien paid for land which was then deeded to a citizen, it would be presumed that the transaction was not bona fide but was intended to evade the statute forbidding aliens to own real estate, and that the land would therefore be declared forfeit to the State. Four of the nine justices wished to overrule *Terrace* v. *Thompson* expressly and declare the entire Alien Land Law unconstitutional; but the majority deemed it unnecessary to pass on this question, and held that the effect of the statute was to discriminate against citizens who receive land paid for by aliens. It is probable that, should the question be presented squarely, the Court would overrule *Terrace* v. *Thompson* and invalidate laws barring aliens from acquiring real estate. State courts in California and Oregon have so held after the Takahashi and Oyama cases were decided.

EQUALITY AMONG CITIZENS

A later chapter of this book is devoted to a consideration of unequal treatment of citizens because of race. That chapter concerns itself largely with unequal treatment of Negro citizens. Here a brief discussion is in order of two other aspects of the subject of unequal treatment of citizens: inequality based upon foreign birth and inequality based upon foreign ancestry.

It would be gratifying to Americans completely committed to egalitarian and democratic principles to be able to say that the Constitution does not recognize two classes of citizens, the native and the naturalized, but treats all exactly alike. Unfortunately, this is not so. Article II, Section I, of the Constitution, which limits eligibility to the Presidency to native-born citizens, in one respect makes a distinction between native and naturalized citizens.

There are two ways of looking at this constitutionally expressed distinction. One could say that, by asserting a distinction only in respect to eligibility to the Presidency, the framers of the Constitution implicitly foreclosed all other distinctions between native and naturalized citizens. Or one could say that, by asserting a distinction between the two classes in one situation, the fathers of the Constitution recognized that in certain situations a distinction between the classes can be reasonable and therefore valid, and thus sanctioned further distinctions by Congress or the States so long as the distinctions are reasonable in the situations in which they are imposed.

Again, it would be gratifying if one could say that the former is the view accepted by the Supreme Court. Unfortunately, this cannot be said with any degree of certainty. Indeed, it is at least equally likely that the Court would refuse in many cases to upset a distinction between native and naturalized citizens declared by Congress to be a reasonable exercise of its constitutional power to regulate naturalization.

It is true that as long ago as 1824 John Marshall expressed the view in *Osborn* v. *Bank of the United States* that the Constitution does not recognize distinctions between naturalized and native citizens; and that, although Congress, under its power to establish a uniform rule of naturalization, may impose any prerequisites to acquiring citizenship that it wishes, once these prerequisites are satisfied and the alien becomes a citizen he stands upon equal footing with native citizens. It is also true that in 1946 Justice Douglas made a similar statement in *Knauer* v. *United States,* asserting that citizenship obtained through naturalization is not a second-class citizenship but carries with it the privilege of full participation in public affairs.

Congress, nevertheless, has not accepted these dicta. The Internal Security Act of 1950 provides that any naturalized citizen who joins a subversive organization within five years after he obtains his citizenship may thereby lose his citizenship, although a native citizen would suffer no similar penalty for the same act. Congress has also provided that a naturalized citizen who remains out of this country for more than five years thereby loses his American citizenship, even though a native American citizen may live outside the United States all his adult life without forfeiting his citizenship. The constitutionality of the latter statute was upheld by the Federal Court of Appeals in a decision which the Supreme Court, in 1949, refused to review, giving no reason for its refusal. This and other decisions leave it doubtful that the Court would upset all Congressional distinctions between native and naturalized citizens.

While the Court has not passed expressly and specifically on this question, it has upheld distinctions among even *native* citizens on the basis of their racial or national ancestry. The cases arose out of the panic that gripped the United States and particularly the West Coast after Pearl Harbor.

About two months after the Japanese attack President Roosevelt authorized the military commander of the West Coast to impose restrictions upon the right to enter, remain in, or leave the military district of the West Coast. This act of the President was shortly thereafter ratified and approved by an act of Congress, which made it a criminal offense to violate any regulation of the military commander. Acting pursuant to this authority, the military commander, General De Witt, imposed a curfew requiring all persons of Japanese descent, whether citizens or non-citizens, to be and remain at home between the hours of 8 P.M. and 6 A.M. every day.

In *Hirabayashi* v. *United States* the Supreme Court unanimously upheld the conviction, under the act of Congress, of an American-born college student of Japanese ancestry who was found outside his apartment after 8 P.M. one evening. Hirabayashi attacked the validity of the curfew regulation on the ground that it discriminated against certain citizens. If the military authorities felt that security required imposition of a curfew they should have imposed the curfew against all. Singling out citizens of Japanese descent constituted an act of inequality.

Although nothing in the Constitution or the Bill of Rights expressly forbids the Federal government from denying to any person the equal protection of the laws, the Court had no hesitation in assuming that, if there was no reasonable basis for distinguishing between citizens of Japanese ancestry and other citizens, the regulation and conviction would be unconstitutional. It should also be noted that there was no evidence that Hirabayashi was engaged in any act of sabotage or espionage when he was apprehended or that he was in any way disloyal to the United States; indeed, it was not claimed that he was anything but a completely loyal American citizen.

Yet the Court found that the curfew limited to Japanese-Americans was reasonable. Distinctions among citizens because of differences in race or ancestry, said the Court, are ordinarily by their very nature odious to a free people whose institutions are founded upon the doctrine of equality. Ordinarily, therefore, legal discriminations based upon racial differences are unconstitutional denials of the equal protection of the law. But in wartime grounds that in peacetime are insubstantial may be reasonable, and the grounds upon which General De Witt acted were in that category. For espionage by pro-Japanese had been found particularly effective in the attack upon Pearl Harbor. In addition, the concentration of Japanese on the West Coast constituted a particular source of danger. The social, economic, and political conditions to which Japanese had been subjected (including bars to immigration or citizenship, alien-land laws, anti-miscegenation statutes, and economic discrimination) might have made them bitter against the United States, intensified their solidarity, and prevented their assimilation. For these and other reasons the Court concluded that the distinction between citizens of Japanese descent and other citizens was not unreasonable or unconstitutional.

Imposition of the 8 P.M. curfew undoubtedly caused inconveniences, but the next step taken by General De Witt was far more serious. Five months after Pearl Harbor he issued an order giving all Americans of Japanese ancestry, citizens as well as aliens, five days to get out of the West Coast and the inland States of Idaho, Montana, Nevada, Utah, and Oregon.

In *Korematsu* v. *United States* this order was likewise upheld by the Supreme Court against an American-born Japanese whose loyalty to the United States was unquestioned. (This time, however, three of the justices were not able to agree with the decision.) Because of pressing public necessity and the gravest imminent danger to the public safety, the majority held, some restrictions upon the liberties of a particular racial group, motivated not by racial prejudice but by military necessity, must be tolerated. The power of the government to protect the nation must be commensurate with the danger that threatens the nation.

On the same day in 1944 that the Korematsu case was decided, the Court called a halt in *Ex parte Endo*. Curfew and evacuation it could with difficulty accept; internment of loyal American citizens in concentration camps solely because of the accident of racial descent was too closely akin to what the Nazis (whom we were fighting) were doing for the Court to acquiesce in, even under the claim of military necessity.

The Court, however, did not declare the entire internment program unconstitutional. It held only that neither the order of the President nor the act of Congress authorized the continued detention of citizens who were admittedly loyal to the government (as was Mitsuye Endo), even if temporary detention to separate the loyal from the possibly disloyal was authorized. Once the military authorities determined that a particular Japanese-American citizen was loyal, they were not authorized, either by the act of Congress or by the executive order of the President, to detain him any further — although they could, according to the Korematsu decision, prohibit him from returning to his home on the West Coast or in the Rocky Mountain States.

All the justices concurred in the decision. But two of them (Murphy and Roberts, who with Jackson had dissented in the Korematsu case) would have gone further and declared the internment program not only unauthorized but unconstitutional, at least as applied solely on racial grounds against loyal American citizens. It is perhaps unfortunate that the Court did not meet the constitutional issue squarely, because the first experience our nation has had with concentration camps has apparently not dissuaded our government from ever resorting to that essentially totalitarian device again. The McCarran Internal Security Act of 1950 authorizes the President, when the nation is at war, to declare an "internal security emergency" and to apprehend and detain indefinitely any person, citizen or non-citizen, who may reasonably be believed to be a probable conspirator, spy, or saboteur. It is fervently to be hoped that the Supreme Court will never have occasion to pass upon the constitutionality of this provision.

THE RIGHT TO GO

The right of a citizen to move freely from State to State is one of the liberties of an American. The Supreme Court so held in *Edwards* v. *California*, where it invalidated an "anti-Oakie" statute that made it a penal offense to bring into the State destitute persons from other States. Although the case was decided on the narrow ground that the statute was an unconstitutional interference with interstate commerce, it did establish that a citizen's right of mobility is constitutionally protected from interference by the States.

While the Court did not find it necessary to decide whether a similar statute enacted by Congress (which *is* empowered to regulate interstate commerce) would also be unconstitutional, it is probable that the Court would so hold. This seems to be implicit in the Korematsu case, where the Congress-authorized regulation excluding Japanese-Americans from the West Coast was sustained only because it was an emergency measure in a period of grave national danger. All American liberties must on occasion be restricted where the restriction is clearly and immediately necessary to protect a superior communal interest, and the liberty to go where one wills is likewise subject to that rule. But in the absence of such an extreme emergency it seems clear that an act of Congress restricting the mobility of Americans would be held an unconstitutional deprivation of liberty without due process of law.

The liberty of free mobility is possessed exclusively by citizens. Since aliens are here only by sufferance and may be expelled at any time for any reason or no reason, it would follow that Congress has the power to restrict their movements within the United States.

Federal restrictions, through Congressional acts or Executive regulations, upon the movement of aliens are common, and their constitutionality does not appear ever to have been seriously challenged.

Is the right to leave the country a liberty of Americans? During most of the history of our republic citizens were free to leave the country and travel abroad as they wished and whenever they wished. While would-be travelers usually sought and obtained passports from the State Department, the purpose of the passport was to certify that the traveler was an American citizen entitled to the protection of American diplomatic and consular officers abroad; it was not considered a permit without which the citizen could not legally leave the country.

An act of Congress in 1946, however, for the first time made it a penal offense to travel abroad without a passport. For a number of years now the State Department has taken the position that travel abroad is not a right but a privilege and that the Department has uncontrolled discretion in granting or withholding the privilege. In 1955 a Federal Court of Appeals rejected this claim and held that the right of an American to leave the country is a liberty of which he may not be deprived without due process of law. The least to which he is entitled, the Court said, is notice of the grounds for the denial of a passport and a hearing at which he might have an opportunity to refute those charges. The State Department decided not to appeal this ruling, and accordingly the Supreme Court has not had occasion to rule on the question. Nevertheless, it is fairly safe to predict that the Court would not accept the State Department's claim that travel abroad during peacetime is a privilege rather than a right, and that a passport may be withheld at will and without review by the courts.

Is the privilege not to be an American a liberty of Americans? In other words, do American citizens have a right to renounce their citizenship and become nationals of other countries? The English common law in the nineteenth century did not recognize the right of a born Englishman to renounce his allegiance to Britain except with the consent of the British government, and Continental European countries took the same position. European rulers, losing subjects, particularly seamen, to the New World, adhered fiercely to the old doctrine. Conversely, the United States, prospering from the migrant's freedom of choice, became champion of the individual's right to expatriate himself. Indeed, we went to war with England in 1812 largely to secure that right.

Surprisingly enough in view of this history, the Supreme Court has never held that there is a constitutionally protected right to renounce American citizenship. On the contrary, in *Shanks* v. *Dupont* the Court followed the English common-law rule of perpetual and unchangeable allegiance to the government of one's birth. However, in 1868 Congress abrogated the holding of that case when it enacted a law declaring that the right of expatriation is a natural and inherent right of all people, indispensable to the enjoyment of the rights of life, liberty, and the pursuit of happiness, and that any contrary decision is inconsistent with the fundamental principles of the American government.

This statute, which has never been repealed, makes it unnecessary for the Supreme Court to decide whether *Shanks* v. *Dupont* should be followed today. Yet here again it is safe to suggest that, if the 1868 statute were repealed and the issue were squarely put before the Court, it would probably hold that the 1868 Congress truly expressed American constitutional principles, and that the free choice not to be an American is a constitutionally protected liberty of Americans.

CHAPTER 9. *Liberty and Equality*

UP FROM SLAVERY

It cost this nation thousands of lives in a bloody civil war, and the arousal of hatreds, bitterness, and passions that have not yet been extinguished, to establish as part of our basic law the proposition that a human being is not a chattel that can be owned by another human being. The legal command of the Thirteenth Amendment — "Neither slavery nor involuntary servitude, except as punishment for crime whereof the party shall have been duly convicted, shall exist within the United States" — was not new in 1866. The Amendment simply reproduced the historic words of the Northwest Ordinance of 1787. The effect of the Amendment was simply to make it a categorical imperative, universally applicable throughout the United States and in any place subject to its jurisdiction.

We have paid a heavy price for the Thirteenth Amendment and the outlawing of slavery. We therefore have the right to expect that we have received what we have so dearly paid for, and that involuntary servitude has indeed disappeared from the land. Unfortunately, this is not so. In 1947 the President's Committee on Civil Rights, in its historic report *To Secure These Rights,* indicated that peonage and involuntary servitude were still to be found in our country, almost a century after the Civil War.

One instance cited in the report was the case of a Mississippi farmer who held a Negro woman and her 10-year-old son in captivity. Forced to work on the farm by day, they were locked in a crude, windowless, chimneyless cabin at night. The mother had made three unsuccessful efforts to escape before Federal authorities finally learned of the situation and released her.

This case is by no means unique, but individual instances of lawlessness or depravity, regrettable as they are, present no serious threat to American liberties. What are of grave concern are the unfortunately far-from-infrequent attempts by Southern States and municipalities to evade the letter and spirit of the Thirteenth Amendment by legal devices more indicative of legislative ingenuity than of devotion to American principles of freedom and liberty. It was not long after the ink became dry upon the signatures to the Thirteenth Amendment that attempted legalistic evasions began to crop up, and as late as 1944 the Supreme Court was still engaged in striking them down.

Two points should be noted about the Thirteenth Amendment. Unlike the Fourteenth and Fifteenth Amendments it is not addressed merely to government; its command is absolute. It forbids all, governments and private individuals alike, to subject any person to slavery or involuntary servitude. Hence — again unlike the Fourteenth and Fifteenth Amendments — the second section, empowering Congress to enforce the Amendment by appropriate legislation, authorizes Congress to make it a Federal crime for any person to subject another to involuntary servitude. Accordingly, as early as 1867 Congress enacted a statute, still on the books, prohibiting peonage and subjecting to criminal punishment persons returning anyone to a condition of peonage.

The second point to be noted is that the Amendment, though primarily intended to emancipate the Negro slave, is not limited to Negroes. The Thirteenth Amendment, the Supreme Court held in *Hodges* v. *United States*, is not a declaration in favor of a particular group. It reaches every race and every individual. Slavery or involuntary servitude of the Chinese, the Italian, or the Anglo-Saxon is as much within the compass of the Amendment as slavery or involuntary servitude of the African.

Despite this, Negroes remain the chief beneficiaries of the Amendment and the chief victims of attempted legal evasions, most of which have arisen in the South. The usual attempted method of evasion has been by statutes providing for imprisonment for breach of contract (generally, a sharecropper contract) or failure to pay a debt, thus, in effect compelling the sharecropper, who usually could not clear himself of debt, to continue working or face criminal prosecution. Another method has been the enactment of laws permitting the court to allow petty offenders to satisfy their fines by working for private persons — who wait around the courtroom, somewhat reminiscent of the plantation owners who used to wait around the courthouse for the slave auction to begin. The Supreme Court has consistently invalidated these and similar techniques as palpable attempts to evade the Thirteenth Amendment.

The right to be free from involuntary servitude, like other American liberties, must occasionally yield for the immediate protection of a paramount social interest. During World War I the Supreme Court held in *Arver* v. *United States,* known as the Selective Draft Law Cases, that, in spite of the Amendment, Congress could compel military service by able-bodied citizens, although this admittedly constitutes involuntary servitude. Similarly, there can be little doubt that a State could compel all able-bodied men to work on embankments or other structures in order to ward off the dangers of an approaching flood. Finally, in 1949, the Court in *International Auto Workers* v. *Wisconsin Board* held that an injunction against a strike or labor stoppage did not violate the Thirteenth Amendment ban on involuntary servitude.

INEQUALITY — THE BADGE OF SLAVERY

The Reconstruction Congress is probably the most maligned Congress in American history. Our post-Civil War history has often been written in a way that casts that Congress and its leaders, Stevens, Howard, Bingham, and others, in the role of vindictive villains whose sole purpose was to wreak vengeance upon the white South, and incidentally to create lucrative political offices for Northern carpetbaggers. Not only was the lawlessness of the Ku Klux Klan excused and justified, but the Klan itself was romanticized as a valiant defender of American culture. The present writer was a youth during the period following World War I which saw the revival of the Klan; he remembers vividly how the better elements in the community deplored this development and gravely warned the community not to confuse that Klan with the earlier Klan whose exploits had been so beautifully depicted in the motion picture *Birth of a Nation.*

Undoubtedly there were men in the Reconstruction Congress — as in every other Congress — motivated by vindictiveness, and perhaps some motivated by venality. But it is an unjust libel so to characterize the whole Congress or its leaders. Their purpose was to secure for the Negro full liberty and equality — not to punish the South or to milk it. Perhaps their purpose could have been better served if they had adopted the more moderate approach urged by Lincoln and Johnson. (Yet it should be remembered that Lincoln considered secession a greater evil than slavery and would have sacrificed the slaves' freedom to preserve the political Union, and that Johnson's primary concern was the winning back of the South and the rapid healing of the war wounds.) If so, they were guilty at most of an error of judgment, an error for which they cannot be too harshly condemned in view of the absence among the responsible Southern leaders of any expression of opinion that the war's verdict was accepted and that the Negro would gradually be accorded full equality. On the contrary, responsible Southern leadership took the exactly opposite position. The guns had barely become silent when throughout the South "Black Codes" were enacted to keep the Negro in his place by force of law. Adoption of a laissez-faire attitude by the Congress would have meant that those who had given their lives between Fort Sumter and Appomattox had indeed died in vain.

Whatever else may be said of the Reconstruction Congress, it clearly did not consider its ends accomplished with the emancipation of the slaves and the adoption of the Thirteenth Amendment. It sought to abolish not only slavery but the badge of slavery — inequality. Immediately after the Thirteenth Amendment became effective, Congress adopted a Civil Rights or Enforcement Act. Based upon the second section of the Thirteenth Amendment, which empowers Congress to enforce the first section by appropriate legislation, its aim was to outlaw the "Black Codes" by securing equality to all persons in the enjoyment of civil rights; these included making contracts, suing in court, acquiring property, and enjoying the security of the law — rights previously denied to Negro slaves. The underlying premise of this statute was that inequality is a symbol or badge of slavery, and the power conferred upon Congress to enforce the abolition of slavery implicitly empowered it to abolish the badges of slavery.

Doubts were expressed by a number of Congressmen as to the constitutionality of this statute, and in the Civil Rights Cases of 1883 the Supreme Court did in fact reject the "badge of slavery" theory, holding that the Thirteenth Amendment did no more than outlaw slavery itself. In an effort to remove these doubts, Congress proposed the Fourteenth Amendment (and later the Fifteenth), which became effective in 1868; and thereafter Congress re-enacted the Civil Rights or Enforcement Act, adding provisions designed to protect the newly granted right of Negroes to vote. In 1871 Congress enacted the Ku Klux Klan or Anti-lynching Law, which penalized action under color of law that deprived persons of their rights under the Constitution. Finally, in 1875 Congress passed the Civil Rights Act, which was designed to guarantee to Negroes equal accommodations with whites in all inns, public conveyances, theaters, and other places of public amusement.

THE FOURTEENTH AMENDMENT

The Fourteenth Amendment, as we have seen, first confers citizenship upon all persons born or naturalized in the United States. It then provides: "No State shall make or enforce any law which shall abridge the privileges or immunities of citizens of the United States; nor shall any State deprive any person of life, liberty, or property, without due process of law; nor deny to any person within its jurisdiction the equal protection of the laws." Three other sections, dealing with representation in Congress, disqualification from Federal office of participants in the Rebellion, and renunciation of the Confederate public debt, do not concern us here. The last section empowers Congress to enforce the Amendment by appropriate legislation.

As we saw in the first chapter, at least some of the Congressional leaders who framed and led the campaign for the adoption of the Fourteenth Amendment understood that it would make applicable as against the States the liberties guaranteed to Americans against Federal infringement by the first eight Amendments. That this was the purpose or effect of the Fourteenth Amendment has consistently been denied by the Supreme Court, with today only Black and Douglas dissenting. Whichever view is historically correct, there can be no question that such was not the primary objective of the Congress that formulated the Fourteenth Amendment. Without doubt, its principal purpose was to secure equality for the newly freed Negroes.

To achieve this end the Amendment imposed three restrictions upon the States: it forbade them to abridge the privileges or immunities of citizens, to deprive any person of life, liberty, or property without due process of law, and to deny to any person the equal protection of the laws. Within five years after the Amendment was adopted, the Supreme Court, in a decision by a bare majority, which nevertheless has never been overruled and has frequently been reaffirmed, rendered the " privileges or immunities " clause a practical nullity. In the Slaughter-House Cases (discussed in the first chapter) the Court rejected an interpretation of that clause which, it said, would have had the effect of transferring the security and protection of all civil rights from the States to the Federal government and of constituting the Supreme Court a perpetual censor upon all legislation of the States with authority to nullify such State laws as it did not approve. The effect of such an interpretation would be to fetter and degrade the State governments, a consequence which the Court (or five of the nine justices thereof) was sure neither Congress nor the ratifying States could have intended.

The vitiation of the " privileges or immunities " clause served only briefly to prevent the Supreme Court from becoming the perpetual censor of State legislation. As the significance of that clause disappeared, the importance of the " due process " clause increased, and it soon became by far the most important provision of the Amendment. The " due process " clause has had three major effects: in chronological order, it has enabled the Supreme Court to nullify economic legislation of which it disapproved; it imposed upon the States the substantive restrictions of the First Amendment; and it secured to Americans the basic elements of fair play in State court criminal trials. The first effect is outside the scope of this book; the second and third have already been discussed.

It would not be accurate to say that the " due process " clause has played no role in the Negro's struggle for equality. In the first place, as the Scottsboro cases and *Moore* v. *Dempsey* show, Negroes in the South are frequently the beneficiaries of the fair-trial requirements of " due process." In the second place, the " due process " clause has occasionally been used to invalidate laws that discriminate specifically against Negroes, as the racial zoning law invalidated in *Buchanan* v. *Warley*, which will be considered later in this chapter.

Despite this, the utility of the " due process " clause in achieving equality for the Negro has been comparatively minor. The chief weapon in the struggle for equality has been the clause prohibiting the States from denying to any person the equal protection of the laws.

THE EQUAL PROTECTION OF THE LAWS

A number of observations about the " equal protection " clause are pertinent here.

(1) Like the Thirteenth Amendment, the Fourteenth makes no specific reference to Negroes. Its mantle protects all persons — whites, Negroes, Asians, American Indians, Catholics, Jews, Jehovah's Witnesses, and all others. For example, in *Skinner* v. *Oklahoma* the Supreme Court in 1942 declared unconstitutional, as a denial of equal protection, a statute providing for the sterilization of certain habitual criminals, such as those convicted of larceny, but not of others, such as those convicted of embezzlement. Moreover, like the " due process " clause and unlike the " privileges or immunities " clause, it does not refer to citizens, and therefore its protection encompasses aliens as well as citizens; the Takahashi case, discussed in the previous chapter, invalidated under the " equal protection " clause a statute restricting fishing licenses to citizens, and *Yick Wo* v. *Hopkins* (1886) invalidated under the same clause a municipal practice of denying laundry licenses to Chinese aliens.

(2) The term " equal protection of the laws " has a much broader meaning than a literal interpretation would indicate. It is not limited to laws that accord protection, but extends as well to laws that confer rights or privileges. A State, for example, may not grant the privilege of a free higher education to whites while withholding it from Negroes. The equal protection of the laws really means the protection of equal laws, or, better yet, equality under law, and its purpose is to forbid discrimination by law.

(3) Not all legal distinctions between persons and classes constitute a denial of equal protection. The test is reasonableness: if the difference of treatment is based upon a reasonable classification, it is constitutional; otherwise it is not. It is reasonable that only citizens be appointed to public office or be permitted to practice law; therefore, a law excluding aliens from public service or from admis-

sion to the bar does not unconstitutionally deny them the equal protection of the laws.

A legal distinction based upon race would probably be deemed by most enlightened persons to be by its very nature unreasonable and unconstitutional. One could have expected the Supreme Court in any event to take that position. Perhaps it would have done so if the issue had not come to it in the midst of the great fear that followed the attack upon Pearl Harbor. Unfortunately, the issue did come up at that time, and the result was the Japanese curfew and relocation cases, discussed in the preceding chapter, with their holding that under extraordinary circumstances discriminatory treatment by law on the basis of racial difference may be constitutional. Nevertheless, the Court stressed, such a distinction is *prima facie* unreasonable and will be sustained only in the most extraordinary circumstances and upon the clearest proof that it is motivated by bona-fide considerations and not racial prejudice.

(4) While the " due process " clause of the Fourteenth Amendment is found also in the Fifth as a command to the Federal government, neither the Bill of Rights nor the Constitution contains any provision expressly prohibiting the Federal government to deny to any person the equal protection of the laws. As has been indicated, however, it is probable that the omission is of little significance, and that unreasonable discrimination between classes would be invalidated by the Supreme Court under the " due process " or other clause applicable to the Federal government, or by other means.

For example, in *Steele* v. *Louisville & Nashville Railroad* (1944) the Court held that a labor union, which by Federal law was made the exclusive bargaining agent for all employees, could not legally discriminate against Negro employees and favor whites in its negotiations with the employer. If the law had been a State statute, interpreted by the State courts to permit such discrimination, the Court would probably have invalidated it as a denial of the equal protection of the laws by analogy to the white primary cases. Since the law involved was a Federal statute, the Court reached the same result by interpreting it as not permitting such discrimination. But the Court noted that, if it were not so interpreted, there would be grave doubts as to its constitutionality. In *Hurd* v. *Hodge,* discussed later in this chapter, the Court used a different device to require equality of treatment by the Federal government, even though it is not bound by an express " equal protection " clause in the Constitution or Bill of Rights.

(5) The last section of the Fourteenth Amendment empowers Congress to enact legislation deemed by it necessary for the enforcement of the Amendment. This authorized Congress after the Civil War to enact the Civil Rights Laws, making it a Federal criminal offense for State officials to deprive Negroes of their civil rights or deny them the equal protection of the laws. But even aside from such statutes the Amendment is self-operating. A State statute denying to Negroes the equal protection of the laws is invalid by the operation of the Amendment even in the absence of any Congressional action.

(6) The horror expressed by the Supreme Court in the Slaughter-House Cases at the idea of transferring to the Federal government the security and protection of civil rights manifested an intent to leave largely to the States the responsibility for carrying out the objectives of the Fourteenth Amendment. The Reconstruction Congress which wrote the Fourteenth Amendment refused to adopt this let-the-South-do-it approach; the statutes enacted by it between 1866 and 1875 indicated clearly its belief that the Southern States could not be relied upon to grant equality to the Negro and that the Federal government should continue to shoulder that responsibility. Congress adhered to this view until the settlement of the Hayes-Tilden disputed election of 1876, which was effected — at least, so many believe — on the basis of the *quid pro quo* that the Republican Party would give up all further efforts to legislate equality for the Southern Negro.

Whether or not this understanding is historically accurate, it is true that the disputed Southern electoral votes were all given to the Republican Hayes, and after 1875 no more civil-rights laws were enacted by Congress — unto this very day. If there was a bargain, the Supreme Court appears to have ratified or at least acquiesced in it. In any event, until the Roosevelt Court and its successors rediscovered the " equal protection " clause in the 1930's, '40's, and '50's, the Court seems to have stuck closely to the path pointed out in the Slaughter-House Cases and, except for invalidating some Southern State efforts to restrict the Negro's access to the ballot, has left largely to the States the responsibility for according equality to the Negro.

The Court accomplished this in three ways. The first was in effect to repeal that part of the Fourteenth Amendment that sought to secure to Negroes the privileges or immunities of citizens. The second was to interpret literally the first two words of the second sentence of the Amendment, "No State" — refusing to interpret them to mean "No person." The third was to interpret the word "equal" to mean not identical, but equivalent. The first way has already been discussed and need concern us no further. The latter two are the subject of consideration in the remainder of this chapter.

STATE ACTION

The last civil-rights law passed by Congress was the Civil Rights Act of 1875, enacted under the enforcement clause of the Fourteenth Amendment. It declared that all persons within the United States are entitled to the full and equal enjoyment of public accommodations, such as public carriers, inns, theaters and other places of public amusement, without discrimination because of race or color, and that refusal to accord any person such accommodations because of his race or color shall constitute a punishable Federal crime.

The Civil Rights Cases, decided by the Supreme Court in 1883, involved criminal prosecutions under this statute against hotel and theater owners in San Francisco and New York, as well as a non-criminal action against a Tennessee railroad for refusing to allow a Negro woman to ride in a railroad car. The Supreme Court threw out the indictments and declared the 1875 act unconstitutional.

The enforcement clause of the Fourteenth Amendment, the Court held, can be no broader in operation than the Amendment itself, for a river can rise no higher than its source. The first section of the Amendment declares that no *State* shall deny to any person the equal protection of the laws. The Amendment invalidates State laws and State acts that deny the equal protection of the laws and authorizes Congress to enact legislation to implement that invalidation. It does not, however, invest Congress with power to legislate upon subjects which are within the domain of the States or to create a code of law for the regulation of private rights. Redress for the infringement of civil rights by *private individuals* acting in their private capacities and unrelated to the State government must be sought under State, not Federal, law.

(There was also an attempt to justify the Act under the Thirteenth Amendment, which is not limited to State action. But, as we have seen, the Court held that mere discrimination on account of race or color cannot be regarded as a badge of slavery and therefore is not within the scope of the Thirteenth Amendment.)

The decision in the Civil Rights Cases has been followed consistently by the Supreme Court. The issue in many if not most of the racial civil-rights cases coming to the Supreme Court since 1883 has been whether the act of discrimination involved in the case was purely private action, or could properly be called State action. Out of these cases have evolved a number of principles, which may now be considered.

STATE ACTION AND STATE OFFICIALS

State action subject to the restrictions of the Fourteenth Amendment is not limited to laws enacted by the State legislature. It encompasses all action under authority or color of State law. It includes decisions by State courts and official action by State judges. For example, in *Ex parte Virginia*, decided in 1880, the Supreme Court upheld an indictment under the Civil Rights Acts against a judge in a Virginia State court who excluded Negroes from juries in his court. As we have seen in an earlier chapter, such conduct deprives Negro defendants in the court of the equal protection of the laws and renders their conviction reversible by the Supreme Court.

The Fourteenth Amendment extends also to the acts of all other State officials, from the governor down to an ordinary State trooper. Moreover, State action encompasses the acts not merely of the State government or officials, but also those of municipalities, counties, and similar political subdivisions of the State. The action of the principal of a public school in excluding a Negro child is State action within the compass of the Fourteenth Amendment.

STATE ACTION AND PERSONAL SECURITY

Aside from any Amendment, Congress has inherent power to protect rights which are conferred by the Constitution or by a Federal statute, and may do so by penalizing even private infringements of such rights. As we have seen, the right of a citizen to vote for members of Congress is a Federal right growing out of the Constitution, and Congress may make it a penal offense for private individuals — even if they are unconnected with any State — to infringe upon a citizen's right to vote at a Federal election.

Similarly, in *United States* v. *Waddell* (1884) the Court upheld the conviction of private individuals who, by the use of violence, drove a homesteader off land upon which he had settled under the Federal Homestead Act. Since the homesteader's right was created by the Federal government, it could be protected by the Federal government against infringement by any person, private individual or State official. So, too, in *Logan* v. *United States* the Court upheld the conviction of members of a lynch mob who attacked prisoners who were charged with a Federal offense and who were in the custody of a Federal marshal. The Court held that the prisoners had a Federal right to a fair trial in a Federal court for violation of a Federal law, and that the action of the lynch mob infringed upon that right. Finally, in *Motes* v. *United States* the Court upheld a Federal indictment charging defendants with having murdered a person because he had informed Federal revenue agents about their illegal operation of a distillery in Alabama.

However, the general right to personal security is not a Federal but a natural right; it does not arise out of the Constitution or any act of Congress. Hence, invasions of such right are punishable only by the States, and the Federal government has no power to make such infringements a Federal crime except to the extent authorized by the Thirteenth and Fourteenth Amendments — i.e., infringements upon the right to be free from involuntary servitude, or other infringements upon personal security committed by a State or State official or one acting under color of State law.

Thus, the right of Americans peaceably to assemble is a natural right. It is secured by the First Amendment against infringement by the Federal government and by the Fourteenth against infringement by the States. But it is not created or conferred by either Amendment or by any other part of the Constitution nor by an act of Congress. Hence, as the Court held in *United States* v. *Cruikshank* in throwing out an indictment under the Ku Klux Klan Act of 1870, violation of the right of peaceable assembly by private persons who commit violence against Negroes attempting to exercise that right cannot be made a Federal crime; it must be left to the States for punishment.

Following the Cruikshank case, the Court held in *United States* v. *Harris* that no Federal offense was committed by twenty members of a Tennessee lynch mob who killed one person and seriously injured three others held in custody by a *State* deputy sheriff on charge of having committed a *State* crime. The Harris case was followed, and the same result reached, in 1887 in *Baldwin* v. *Franks;* here the Court threw out an indictment against a person charged with assaulting Chinese citizens and driving them out of a California town. (The Court did indicate that a properly framed indictment might have been sustained if it had proceeded on the theory that the Chinese citizens were protected by a treaty between the United States and the Government of China, since such protection is a right conferred by the Federal government.) Finally, in *Hodges* v. *United States* the Court invalidated an indictment charging defendants with intimidating and driving from work a group of Negro mill hands hired by a lumber mill. The right to work and to contract to work, the Court said, is a natural right and not one created or conferred by the Federal government. It is because of these decisions that the Federal Department of Justice has been unable to take any action in respect to the recent brutal slaying of Eustace Till in Mississippi and other Negroes in the South.

But if the violation of a Negro's rights is committed by a State official it may be State action within the scope of the Fourteenth Amendment and Congressional enforcement legislation even if the official's act also violates State law and is punishable by the State. Consider the case of *Screws* v. *United States,* decided by the Supreme Court in 1945.

Screws was sheriff of Baker County in Georgia. He enlisted the assistance of a policeman named Jones and a special deputy named Kelley in arresting Robert Hall, a 30-year-old Negro, who, Screws said, had stolen an automobile tire. Screws, Jones, and Kelley drove to Hall's home late at night and, exhibiting a warrant for his arrest, handcuffed him and took him by car to the local courthouse. As Hall alighted from the car, Screws, Jones, and Kelley began beating him with their fists and with a solid-bar blackjack; they later claimed that Hall (still handcuffed) had reached for a gun and had insulted them as he alighted. For some fifteen to thirty minutes as he lay on the ground they continued beating him until he became unconscious. They then dragged him, feet first, through the courthouse yard into the jail and threw him upon the floor. Later an ambulance was called to take him to a hospital, but he died without regaining consciousness. It later appeared that Screws had held a grudge against Hall and had threatened to "get" him.

Screws, Jones, and Kelley, all respected white citizens of Baker County, were indicted under a section of one of the Reconstruction Congress's Civil Rights Acts, which made it a Federal crime for persons "under color of any law" of a State willfully to deprive any person of any rights, privileges, or immunities secured or protected by the Constitution. The indictment charged that the defendants had deprived Hall of the right, protected by the Fourteenth Amendment, not to be deprived of life without due process of law, and of the right to a fair trial and to punishment, if convicted, in accordance with the laws of Georgia.

The defendants denied that they acted "under color of" State law. On the contrary, they argued, what they did was to commit murder, an act directly in violation of State law. But the Supreme Court, in upholding the indictment, refused to accept this argument. The defendants, the Court held, were acting under and by virtue of their official authority as State officers in arresting Hall. Neither the fact that they violated the law under which they acted nor the fact that their conduct was criminal and punishable under State law made it any the less an act under color of State law and punishable under Federal law.

Neither of these propositions is particularly startling. Considering the second one first, it may be noted that often a single act is simultaneously a violation of State and Federal law and punishable under both. A person who heaves a brick through a post-office window, or robs a member bank of the Federal Reserve System, or shoots a Federal revenue agent commits at one time a State and a Federal crime and can be punished for both. As for the first proposition, it simply is an application of a well-known and long-standing rule of the civil laws of agency. An employer may have an absolute rule forbidding his drivers to exceed a certain speed limit and making them subject to immediate dismissal if they violate the rule. Yet a chauffeur who violates the rule and injures a pedestrian by his excessive speed still acts within the course of his employment, so that the employer becomes responsible to the injured pedestrian. The test is not whether the wrongdoer — State sheriff or private chauffeur — violated a rule of his employer, but whether he was acting within the scope of his employment, office, or authority.

The postscript to the Screws case is interesting. Although the indictment was sustained, the conviction was set aside and a new trial ordered because of an error in the judge's charge to the jury. By the time the new trial was held, the indignation of the good people of Baker County had cooled off considerably; in the second trial Screws, Jones, and Kelley were acquitted. It need hardly be added that none of them was ever prosecuted under State law.

Yet even here some progress is evident. The recent slayings of Eustace Till and of Clinton Melton were in each case followed by prosecutions for murder in Sumner, Mississippi. Although in both cases the all-white juries speedily acquitted the white defendants, the fact that national public opinion compelled Mississippi to prosecute the defendants is an encouraging sign.

Nevertheless, deplorable as it is, it remains true that the South does not appear ready to accord to Negroes the equal protection of the laws, and that Federal intervention is still necessary to protect many Negroes from violence on the part of lawless police officers and State officials. It is hardly open to doubt that, but for Federal prosecution, not a few brutal violations of Negroes' rights would go unpunished. An illustrative case occurred in 1947 when a constable who whipped a Negro prisoner and forced him to jump into a river, so that he drowned, was prosecuted and convicted for violation of the Federal Civil Rights Act. In 1951 a conviction under Federal law — a conviction which the Supreme Court in *Lynch* v. *United States* refused to disturb — was obtained against police officials for surrendering some Negro prisoners to a Ku Klux Klan mob, who then administered a severe beating to the Negroes. Although the penalties that may be imposed under the Federal Civil Rights Acts are comparatively light in relation to the gravity of the offense, they are often the only penalties available in practice; and fear of even these light penalties probably acts as a substantial deterrent, thus saving many Negroes their lives and limbs.

STATE ACTION AND RACIAL GHETTOS

Invocation by Negroes of the Fourteenth Amendment in support of their efforts to break out of their racial ghettos and acquire houses in neighborhoods closed to them presents perhaps the best case history of the expanding meaning of "State action." Even today the prospect of a Negro moving into a white block throws panic into the hearts of most white residents, all of whom without doubt consider themselves completely free of prejudice and bigotry. Throughout the past half-century, and particularly since World War I, there has been a steady migration of Negroes from the South and a steady improvement of their economic standing, so that larger numbers of them are able to pay the purchase price demanded by white sellers of houses in white neighborhoods. During the same period real-estate lawyers, with the cooperation of zoning boards and other municipal agencies, have been exercising extreme ingenuity in devising ways to keep Negroes from moving into white neighborhoods. As each device is frustrated by a decision of the Supreme Court, the lawyers, carefully studying and weighing every word of the Court's opinion, devise new methods to get through or around the decision. The over-all picture is not unlike the chess game for the Negro's right to vote, described in an earlier chapter.

The most obvious and undoubtedly the most effective way of preventing Negroes from moving into white neighborhoods is the simple one of prohibiting them by law from doing so. This was, indeed, the first method tried, or at least the first to come before the Supreme Court. In 1917 the Court countered the move by declaring it unconstitutional.

The case was *Buchanan* v. *Warley*. It involved a municipal ordinance that simply forbade Negroes to occupy houses in blocks the majority of whose residents were white. To show their impartiality, the city fathers also forbade white persons to occupy houses in blocks the majority of whose residents were colored — a delicate touch reminiscent of Anatole France's admiration of the fine impartiality of French law, which prohibits the rich and poor equally to sleep under bridges.

The ordinance was attacked, not by a Negro wishing to buy a house in a white neighborhood, but by a white desiring to sell to a

Negro. His claim was that the right to sell one's house to whomever one wills is property of which one may not be deprived without due process of law. The ordinance seeking to bar him from selling to a Negro, though there might be no white purchaser willing to buy his house at the price offered by the Negro, was State action violating the "due process" clause of the Fourteenth Amendment.

The ordinance was defended as an exercise of the police power to maintain the purity of the races, prevent race riots, and preserve interracial tranquillity, which would be endangered if Negroes were allowed to move into white neighborhoods. The Supreme Court refused to accept this argument. The serious and difficult problems arising from a feeling of race hostility, the Court said, cannot be solved by depriving citizens of their constitutional rights and privileges.

Checked by this decision, the real-estate lawyers tried a slightly different approach. Instead of absolutely forbidding Negroes to move into white neighborhoods, they made it a matter of democratic choice. They devised an ordinance that forbade any Negro to establish a home in a white neighborhood except on the written consent of a majority of the white inhabitants of the neighborhood. Again to be fair and impartial, they also forbade whites to move into colored neighborhoods except on the written consent of a majority of the Negro residents.

The theory of this approach was that the discriminatory exclusion was not action by the State but the voluntary private action of the majority of the residents of the neighborhood. The Supreme Court was not impressed. The voluntary choice of a majority of the residents would have no practical effect upon the dissenting minority except by operation of the ordinance. In *Harmon* v. *Tyler* the Court, in 1927, unanimously declared the ordinance unconstitutional.

The ineffectuality of racial zoning ordinances to prevent the sale of houses by white owners to Negro purchasers set the real-estate lawyers off on a different tack. This time they employed the restrictive covenant, a device having a sanction of many centuries in real property law. Before the advent of zoning laws the residential character of neighborhoods was maintained by means of agreements among the owners not to use their properties for industrial or commercial purposes and not to sell their properties to persons who would use them for other than residential purposes. These restrictive covenants have always been enforced by the courts, not only against those who signed them but also against those who acquired land that was subject to the covenants. Real-estate lawyers in white neighborhoods accordingly began drafting restrictive covenants whereby the owners agreed for themselves, their heirs, and their assigns not to sell their houses to Negroes or allow Negroes to live in them except as domestic servants.

For twenty years it appeared that the lawyers had finally hit upon the answer to their problem. In *Corrigan* v. *Buckley* the Supreme Court, in 1926, upheld such restrictive covenants. The case arose in the District of Columbia, which is governed by Congress. Hence, enforcement of the racial restrictive covenant was opposed not under the " equal protection " clause, but on the ground that by enforcing it the Federal courts would be depriving the white sellers of property without due process of law. This attack had proved successful in *Buchanan* v. *Warley*, but it failed here. The Court held that the " due process " clause restricted only governmental action, not the voluntary action of private individuals. Accordingly, the Court upheld the issuance of an injunction forbidding a white owner who was subject to the racial restrictive covenant to sell his house to a Negro.

Since the " equal protection " clause also restricts only governmental action and does not affect the voluntary action of private individuals, it was clear that State court enforcement of racial restrictive covenants was likewise constitutional. At least the State courts so assumed. For twenty years they uniformly issued injunctions against white owners who threatened to sell their houses to Negroes in violation of such covenants and against Negroes who sought to buy the houses and move into them.

The real-estate lawyers therefore experienced a rude and unexpected awakening in 1948, when in *Shelley* v. *Kramer* and *Hurd* v. *Hodge* the Supreme Court in effect overruled *Corrigan* v. *Buckley* and unanimously held racial restrictive covenants unenforcible in both State and Federal courts. The former case involved a covenant affecting land within a State, the latter, land within the District of Columbia. The former was invalidated under the " equal protection " clause. The Court held that, while the Fourteenth Amendment did not require a white owner to sell to a Negro if he did not wish to do so, nor did it invalidate the voluntary agreements of private individuals, it did restrict State action giving legal effect to such agreements. As in *Harmon* v. *Tyler*, the voluntary agreements not to sell to Negroes would have no practical effect unless the State enforced them by its action. Courts, said the Supreme Court, are agencies of the State no less than legislatures and executive officials. An injunction issued by a State court enforcing a racial restrictive covenant is discriminatory State action barred by the " equal protection " clause, no less than a State statute or municipal ordinance forbidding Negroes to move into white neighborhoods.

The Supreme Court made short shrift of the claim that, since the State courts would also enforce racial restrictive covenants executed by Negroes to exclude whites from colored neighborhoods, both races were treated equally and neither race was denied the equal protection of the laws. The Fourteenth Amendment, the Court said, protects individuals, not races, and each individual Negro is entitled to equal treatment under law. Equal protection of the law is not achieved through indiscriminate imposition of inequalities.

In the Hurd case the Court held the covenant unenforcible in the Federal courts on the ground that the Civil Rights Act of 1866 — which is constitutionally applicable to the District of Columbia even if not to the States — assured to Negroes the same rights as whites to purchase, acquire, and own real property. The Court also held that enforcement of the covenant would violate Federal judicial policy.

Their heads bloody but unbowed, the real-estate lawyers refused to accept defeat. If they could not call upon courts to enforce racial restrictive covenants by enjoining whites from selling to Negroes and Negroes from purchasing from whites, they would make it unprofitable to do so, or at least make the white rebels pay for their ungentlemanly conduct. Accordingly, instead of suing for injunctions, they began to bring action for damages for breach of contract, claiming that the breach of the covenant depreciated the value of the near-by previously all-white property. In addition, they inserted in racial restrictive covenants provisions for payment of large sums to neighboring owners as liquidated damages should any signer breach the covenant.

With only Chief Justice Vinson dissenting, the Supreme Court in *Barrows* v. *Jackson* held that a verdict for damages for breach of a racial restrictive covenant would be unconstitutional State action in violation of the " equal protection " clause. The State would be accomplishing indirectly what it could not constitutionally do directly; for the fear of being required to pay damages would undoubtedly deter many willing white owners from selling to Negroes. This could be just as effective as a racial zoning ordinance or a court injunction and is just as unconstitutional.

Real-estate lawyers have recently experimented with another device, this time again borrowing from the old common law of real property. For perhaps a thousand years parcels of land have been conveyed in England and America subject to reversionary interests retained by the grantors. A grantor would convey land for as long as the grantee lived, or as long as he remained single, or upon a similar contingency. Upon the grantee's death or upon his marriage, title to the land automatically reverted to the grantor without the execution of any additional deeds or documents and without the necessity of obtaining a court decree declaring that the land had reverted.

In North Carolina land was recently conveyed to a municipality to be used as a public park for whites. The deed declared that, as soon as Negroes were admitted, the title would automatically revert to the grantor. If valid, the same device can easily be used to keep Negroes out of new residential developments. The developer need only put in his deed a provision that, when any parcel is no longer owned or occupied by a white, title to it shall automatically revert to the developer. The North Carolina supreme court has upheld the reverter device on the theory that the reversion is automatic and not the result of State action; but it is reasonably safe to predict that, when the Supreme Court is called upon to pass on the question, this device will prove as constitutionally vulnerable as the others. For better or worse, white owners who tremble at the thought of having a Negro family move in next door will in all probability just have to rely upon the voluntary restraints imposed by their neighbors' similar prejudices.

SEPARATE BUT EQUAL

The third major instrument employed after the Civil War by the Supreme Court to frustrate the objectives of the Reconstruction Congress and to leave to the States the responsibility for securing equality for the Negro was the " separate but equal " doctrine. Though developed somewhat later than the other two — vitiation of the "privileges or immunities" clause, and restriction of the Fourteenth Amendment to State action — it proved effective for more than half a century. The Roosevelt Court, in its rediscovery of "equal protection," began picking away at it; the Vinson Court accelerated the pace of disintegration, and the Warren Court administered the final blow.

The "separate but equal" doctrine was announced by the Court in 1896 in the case of *Plessy* v. *Ferguson.* Louisiana enacted a law requiring all railroads to have separate coaches for white and colored passengers, and made it a criminal offense for a person of one race to sit in a coach reserved for members of the other race. A man named Plessy, who was all of one-eighth Negro — one of his eight great-grandparents having been of African descent — entered a coach reserved for whites; the conductor ordered him to sit in the coach for colored passengers. When Plessy refused, he was arrested for violation of the law. With only one justice dissenting, the Supreme Court upheld the validity of the law.

Plessy argued first that enforced racial segregation was a badge of slavery and thus prohibited by the Thirteenth Amendment. This argument was futile for, as we have seen, the Court had earlier interpreted the Amendment to bar no more than involuntary servitude. His second and principal argument was that legally enforced separation of Negroes from whites necessarily implied inferiority of Negroes to whites and thus denied to Negroes the equal protection of the laws.

Only Justice Harlan (who thirteen years earlier had also been the lone dissenter in the Civil Rights Cases) found this argument acceptable. To the other eight justices, laws separating Negroes and whites do not imply the inferiority of Negroes any more than they imply the inferiority of whites. If enforced separation stamps the colored race with a badge of inferiority, it is not because of anything in the law but because the colored race chooses to put that construction on it. Legislation is powerless to overcome social prejudices or to eradicate racial instincts. If one race is inferior to the other socially, the Constitution of the United States cannot put them on the same plane. So long as the Louisiana statute did not require the railroad to put Plessy in a coach whose accommodations were physically inferior to those of coaches reserved to white passengers, Plessy was not discriminated against or denied the equal protection of the laws; and therefore he had no cause to complain to the Supreme Court.

SEGREGATED SCHOOLS: SEPARATE AND UNEQUAL

For more than forty years *Plessy* v. *Ferguson* and the " separate but equal " doctrine reigned supreme. It was in the field of education that the doctrine received its first setback, and it was in that field that it suffered its final defeat.

In 1927 the Supreme Court was not yet prepared to question the doctrine. A child of Chinese parentage was excluded from a white school under a State segregation law and assigned to a Negro school. In *Gong Lum* v. *Rice* the Court felt itself bound by *Plessy* v. *Ferguson* and the decisions that followed it. The Court held further that the question whether a Chinese child is to be considered a white or a Negro under a segregation law which apparently had not contemplated that children of any other races would enter public schools was exclusively for the State courts to decide, without interference from the United States Supreme Court.

The major attack upon the Plessy doctrine was launched in 1938, when the Supreme Court indicated that it would hold the States strictly to the " but equal " part of the formula. Earlier the Court had been more tolerant. In 1899 a local school board, finding that maintenance of separate high schools for whites and Negroes was expensive and imposed a severe burden upon taxpayers, decided temporarily to suspend the colored high school — although, of course, it did not permit the colored children to attend the white school. In *Cumming* v. *Richmond County Board* the Supreme Court held that the evidence did not conclusively establish that the school board had acted out of hostility to the colored race or out of the belief that in any event a primary-school education is all that Negro children should have. Accordingly, the Court declined to interfere with the school board's decision.

The Roosevelt Court adopted a sterner attitude. Racial prejudice is an expensive luxury; if Southern white taxpayers wanted it, they would have to pay the full price for it. The Court made this clear in

Missouri ex rel. Gaines v. *Canada,* which began the process of chipping away at the constitutional wall erected in *Plessy* v. *Ferguson* to separate the races.

Missouri, like most border States and all Southern States, did not admit Negroes to its free State university. Instead it established a separate college, Lincoln University, for Negroes. The State university maintained a law school, but there was none at Lincoln. In view of the small number of Negroes seeking a law degree, the cost of maintaining a separate law school for them would have been prohibitive. The States adjacent to Missouri on the north and west — Kansas, Nebraska, Iowa, and Illinois — permitted Negroes to attend their State universities, all of which included law schools. So Missouri passed a law providing that any Negro resident desiring a law degree could attend any of the adjacent State universities, and the tuition charged by them to out-of-State students would be paid by the State of Missouri.

This the Supreme Court refused to accept as equal treatment. To permit whites to obtain their legal education in Missouri and compel Negroes to travel to another State for theirs was not equality. Missouri would have to admit young Lloyd Gaines to the State law school or establish a law school for him within the State, even if no other Negro applied for admission thereto.

Although it was not then appreciated, the Gaines case foretold the ultimate doom of enforced racial segregation. The equality of separate facilities had long been little more than a fiction. Negro schools were almost invariably inferior to schools for whites. The physical facilities were worse, the teachers were paid less, fewer teachers were hired, more children were crowded into classrooms, equipment was inferior; on the average, at the time of the Gaines decision, the South probably spent on the education of each colored child half of what it spent for the education of each white child. Only thus was the South able to maintain its wasteful dual education system. The victims were not only the colored children but, to a lesser yet substantial extent, the white children who also had to be satisfied with an inferior schooling in order to satisfy their parents' prejudices.

If, however, the courts were going to insist upon actual equality of white and Negro schools, it was only a matter of time before the dual system would collapse under the weight of its unbearable economic burden. To a substantial extent it was the realization, on the part of at least the more realistic and forward-looking Southern leaders, that racial segregation in education was a luxury that could not indefinitely be carried by the South that made it possible for a unanimous Supreme Court in 1954 to declare it unconstitutional.

Exhibiting a degree of judicial statesmanship nourished by a century and a half of experience in issuing decisions violently unpopular in some segment of the American community, the Court wisely approached its ultimate objective through an attack upon segregation in higher education. For many reasons, resistance to racial integration at the university level was bound to be considerably more moderate than at the elementary school level.

After permitting the South to live with the Gaines decision for a decade, the Court resumed the attack with its decision in *Sipuel* v. *Board of Regents*. There a Negro sought admission to the law school at the State university. He was told that under the State's compulsory racial-segregation law he could not be admitted, but that he should be patient since a separate law school for Negroes was in the process of formation. The Supreme Court held that the Fourteenth Amendment did not impose an obligation of patience upon Negro youths seeking a legal education. To open the doors of the law school to whites while Negroes were required to wait was to deny Negroes the equal protection of the laws. The State of Oklahoma, the Court held in the follow-up case of *Fisher* v. *Hurst* decided in the same year, had the choice of admitting Negroes to the law school or closing the school to white applicants until the school for Negroes was ready to open.

Two years later in *Sweatt* v. *Painter* the Supreme Court interpreted the equality obligation in such a way as to make separate professional school legally impossible. Under the pressure of lawsuits the State of Texas had established a law school for its Negro residents. It had a student body of 23 (the white law school had 850), 5 faculty members (the white school had 19), and a library of 16,000 volumes (the white school had 65,000).

The Supreme Court unanimously held that this did not constitute equality. Far more important, the Court also held that a law school that excludes members of the racial group that numbers 85 per cent of the State's population — including most of the lawyers, judges, witnesses, jurymen, and court officials with whom the Negro law student will deal when he becomes a lawyer — does not and cannot accord to the Negro students the advantages and benefits accorded to students attending the white school. Put simply, the Court held that racial segregation in law schools is by its very nature inequality.

Clearly, the reasoning applicable to law schools is equally applicable to all professional schools. The legal effect of the Sweatt case, therefore, was to outlaw racial segregation, at least at the level of university professional schools.

On the same day that the Sweatt decision was announced, the Court handed down the decision in *McLaurin* v. *Oklahoma State Regents*. The decision held in effect that Negroes admitted to white universities may not be segregated within the school. McLaurin, a Negro candidate for a doctorate in education, succeeded in gaining admission to the University of Oklahoma; but his troubles had only begun. First he was required to sit at a designated desk in an anteroom, adjoining the classroom, from which he could hear though not see the professor. He was not permitted to use the regular desks in the reading room, or to eat in the school cafeteria at the same time as the other students. Then, as he started a lawsuit to remove these restrictions, the university officials altered them. He was allowed to sit in the classroom, but a rail and low curtain were placed around his seat, and a sign was hung on it, reading: "Reserved for Colored."

McLaurin's white fellow students, becoming somewhat exasperated with both the university officials and the Oklahoma segregation laws, took matters in their own hands and forcibly removed the railing, curtain, and sign. Thereupon the university officials, no doubt embarrassed but feeling bound by the State's segregation laws, required McLaurin to sit in a row specified for colored students and at specified tables in the library and cafeteria.

Even this nominal and purely symbolic separation was unacceptable to the Supreme Court. The conditions under which McLaurin was required to receive his education, it held, deprived him of the equal protection of the laws. Having been admitted to a State-supported graduate school, he must receive the same treatment at the hands of the State as students of other races. Equal protection means equality, not something less.

The Sipuel, Sweatt, and McLaurin decisions raised little more than a ripple of discontent in the South. Within two years over a thousand Negroes were attending Southern graduate and professional schools with no visible ill effects. On the contrary, campus newspapers in a number of white colleges openly called for integration. The stage was set for outright invalidation of racial segregation in its most prevalent form, segregated elementary-school education, and abrogation of the " separate but equal " doctrine of *Plessy* v. *Ferguson.*

This the Supreme Court accomplished in 1954 by its unanimous decision in *Brown* v. *Board of Education.* Brushing aside all questions as to the relative physical superiority or inferiority of the schools attended by these colored children, the Court hit at the heart of the problem. In effect it adopted the " badge of slavery " concept rejected by all but Justice Harlan in *Plessy* v. *Ferguson.*

Segregation of white and colored children in the public schools, the Court said, has a detrimental effect upon the colored children. The impact is greater when it has the sanction of law; for the policy of separating the races is usually interpreted as denoting the inferiority of the Negro group. A sense of inferiority affects the motivation of a child to learn. Segregation with the sanction of law, therefore, has a tendency to retard the educational and mental development of Negro children and to deprive them of some of the benefits they would receive in a racially integrated school system.

In the field of public education, the Court concluded, the doctrine of " separate but equal " has no place. Separate educational facilities are inherently unequal and are therefore unconstitutional as a denial of the equal protection of the laws.

At the same time that this decision was handed down, the Court held in *Bolling* v. *Sharpe* that racial segregation in the public schools of the District of Columbia was likewise unconstitutional. Since the Federal government is not subject to the " equal protection " clause, the result was based on the " due process " clause of the Fifth Amendment.

TRANSPORTATION AND THE DEMISE OF PLESSY

In the Brown case the Court did not by express language completely overrule *Plessy* v. *Ferguson.* It held only that the doctrine of " separate but equal " could not constitutionally be applied to education. The Plessy case itself had involved segregation in transportation on railroad coaches. But while the Court was outlawing racial segregation in education it was, by a somewhat different method, outlawing legally enforced racial segregation in transportation.

During the Reconstruction era the legislature of Louisiana enacted a law *prohibiting* railroads and other public carriers to discriminate against any passenger on account of race and color. In 1878, after the settlement of the Hayes-Tilden election dispute, the Supreme Court in *Hall* v. *DeCuir* held this statute unconstitutional in so far as it affected trains traveling between States, on the ground that it interfered with interstate commerce. Since a neighboring State might pass a law *requiring* racial segregation of passengers, the result would be that the free flow of interstate commerce would be seriously hampered by wholesale shifting of passengers as the train reached the State border.

In 1946, in *Morgan* v. *Virginia* the Supreme Court ruled that what was sauce for the goose was equally sauce for the gander. It invalidated, in so far as it was applicable to passengers traveling between States, a Virginia law requiring the segregation of white and colored passengers. If, said the Court, a State law *prohibiting* segregation on interstate carriers is an unconstitutional burden on interstate commerce, so too is a State law *commanding* such segregation.

The Morgan case held only that a State could not constitutionally require racial segregation on interstate carriers; it did not hold that the railroad companies themselves could not legally segregate their colored passengers. However, interstate carriers are subject to the Federal Interstate Commerce Law, one section of which makes it unlawful for any interstate carrier to subject any person to any undue or unreasonable prejudice or disadvantage in any respect whatsoever.

In *Mitchell* v. *United States,* decided in 1941, a Negro passenger named Mitchell, who held a first-class ticket, was denied a Pullman seat, although such a seat was unoccupied and would have been available to him if he had been white. The rules of the railroad had allotted a limited amount of Pullman space for Negro use; as all that space was occupied, Mitchell was required to ride in a second-class coach. The Supreme Court held that he had thereby been subjected to an unreasonable disadvantage in violation of the Interstate Commerce Law.

In *Henderson* v. *United States* the Court applied to transportation the reasoning it had in the same year employed in *McLaurin* v.

Oklahoma to require equal treatment of Negroes admitted to a State university. In the Henderson case the Court held it an unreasonable disadvantage under the Interstate Commerce Law to compel a Negro passenger to wait until a seat became vacant at a dining-car table set aside for Negro passengers, if at the time unoccupied seats were available at other tables. But the Court went even further; it held that curtains, partitions, and signs employed to set off the Negroes' tables from the whites' subjected the Negroes to unreasonable discrimination in violation of the Law.

The effect of the Henderson decision was to hold segregation in trains to be discrimination. If it is discrimination, then obviously under the " equal protection " clause it may not constitutionally be compelled by a State law. The substantial result of the Henderson case, therefore, was to overrule *Plessy* v. *Ferguson*, even though that case was not even mentioned in the Henderson decision.

When the Henderson case is considered along with *Brown* v. *Board of Education*, it is safe to say that the " separate but equal " doctrine is now of little more than historic significance. If enforced segregation in transportation and enforced segregation in education are both acts of unconstitutional discrimination, there is no reason to believe that the Supreme Court will sanction enforced segregation in any other area. *Plessy* v. *Ferguson* may safely be said to have passed away with few to mourn it north of the Mason-Dixon line.

STATE ANTI–DISCRIMINATION LAWS

The decisions discussed in this chapter have held only that the Fourteenth Amendment prohibits racial discrimination and segregation by State law or action of State officials or agencies. The Amendment does not bar racial discrimination or segregation by private individuals unconnected with government. The Civil Rights Cases denied to Congress the power to enact legislation outlawing racial discrimination by private persons. The decision, however, left the States free to enact such laws. Accordingly, immediately after the decision in that case, the Northern States began enacting laws prohibiting various types of racial and religious discrimination by private persons. These statutes followed the pattern of the Civil Rights Act of 1875 and were limited to outlawing racial discrimination in places of public accommodation — inns, public conveyances, theaters, and the like. Over the years, however, the definition of "public accommodation" has been steadily broadened in many of these statutes so as to include a wide variety of places, such as retail shops, libraries, restaurants, and others. The constitutionality of these statutes was upheld by the Supreme Court in 1948 in the case of *Bob-Lo Excursion Co.* v. *Michigan.*

Beginning in 1945 the Northern States began enacting laws banning racial and religious discrimination in private employment. These statutes, known as Fair Employment Practices Acts, are spreading rapidly, and today about one-quarter of all the States in the Union have such laws. While the constitutionality of these statutes has never been directly passed upon by the Supreme Court, its decision in *Railway Mail Association* v. *Corsi,* upholding a New York law prohibiting racial or religious discrimination by labor unions, makes it clear that Fair Employment Practices Acts would undoubtedly be held constitutional.

Recently, the pattern of Fair Employment Practices Acts has been extended to other areas. A number of States in the Northeast have enacted Fair Education Practices Acts, prohibiting racial or religious discrimination in admission to private schools and colleges. It is only a question of time before Fair Housing Practices Acts will likewise be adopted among the Northern States. The past decisions of the Supreme Court give no reason to fear for the constitutionality of these and similar State anti-discrimination laws.

There is unfortunately little reason to expect or even hope that similar laws will be enacted to any appreciable extent in the Southern States within the foreseeable future. Negroes there must still look to the Federal government and to enlightened public opinion for the protection of their civil rights. Thus, protection and preservation of the liberties of Negroes is the common responsibility of the Federal government, the States, and the American people — which, after all, is equally true of the liberties of all Americans.

CHAPTER 10. *Today and Tomorrow*

Madison, it will be remembered, was dubious about the efficacy of a bill of rights, which, he thought, might be little more than a "parchment barrier." A constitutional declaration of rights would be of value only if "independent tribunals of justice" would "consider themselves in a peculiar manner the guardians of those rights."

More than eight score years have passed since the Bill of Rights was added to the Constitution — a length of time sufficient to justify an estimation of the validity of Madison's prediction. Has the Bill of Rights been effective in protecting the liberties of Americans, or has it been only a parchment barrier of merely exhortatory value? To what extent has the highest independent tribunal of justice in the nation considered itself in a peculiar manner the guardian of the Bill of Rights, and to what extent has it been effective in that role? Before an answer to these questions is essayed, some evaluation is necessary of the state of civil liberties today and of their outlook in the immediate future.

LIBERTY OF BELIEF AND DISBELIEF

Despite occasional restrictions upon the free exercise of religion, it is probably true that, of all liberties of Americans, freedom of worship is most esteemed and most secure. Even the Cold War, which seriously affected other liberties, has done little damage to religious liberty, as the Russian Orthodox Church case testifies. Nor is there anything now visible on the horizon that threatens this enviable state of affairs. It is fairly safe to predict that the free exercise of religion in the United States will not be subject to serious governmental restriction in the foreseeable future.

Unfortunately, so sanguine a prediction cannot be made in respect to the no-establishment aspect of the First Amendment — at least not as it has been interpreted by the Supreme Court in the McCollum case. A substantial segment of organized religion has not made its peace with that case or accepted its broad principle of the separation of church and state. The Roman Catholic Church in particular is unable to reconcile itself to the concept of governmental neutrality between belief and disbelief.

The arena in which the attack upon the broad principle of separation is likely to be most severe in the immediate future is religion in public education. This is hardly surprising, for our public schools are at the same time a major medium for the transmission of our culture and a major instrumentality for the shaping of that culture. The McCollum decision cast the mantle of constitutional protection on the secularity of our public-school system, and many religiously motivated persons fear that unless the decision is overruled or substantially modified the inevitable result will be the secularization of our culture.

The tremendous expansion of religious institutions and particularly the advances in religious education during the past several years would seem to cast doubt on the validity of this fear. But the point is not whether the fear is justified; the point is that it is real and deep-seated. So long as it exists the public schools will continue to be subjected to pressures to involve themselves in the field of religious education. Means will be sought to evade or even frustrate the McCollum decision.

The ultimate goal of these religiously motivated persons and particularly the Roman Catholic Church is the abrogation of the McCollum decision by the Supreme Court itself. The Court had an opportunity and was called upon to do just that when the Zorach case was before it. Notwithstanding some ambiguous language in that decision, it is now quite clear that the Court rejected the opportunity and that the principles of the McCollum decision are still the law of the land, and will probably remain so for some time.

LIBERTY OF SPEECH AND SILENCE

Freedom of political expression is not secured through the use of a formula — even so liberal a formula as the " clear and present danger " test. The use of that test by the Roosevelt Court manifested rather than was the cause of the Court's liberal approach toward freedom of speech. Conversely, use by the post-World War I Court of the "evil intent" or the "evil tendency" test was merely an indication of its restrictive views on the protection accorded to speech by the First Amendment. When the Vinson Court, in upholding the constitutionality of the Smith Act in the Dennis case, modified the language of the "clear and present danger," it indicated an intent to retreat from the liberal approach of the Roosevelt Court. The fact that it did not rely on "evil intent" or "evil tendency" showed that it was not prepared to retreat all the way to the position of the post-World War I Court.

To what extent the Dennis decision represents the present thinking of the Court is difficult to judge. Chief Justice Vinson's opinion, concurred in by only three other justices, never represented the expressed view of a majority of the Court. After the decision was handed down Vinson died and was replaced by Chief Justice Warren, who in other instances has manifested a significantly more liberal attitude toward political liberties. As of this writing the Warren Court has not had to pass on the question of how far political expression is constitutionally protected, nor has it expressed its views on the "clear and present danger" test. Nevertheless, there is more than a fair chance that, barring unfavorable circumstances such as a revival of violent McCarthyism, the Court's free-speech decisions in the near future will signify a more liberal attitude than that expressed in the Dennis case.

The Warren court has given an indication of its attitude to one aspect of the speech clause of the First Amendment — freedom of silence. In the Quinn case it went out of its way to express the view that the power of Congress to investigate is not unlimited and that accordingly a witness is constitutionally entitled to keep his silence where a Congressional committee seeks to pry into his private affairs for a purpose unrelated to a valid legislative function. The full meaning and implication of this dictum must await the time when the Court is called upon to review the contempt conviction of a private citizen who pleads only the First Amendment in refusing to answer a question relating to affiliation with the Communist Party.

It is probable that for the present and in the immediate future the real danger to freedom of political speech will lie not so much in government restraints or punishments as in action by private groups and individuals. Except to the extent that political expression was involved in prosecutions based upon affiliation with the Communist Party, prosecutions for speech were rare even at the height of the McCarthy nightmare. Then as now, the major restraint upon free political expression was not the fear of criminal prosecution. It was, first, fear of non-criminal sanctions, such as loss of employment and social ostracism; and, second, inability to obtain a forum for the expression of unpopular political views. Not only civil-service employees but even employees in many private industries are still fearful of expressing political views that might be considered subversive by their employers; proponents of unconventional or unpopular political views are still frequently unable to "hire a hall" to express these views or to obtain time on radio or television for that purpose. In the foreseeable future, private action, which is not subject to the Bill of Rights, is likely to be a more potent deterrent upon free political speech than government restraints.

LIBERTY OF PETITION, ASSEMBLY, AND ASSOCIATION

The Dennis decision was followed by the prosecution and conviction under the Smith Act of a group of "second-string" Communists, and this was followed by the prosecution and conviction of "third-string" Communists. In all these cases prosecution was based not on mere membership in the Party but on active participation in its affairs and in the furtherance of its objectives. The Supreme Court has consistently refused to upset these convictions.

With the approaching exhaustion of available active Communists — first, second, or third string — some Federal prosecuting attorneys have turned their attention to passive Communists. Prosecutions have been undertaken and convictions obtained under the provision of the Smith Act making it a crime to be a member (with knowledge of its purposes) of an organization engaged in advocating the violent overthrow of the government. The Supreme Court has as yet not had occasion to pass on the constitutionality of the "membership" provision of the Smith Act, although a consideration of that issue by the Court cannot be long delayed. When that happens, the Court may well have to commit itself either to the Jackson view that the Communist Party is a criminal conspiracy whose members are to be treated as criminal conspirators with no rights protected by the First Amendment, or to the Black-Douglas view that it is a radical political party within the tradition of American radical political movements.

Whether or not the Court will sustain criminal punishment for Communist Party affiliation, there are no lack of non-penal sanctions, and these will probably continue for many years. There is hardly a government agency, Federal, State or municipal, which does not bar Communists from employment. Private industries engaged in defense work likewise bar Communists from employment. The doors of the legal and many other professions are closed to them in most if not all States. Communists are barred from election to public office in many States, are excluded from participating in the benefits of public housing, are disqualified from labor-union leadership and often membership, and are forbidden to travel abroad. If aliens they are subject to deportation — if drafted, to dishonorable discharge. Whatever the Supreme Court should decide, it is clear that in the eyes of the general American community the Communist Party is a criminal conspiracy and its members the equivalent of criminals. Barring the eruption of another war in which the United States and Soviet Russia will again be allies against a common enemy, it is not likely that this situation will change substantially in the near future.

Already, however, there has set in a noticeable amelioration of the condition of *former* Communists, even those who have not become vociferous anti-Communists, and of non-Communists who had cooperated with the Communists in furtherance of common objectives. Membership in an organization on the Attorney General's list entails noticeably less serious consequences than it did in 1952. Should the relaxation of international tensions that followed the Geneva Conference and the softening of Soviet international policies continue, an even more tolerant approach to freedom of association may be predicted.

LIBERTY OF KNOWLEDGE AND LEARNING

What was said of freedom of political expression is equally true here: the danger to freedom of intellectual inquiry and artistic expression lies not so much in government restraints or punishments as in the action of private groups and individuals. Fear of government reprisal for non-conformist writing and teaching has by no means altogether disappeared. Teachers in public educational institutions still do not subject American economic, political, and social institutions to objective scrutiny to anywhere near the same extent as twenty or even ten years ago. The investigation by Senator James Eastland of subversion in the New York press was without doubt intended to put the fear of the Senator into the hearts of the editors of the New York *Times,* just as the earlier investigation by Senator McCarthy was intended to have a similar effect on the editors of the New York *Post.* The recent investigation of tax-exempt foundations was similarly motivated.

Nevertheless, the major danger of restraint probably lies in the area of private censorship, suppression, and boycott, as Paul Blanshard's recent book *The Right to Read* clearly indicates. Senator Eastland's efforts to change the editorial policies of the New York *Times* proved as futile as Senator McCarthy's attempt to change the editorial policies of the New York *Post.* There has been no noticeable change in the activities of the Fund for the Republic or other tax-exempt foundations. The Supreme Court's decision in the *Miracle* and other motion-picture cases has been followed by State court decisions invalidating a number of movie-censorship statutes. Government restraints appear to be lessening on all fronts.

Private suppression, on the other hand, appears to be on the increase. Motion pictures that government censors are constitutionally prohibited from suppressing are often kept from the public because of fear of organized private boycott. Private "legions of decency" police movie houses and neighborhood bookstores. Veteran groups scrutinize the shelves in public libraries.

Attacks on religion, the Supreme Court said in the *Miracle* case, are protected by the First Amendment from government suppression, but the voluntary television and motion-picture codes strongly disapprove of such attacks, and it is a rare television or movie producer who would put on a program that might even remotely be deemed a criticism of religion or clergymen. Radio and television companies studiously avoid programs that are "too controversial." Paradoxically, in this area government sometimes acts as an ally of freedom; for it is only the policy of the Federal Communications Commission to obtain balanced television programs that sometimes insures a forum for less orthodox views of public issues.

FAIR PLAY AND FAIR TRIAL

The Supreme Court's decision in the Quinn case has given new life to the Fifth Amendment privilege against self-incrimination. Indeed, many contend that the privilege is often abused and employed for purposes not intended by the fathers of the Bill of Rights — as where it is used to avoid being compelled to name names. Whether or not this is so, courts and government investigating agencies have interpreted the Quinn decision as conferring a fairly broad immunity from testifying by one who asserts the privilege.

The Court's holding in the Quinn and Slochower cases that assertion of the privilege does not constitute an admission of guilt is likely also to have some salutary effects. Before the Slochower decision a government employee — Federal, State, or municipal — who asserted the privilege faced almost certain immediate discharge. The same was probably true of workers in defense plants, radio and television studios, newspapers (even the New York *Times* discharged employees who asserted the privilege in the course of Senator Eastland's investigation), and many if not most private colleges and libraries. The full effect of the Slochower decision on this practice cannot yet be predicted with any degree of certainty; but one can hardly doubt that it will have a substantial ameliorative effect.

Lately, too, there has been a considerable improvement in the conducting of government investigations, particularly of subversion. There has been a noticeable decline in the number of these investigations, and it is rare for those that are held to be reported on the front page or to receive considerable newspaper coverage. Recent investigations have manifested a substantial improvement in fairness and in respecting the constitutional rights of witnesses.

Wiretapping and the use of other electronic eavesdropping devices by government agents and particularly law-enforcement officials remain serious problems. It is a difficult task to reconcile the citizen's claim to privacy with the demands of prosecuting officials not to be unduly hampered in obtaining the conviction and punishment of criminals. There is no convincing evidence that the percentage of criminals apprehended by Federal agents and convicted in Federal courts, where wiretap and other illegally obtained evidence is excluded, is lower than that of criminals apprehended by State police officers and convicted in State courts, where illegally obtained evidence is admissible. This fact may well be a major reason on the one hand for the failure of the Department of Justice to obtain Congressional legislation authorizing wiretapping by Federal agents, and on the other hand for the increasing demand in many States for legislation to curb wiretapping by State police officers.

LIBERTY OF FRANCHISE

The steady forward progress of the Southern Negro's struggle toward the ballot box may have been temporarily halted in the wake of the reaction to the school segregation decision. In the Deep South there have been renewed outbreaks of violence and threats of violence against Negroes seeking to exercise their right to vote. Legislators are again casting around for "legal" ways to evade the Supreme Court's decisions outlawing racial discrimination in elections and primaries. It can hardly be doubted that many white election officials conducting literacy or similar tests for new voters are giving considerable weight to the color of the applicant's skin.

The halt, however, is only temporary. Barring a serious break between North and South, which seems highly improbable, the Negro's forward march toward equality of suffrage is certain to be resumed before long. Indeed, the school segregation decision may actually accelerate the march. The decision and the efforts of the South to frustrate it have aroused political awareness among many Southern Negroes who previously eschewed politics, with the result that many more Negroes will seek to exercise the franchise. Simultaneously, the Northern Negro's feeling of unity with his brother below the Mason-Dixon line has been intensified, and the demand for Federal protection of the Southern Negro's right to vote has become nationwide. Even Southern Senators and Congressmen find it necessary to take some cognizance of this demand, as is evidenced by the offer of their leaders to vote for a constitutional amendment outlawing the poll tax.

Abolition of the poll tax is, of course, a minimal reform, particularly in the present period of prosperity. Yet the fact that the South is willing to offer it is a clear indication that the forward progress has not been permanently halted. If there is any liberty which is fairly certain of final achievement within the comparatively near future it is probably the Negro's right to vote.

Achievement of this goal will not mean achievement of equality of franchise. The disproportion in weight between rural and urban votes constitutes a substantial infringement upon liberty of franchise. No satisfactory solution of this problem is in sight. So long as the upper houses of our Federal legislature and most of our State legislatures represent geographical units (States or counties) rather than population units, inequality will remain. The only area where reform is realistically possible is in the selection of members of the lower houses. Proposals for such reform do not appear to be making much headway. It is unlikely too that the Supreme Court will soon overrule its decisions that distribution of the vote between rural and urban areas presents a political rather than a juridical question and therefore is not subject to judicial review. If there is to be any amelioration of the situation it may lie in the continuance of the present movement of populations away from the cities into the suburbs. If the equal vote will not come to the city dweller, perhaps he will move to a place where he can get it.

LIBERTY OF ENTRY, SOJOURN, AND EXIT

There is nothing to indicate any likelihood that the Supreme Court will soon modify its decisions that aliens have no judicially enforcible constitutional rights to enter the country or to become citizens after they enter. Reform and liberalization of our immigration and naturalization laws will remain the primary responsibility of Congress.

A somewhat more optimistic prediction is justifiable in respect to the right to stay and the right to leave. The Supreme Court, it is true, is not likely to interfere with the judgment of Congress as to what shall constitute grounds for deportation of aliens — even the patently unfair and cruel judgment that an alien who has committed an act (such as joining the Communist Party) that was perfectly legal at the time it was committed may be torn from his American wife and children and deported to a country from which he fled to save his life or which he left during infancy. It is, however, quite probable that the Court will exercise increasing scrutiny as to the fairness of the procedure employed by the government in determining whether the alien actually committed the deportable act. It is not unreasonable to expect that at some time in the not too distant future the Court will hold that confidential, unsworn testimony may not constitutionally be used against an alien in a deportation proceeding; that the alien has the right to face and cross-examine his accuser; that he may be represented by counsel; and that he is entitled to other procedural safeguards which together make up the Anglo-American concept of fair play.

An optimistic outlook is also justified in respect to a citizen's right to travel. The State Department has until now avoided a review by the Supreme Court of lower-court decisions that a citizen has a constitutionally protected right to travel and that therefore the Department may not arbitrarily and without a hearing deny a citizen's application for a passport to travel abroad. Should the issue reach the Supreme Court, there is a good chance that the lower-court decisions will be upheld and that the right to travel abroad will be declared to be a liberty of Americans.

LIBERTY AND EQUALITY

Perhaps the most critical issue in civil liberties today is that of racial segregation in the South. The Supreme Court's decision outlawing racial segregation in public elementary schools marked a milestone in the history of Negro–white relations in the United States. The decision itself was clearly foreshadowed by the Court's previous decisions invalidating segregation at the university level, and the school decision came as no great surprise even in the South. For that reason the immediate repercussions were almost unbelievably mild — so mild, in fact, that for a short time it appeared that integration at the elementary and secondary-school level might proceed almost as smoothly as had been going on at the university and professional-school level.

When the Southern reaction did manifest itself more than a year after the decision itself, it was as vigorous as it was delayed. There were renewed outbreaks of violence against individual Negroes, particularly those affiliated with the National Association for the Advancement of Colored People. The association itself became the subject of attack, with its members often barred from public teaching positions or other public employment. Legislatures in the South revived the " interposition " movement of pre-Civil War days and cast about for means to frustrate the Court's decision. Laws were passed authorizing the abolition of the public-school system if implementation of the decision should be attempted, or cutting off public funds from schools not practicing racial segregation.

Cries of defiance could be heard all through the South. In Washington, ninety-six Southern Senators and Representatives issued a declaration attacking the Supreme Court and pledging themselves " to use all lawful means to bring about a reversal " of its decision — which they asserted was " contrary to the Constitution " — and " to prevent the use of force in its implementation." One Senator warned that every nominee to the Federal bench would be examined closely as to his views on segregation and those opposed to it would not be confirmed. James Eastland of Mississippi, chairman of the Senate Judiciary Committee, made it clear that he would block approval of the President's nomination of Solicitor General Simon Sobeloff to the Federal Circuit Court bench because the latter had filed a brief *amicus curiae* with the Supreme Court in support of desegregation.

If these strident cries of defiance were intended to intimidate the Supreme Court or influence its further actions, it is extremely doubtful that they achieved any success. Almost simultaneously with the publication of the proclamation by the ninety-six Congressmen, the Court unanimously ordered the University of Florida immediately to admit a qualified Negro applicant to its law school, and affirmed, also unanimously, a lower-court decision that racial segregation in tax-supported colleges is unconstitutional.

Southern resistance to integration is serious and must be reckoned with. Yet its importance should not be overestimated. Many factors combine to assure substantial racial integration throughout the South within the near future. First is the recognition that, if integration is prevented, substantially equal separate facilities will have to be provided for Negro children at a cost that may well prove prohibitive. The rising tide of Negro political activity is another important factor to be considered. A third is the fact that opposition to integration among Southerners manifests itself in direct proportion to their age; the diehards are to be found mostly among the older generation. Young men who have been drafted into the army and have served and lived together with Negroes for two years or more are less likely to react hysterically at the prospect of having their children go to school together with the children of their colored comrades in arms. The rapidly increasing industrialization of the South is bound to have a similar effect upon whites working in factories side by side with Negroes. The shouting and the tumult in the South are really but the death-cry of a dying system.

That the above view is not merely wishful thinking is evidenced by the significant report of a careful study made by the New York *Times* and released on March 13, 1956, the day after the publication of the Southern Congressmen's declaration. The study shows that, even as the ninety-six Congressmen were proclaiming that they would never yield to integration, integration was actually taking place in many of their own communities. The conclusion reached by the *Times* on the basis of its study was that "some form of compliance with the Supreme Court's order to desegregate the public schools seems inevitable in most Southern states — perhaps in all."

The importance of the *Times* study warrants setting forth here its own summary of the report:

> A majority of Southerners want to deal with the problem of integration by legal means. They usually disavow violence and are afraid of it, although there still may be sporadic outbreaks.
>
> Generally white Southerners seem more troubled, confused and resentful than rebellious. They are troubled by the demand that they make a radical change in their settled and preferred social patterns. They are confused by the dilemma that confronts them — how to preserve the structure of their society and yet comply with the law of the land. They are resentful of badgering by outsiders.
>
> While seeking adjustment, they are resisting drastic change by various devices to nullify, delay or moderate the impact of desegregation.
>
> Southern Negroes likewise are troubled and sometimes resentful. In the main, they want the rights vouchsafed to them by the highest court in the land. In some cases hesitantly, in others resolutely, they are demanding the admission of their children to mixed schools.
>
> The interplay of white and Negro forces has so far produced a patchwork pattern in the eighteen public school systems. The degree of school integration ranges from nil in Mississippi to complete in the nation's capital.

The commonest index to the degree of compliance is the ratio of Negro population to white in any given area. Where the ratio is low integration is proceeding; where it is high there is resistance.

But how long can resistance continue?

White spokesmen talk of staving off the unwelcome day for twenty to twenty-five years. The very fact that they set a limit on their hopes suggests that they foresee eventual integration.

Age-old community alignments and customs are changing in the South. The Negro is gaining political and economic power. Among the whites, youth is less adamant than age.

On the basis of the foregoing summary of the status of civil liberties in the United States today and of their prospects in the immediate future, the following comments may be made on the questions propounded at the beginning of this chapter: Has the Bill of Rights been effective in protecting the liberties of Americans? To what extent has the Supreme Court been an effective guardian of the Bill of Rights?

(1) As democracy is indivisible, so our liberties are interdependent. When one liberty is under attack, the others are endangered. When political liberty is threatened, religious liberty and racial equality are in danger. The statute under which a group of Negroes in Montgomery, Alabama, were indicted for boycotting segregated buses had originally been enacted to restrict labor unions. It is hardly surprising that the Federal government's experiment in investigating and otherwise harassing unorthodox political organizations should be emulated by the South in its treatment of the National Association for the Advancement of Colored People. Conversely, the improvement in Federal trial and investigation procedures has likewise been emulated; the South Carolina statute providing for the dismissal of any public employee who is a member of the National Association for the Advancement of Colored People provides that the employee shall have a fair trial with the right to face and cross-examine his accusers.

(2) The state of our liberties is tied up with the state of our nation. National and international relations cast their reflection on the Bill of Rights. Just as the Bolshevik revolution brought on a crisis in the condition of American liberties in the post-World War I period, so too did Soviet aggression in Europe and Asia bring on a similar crisis in the post-World War II period. The recent improvement in the status of our liberties is attributable to the easing in

world tensions ensuing upon the apparent change in Soviet Russia's international policies, and perhaps also in part to the widespread prosperity with which we are now blessed.

(3) American liberties move in cycles. Periods of liberalism are followed by periods of repression, which in turn are followed by periods of liberalism. If we were to plot the progress of liberties on a graph we would find a succession of hills and valleys rather than a straight line.

(4) Nevertheless, the trend has clearly and definitely been upward. The march of civil liberties in American history has been forward; temporary halts or retreats have been overcome and the forward march resumed. Even the most fanatic defender of segregation does not urge repeal of the Fourteenth Amendment or abrogation of the decisions entitling Negroes to equality in their separate facilities. In the same decision (*Gitlow* v. *New York*) where the Supreme Court upheld the "evil intent" and "evil tendency" test for seditious utterances, it accepted the responsibility of passing upon complaints of denial of liberties against State and municipal officials. The persecution suffered by Jehovah's Witnesses, severe and cruel as it has been, compares favorably with that suffered a century earlier by the Mormons. Persons of Japanese or Chinese descent may become naturalized citizens today; as recently as fifteen years ago they could not. These illustrations could be multiplied; they all show the forward progress of American liberties.

(5) In this forward progress the Bill of Rights has played a crucial role. Even in periods of deep darkness it has been a beacon of light for seekers of liberty. Like the Magna Carta in England, it has been the rallying point for defenders of freedom. It has, as Madison predicted, proved "a good ground for an appeal to the sense of the community." Senator McCarthy's turbulent and now happily-ended excursion in despotism shows that an appeal to the sense of the community will sooner or later be answered.

(6) The Supreme Court, too, has played a crucial role in this forward progress. At times it might perhaps have moved at a faster pace. It may at times have underestimated the good sense of the community. In its endeavor not to advance too far ahead of public opinion, it may have occasionally been too cautious and too conservative. If it had not announced the "separate but equal" rule in the Plessy case in 1896, it would not have had to outlaw racial segre-

gation in 1954, and racial integration would have come a half-century earlier and perhaps with less disturbance. If it had not upheld the sedition convictions in the early 1920's, Congress might not have adopted the Smith Act in 1940 or the Communist Control Act in 1954. If, at the turn of the twentieth century, it had recognized the penal nature of deportation and had accorded to aliens the substantive protection of the Bill of Rights, we would not now have a deportation policy and practice whose Draconian consequences have been vividly portrayed by Will Maslow (in an article in the March 1956 issue of the *Columbia Law Review*).

Nevertheless, the Supreme Court has in large measure fulfilled its responsibilities as guardian of the Bill of Rights. By and large it has kept its head when all others have lost theirs. If the Negro finally achieves equality, it will be by action of the Supreme Court, not of Congress, which has not enacted a civil rights measure for three-quarters of a century. If our public schools are free or relatively free from sectarianism it is because of the Supreme Court's decision in the McCollum case; and if parents dissatisfied with the secularity of public education send their children to parochial schools, it is because the Court secured their right to do so in the Pierce case. Harry Bridges is still in the United States, despite government efforts worthy of a more commendable objective, only because the Supreme Court recognizes its obligation to protect the rights of the unpopular and the despised. Many Jehovah's Witnesses can gratefully testify to that.

Here, too, illustrations could be multiplied. There is no need to do so, for that would merely repeat what is in the rest of this book. An objective appraisal of the history of the Supreme Court cannot but come to the conclusion that by and large it has fulfilled the responsibility committed to it to guard the Bill of Rights and protect the liberties of Americans.

APPENDIX

Liberties Guaranteed by the Constitution and Bill of Rights

Preamble to the Constitution

We the People of the United States, in Order to form a more perfect Union, establish Justice, insure domestic Tranquility, provide for the common defence, promote the general Welfare, and Secure the Blessings of Liberty to ourselves and our Posterity, do ordain and establish this Constitution for the United States of America.

Article I, Section 9

The Privilege of the Writ of Habeas Corpus shall not be suspended, unless when in Cases of Rebellion or Invasion the public Safety may require it.

No Bill of Attainder or ex post facto Law shall be passed.

Section 10

No State shall . . . pass any Bill of Attainder, ex post facto Law, or Law impairing the Obligation of Contracts . . .

Article III, Section 2

The Trial of all Crimes, except in Cases of Impeachment, shall be by Jury; and such Trial shall be held in the State where the said Crimes shall have been committed; but when not committed within any State, the Trial shall be at such Place and Places as the Congress may by Law have directed.

Section 3

Treason against the United States, shall consist only in levying War against them, or in adhering to their Enemies, giving them Aid and Comfort. No Person shall be convicted of Treason unless on the Testimony of two Witnesses to the same overt Act, or on Confession in open Court.

The Congress shall have Power to declare the Punishment of Treason, but no Attainder of Treason shall work Corruption of Blood, or Forfeiture except during the Life of the Person attainted.

Article IV, Section 2

The Citizens of each State shall be entitled to all Privileges and Immunities of Citizens in the several States.

Section 4

The United States shall guarantee to every State in this Union a Republican Form of Government, and shall protect each of them against Invasion; and on Application of the Legislature, or of the Executive (when the Legislature cannot be convened) against domestic Violence.

Article V

. . . no religious Test shall ever be required as a Qualification to any Office or public Trust under the United States.

Amendment I

Congress shall make no law respecting an establishment of religion, or prohibiting the free exercise thereof; or abridging the freedom of speech, or of the press; or the right of the people peaceably to assemble, and to petition the Government for a redress of grievances.

Amendment II

A well regulated Militia, being necessary to the security of a free State, the right of the people to keep and bear Arms, shall not be infringed.

Amendment III

No Soldier shall in time of peace be quartered in any house, without the consent of the Owner, nor in time of war, but in a manner to be prescribed by law.

Amendment IV

The right of the people to be secure in their persons, houses, papers, and effects, against unreasonable searches and seizures, shall not be violated, and no Warrants shall issue, but upon probable cause, supported by Oath or affirmation, and particularly describing the place to be searched, and the persons or things to be seized.

Amendment V

No person shall be held to answer for a capital, or otherwise infamous crime, unless on a presentment or indictment of a Grand Jury, except in cases arising in the land or naval forces, or in the Militia, when in actual service in time of War or public danger; nor shall any person be subject for the same offense to be twice put in jeopardy of life or limb; nor shall be compelled in any criminal case to be a witness against himself, nor be deprived of life, liberty, or property, without due process of law; nor shall private property be taken for public use, without just compensation.

Amendment VI

In all criminal prosecutions, the accused shall enjoy the right to a speedy and public trial, by an impartial jury of the State and district wherein the crime shall have been committed, which district shall have been previously ascertained by law, and to be informed of the nature and cause of the accusation; to be confronted with the witnesses against him; to have compulsory process for obtaining witnesses in his favor, and to have the Assistance of Counsel for his defence.

Amendment VII

In Suits at common law, where the value in controversy shall exceed twenty dollars, the right of trial by jury shall be preserved, and no fact tried by a jury, shall be otherwise re-examined in any Court of the United States, than according to the rules of the common law.

Amendment VIII

Excessive bail shall not be required, nor excessive fines imposed, nor cruel and unusual punishments inflicted.

Amendment IX

The enumeration in the Constitution, of certain rights, shall not be construed to deny or disparage others retained by the people.

Amendment X

The powers not delegated to the United States by the Constitution, nor prohibited by it to the States, are reserved to the States respectively, or to the people.

Amendment XIII, Section 1

Neither slavery nor involuntary servitude, except as a punishment for crime whereof the party shall have been duly convicted, shall exist within the United States, or any place subject to their jurisdiction.

Section 2

Congress shall have power to enforce this article by appropriate legislation.

Amendment XIV, Section 1

All persons born or naturalized in the United States, and subject to the jurisdiction thereof, are citizens of the United States and of the State wherein they reside. No State shall make or enforce any law which shall abridge the privileges or immunities of citizens of the United States; nor shall any State deprive any person of life, liberty, or property, without due process of law; nor deny to any person within its jurisdiction the equal protection of the laws . . .

Section 5

The Congress shall have power to enforce, by appropriate legislation, the provisions of this article.

Amendment XV, Section 1

The right of citizens of the United States to vote shall not be denied or abridged by the United States or by any State on account of race, color, or previous condition of servitude.

Section 2

The Congress shall have power to enforce this article by appropriate legislation.

SUGGESTED READING LIST

1. American Liberties and the Supreme Court

Chafee, Zechariah, Jr. *How Human Rights Got Into the Constitution.* Boston: Boston University Press, 1952.

Emerson, Thomas I., and Haber, David. *Political and Civil Rights in the United States.* Buffalo: Dennis & Co., 1952.

Douglas, William O. *An Almanac of Liberty.* Garden City: Doubleday, 1954.

Konvitz, Milton R. *Bill of Rights Reader.* Ithaca: Cornell University Press, 1954.

Pritchett, C. Herman. *Civil Liberties and the Vinson Court.* Chicago: University of Chicago Press, 1954.

Rossiter, Clinton. *Seedtime of the Republic: The Origin of the American Tradition of Political Liberties.* New York: Harcourt, Brace, 1953.

Rutland, Robert A. *The Birth of the Bill of Rights.* Chapel Hill: University of North Carolina Press, 1955.

Wilcox, Claire, ed. *Civil Liberties Under Attack.* Philadelphia: University of Pennsylvania Press, 1951.

2. Liberty of Belief and Disbelief

Bates, M. Searle. *Religious Liberty: An Inquiry.* New York: International Missionary Council, 1945.

Blau, Joseph L. *Cornerstones of Religious Freedom in America.* Boston: Beacon Press, 1949.

Butts, R. Freeman. *The American Tradition in Religion and Education.* Boston: Beacon Press, 1950.

Johnson, Alvin W. and Yost, Frank H. *Separation of Church and State in the United States.* Minneapolis: University of Minnesota Press, 1948.

O'Neill, James M. *Religion and Education Under the Constitution.* New York: Harper, 1949.

Pfeffer, Leo. *Church, State, and Freedom.* Boston: Beacon Press, 1953.

Stokes, Anson Phelps. *Church and State in the United States.* New York: Harper, 1950.

Torpey, William George. *Judicial Doctrines of Religious Rights in America.* Chapel Hill: University of North Carolina Press, 1948.

3. Liberty of Speech and Silence

Biddle, Francis. *The Fear of Freedom.* New York: Doubleday, 1951.

Carr, Robert K. *The House Committee on Un-American Activities.* Ithaca: Cornell University Press, 1952.

Chafee, Zechariah, Jr. *Free Speech in the United States.* Cambridge: Harvard University Press, 1941.

Meiklejohn, Alexander. *Free Speech and Its Relation to Self-government.* New York: Harper, 1948.

Millar, John O. *Crisis in Freedom: The Alien and Sedition Acts.* Boston: Little, Brown, 1951.

Taylor, Telford. *Grand Inquest: The Story of Congressional Investigations.* New York: Simon and Schuster, 1955.

4. Liberty of Petition, Assembly, and Association

Barth, Alan. *The Loyalty of Free Men.* New York: Viking Press, 1951.

Bontecou, Eleanor. *Federal Loyalty Security Programs.* Ithaca: Cornell University Press, 1953.

Cook, Thomas I. *Democratic Rights, vs. Communist Activity.* New York: Doubleday, 1954.

Gellhorn, Walter. *The States and Subversion.* Ithaca: Cornell University Press, 1952.

Hook, Sidney. *Heresy, Yes; Conspiracy, No.* New York: John Day, 1953.

Palmer, Edward E., ed. *The Communist Problem in America.* New York: Thomas Y. Crowell, 1951.

5. Liberty of Knowledge and Learning

Beale, Howard K. *A History of Freedom of Teaching in American Schools.* New York: Scribner, 1941.

Blanshard, Paul. *The Right to Read.* Boston: Beacon Press, 1955.

Chafee, Zechariah, Jr. *Government and Mass Communications.* Chicago: University of Chicago Press, 1947.

Daniels, Walter M., ed. *The Censorship of Books.* New York: H. W. Wilson, 1954.

Ernst, Morris. *The First Freedom.* New York: Macmillan, 1946.

Gellhorn, Walter. *Security, Loyalty, and Science.* Ithaca: Cornell University Press, 1950.

MacIver, Robert M. *Academic Freedom in Our Times.* New York: Columbia University Press, 1955.

Taylor, Harold. *On Education and Freedom.* New York: Abelard-Schuman, 1954.

6. Liberty and Justice: Fair Play and Fair Trial

Beaney, William M. *The Right to Counsel in American Courts.* Ann Arbor: University of Michigan Press, 1955.

Griswold, Erwin N. *The Fifth Amendment Today.* Cambridge: Harvard University Press, 1955.

Hopkins, Ernest J. *Our Lawless Police.* New York: Viking Press, 1931.

Lowenthal, Max. *The Federal Bureau of Investigation.* New York: Sloane, 1950.

National Commission on Law Observance and Enforcement. *Report on Lawless-*

ness in Law Enforcement. Washington: U.S. Government Printing Office, 1931.

7. Liberty of Franchise

Key, V. O., Jr. *Southern Politics in State and Nation.* New York: Knopf, 1949.

Mangum, Charles S., Jr. *The Legal Status of the Negro.* Chapel Hill: University of North Carolina Press, 1940.

McGovney, Dudley O. *The American Suffrage Medley.* Chicago: University of Chicago Press, 1949.

Moon, Henry Lee. *Balance of Power: The Negro Vote.* Garden City: Doubleday, 1948.

President's Committee on Civil Rights. *To Secure These Rights.* Washington: Government Printing Office, 1947.

8. Entry, Sojourn, and Exit

Grodinz, Morton. *Americans Betrayed: Politics and the Japanese Evacuation.* Chicago: University of Chicago Press, 1949.

Konvitz, Milton R. *Civil Rights in Immigration.* Ithaca: Cornell University Press, 1953.

Konvitz, Milton R. *The Alien and the Asiatic in American Law.* Ithaca: Cornell University Press, 1946.

McWilliams, Carey. *Brothers Under the Skin.* Boston: Little, Brown, 1951.

President's Commission on Immigration and Naturalization. *Whom We Shall Welcome.* Washington: Government Printing Office, 1953.

9. Liberty and Equality

Abrams, Charles. *Forbidden Neighbors: A Study of Prejudice in Housing.* New York: Harper, 1955.

Berger, Morroe. *Equality by Statute: Legal Controls Over Group Discrimination.* New York: Columbia University Press, 1952.

Carr, Robert K. *Federal Protection of Civil Rights.* Ithaca: Cornell University Press, 1947.

Hill, Herbert, and Greenberg, Jack. *Citizen's Guide to Desegregation.* Boston: Beacon Press, 1955.

Johnson, Charles S. *Patterns of Negro Segregation.* New York: Harper, 1943.

Konvitz, Milton. *The Constitution and Civil Rights.* New York: Columbia University Press, 1947.

Myrdal, Gunnar. *An American Dilemma: The Negro Problem and Democracy.* New York: Harper, 1944.

Williams, Robin M., Jr., and Ryan, Margaret W. *Schools in Transition: Community Experiences in Desegregation.* Chapel Hill: North Carolina Press, 1954.

Table of Cases

Gitlow v. *New York,* 268 U.S. 652 (1925): 17, 73, 78, 81, 85, 87, 136, 282

Goldman v. *United States,* 316 U.S. 129 (1942): 175

Gong Lum v. *Rice,* 275 U.S. 78 (1927): 261

Grosjean v. *American Press Co.,* 297 U.S. 233 (1936): 139

Grovey v. *Townsend,* 295 U.S. 45 (1935): 206

Gryger v. *Burke,* 334 U.S. 728 (1948): 180

Guinn v. *United States,* 238 U.S. 347 (1915): 204

Hague v. *C.I.O.,* 307 U.S. 496 (1939): 106, 107, 110, 139

Hall v. *DeCuir,* 95 U.S. 485 (1878): 266

Hamilton v. *Regents of the University of California,* 293 U.S. 245 (1934): 50

Hannegan v. *Esquire, Inc.,* 327 U.S. 146 (1946): 133, 134

Harisiades v. *Shaughnessy,* 342 U.S. 580 (1952): 163, 224, 225

Harmon v. *Tyler,* 273 U.S. 668 (1927): 256, 258

Harris v. *United States,* 331 U.S. 145 (1947): 173

Hawker v. *New York,* 170 U.S. 189 (1898): 164

Heim v. *McCall,* 239 U.S. 175 (1915): 232

Henderson v. *United States,* 339 U.S. 816 (1950): 266, 267

Hennington v. *Georgia,* 163 U.S. 299 (1896): 56

Herndon v. *Lowry,* 301 U.S. 242 (1937): 78, 79

Hirabayashi v. *United States,* 320 U.S. 81 (1943): 234, 235

Hodges v. *United States,* 203 U.S. 1 (1906): 241, 252

Hughes v. *Superior Court of California,* 339 U.S. 460 (1950): 108

Hurd v. *Hodge,* 334 U.S. 24 (1948): 247, 257, 258

Hurtado v. *California,* 110 U.S. 516 (1884): 16, 170

International Auto Workers Union v. *Wisconsin Board,* 336 U.S. 245 (1949): 104, 242

Jackson, Ex parte, 96 U.S. 727 (1878): 133

Jacobson v. *Massachusetts,* 197 U.S. 11 (1905): 55

James v. *Bowman,* 190 U.S. 127 (1903): 203

Jamison v. *Texas,* 318 U.S. 413 (1943): 139

Joint Anti-Fascist Refugee Committee v. *McGrath,* 341 U.S. 123 (1951): 123

Kedroff v. *St. Nicholas Cathedral,* 344 U.S. 94 (1952): 38, 41, 46, 47, 269

Kemmler, Ex parte, 136 U.S. 436 (1890): 15, 196

Kilbourn v. *Thompson,* 103 U.S. 168 (1880): 93, 94

Knauer v. *United States,* 328 U.S. 654 (1946): 234

Knauff v. *Shaughnessy.* See *United States ex rel. Knauff* v. *Shaughnessy*

Korematsu v. *United States,* 323 U.S. 214 (1944): 236, 237

Kunz v. *New York,* 340 U.S. 290 (1951): 54

Kwong Hai Chew v. *Colding,* 344 U.S. 590 (1953): 221, 223

Lane v. *Wilson,* 307 U.S. 268 (1939): 204

Leyra v. *Denno,* 347 U.S. 556 (1954): 184

Logan v. *United States,* 144 U.S. 263 (1892): 251

Louisiana ex rel. Francis v. *Resweber,* 329 U.S. 459 (1947): 196

Lovell v. *Griffin,* 303 U.S. 444 (1938): 138

Index

For references to legal cases, see Table of Cases beginning on page 291.